Hearth & Heritage
ALONG THE CONESTOGA

Hearth & Heritage

ALONG THE CONESTOGA

A collection of stories and recipes
from Caernarvon Township,
Lancaster County, PA

By Historic Poole Forge
and the Caernarvon Fire
Company Ladies' Auxiliary

Hearth & Heritage
ALONG THE CONESTOGA

A collection of stories and recipes from Caernarvon
Township by Historic Poole Forge and the
Caernarvon Fire Company Ladies' Auxiliary

HISTORIC POOLE FORGE
PO Box 127
1940 Main St Narvon, PA 17555
717 445 0472

CAERNARVON FIRE COMPANY
2145 Main St
Narvon, PA 17555
717 445 7310

PUBLISHED BY
The Cookbook Committee from Historic Poole Forge
and Caernarvon Fire Company Ladies' Auxiliary

COPYRIGHT 2009
The Cookbook Committee from Historic Poole Forge
and Caernarvon Fire Company Ladies' Auxiliary

PHOTOGRAPHY
Alex Diem

DESIGN & LAYOUT
Zach Raffensperger

This cookbook is a collection of some favorite recipes,
which are not necessarily original recipes.

ISBN: 978-1-60126-200-4

MANUFACTURED BY
Masthof Press
219 Mill Road
Morgantown, PA 19543
(610) 286-0258

MANUFACTURED IN MORGANTOWN, PA
First Printing 2009
2000 copies

The Fireman's Creed

When I'm called to duty God,
Wherever flames may rage,
Give me strength to save a life,
Whatever be its age.
Help me to embrace a little child,
before it is too late.
Or save an older person from
the horror of that fate.
Enable me to be alert,
To hear the weakest shout,
And quickly and efficiently,
To put the fire out.
I want to fill my calling and
To give the best in me,
To guard my neighbor and
Protect his property.
And if according to your will,
I have to lose my life,
Bless with your protecting hand
My children and my wife.

Mission of Historic Poole Forge

Historic Poole Forge, Inc. actively promotes restoration
and preservation of the property, to provide parks and
recreation facilities for the community. Our goal is to foster
volunteerism, to provide education, appreciation of our
heritage and to support uses to help sustain the property.

About this Cookbook

The Poole Forge volunteers were looking for a fundraising opportunity to involve the community and generate funds for the extensive renovations needed on the property. The fire company Ladies' Auxiliary was also exploring a cookbook idea to support the needs of the volunteer fire company. The creation of "Hearth & Heritage Along the Conestoga" is the collaboration between the volunteers at Historic Poole Forge and the Caernarvon Fire Company Ladies' Auxiliary. This book is a partnership between these volunteer organizations benefiting both the historic landmark and supporting the needs of the volunteer fire company.

At first, the committee was unclear about the theme of the cookbook but knew it was not going to be "just a cookbook." We wanted the Churchtown community and surrounding Caernarvon Township, with its rich farming heritage, strong family ties, historic architecture and spectacular scenery, well documented in the essence of the book. Eventually, the Ladies' Auxiliary and the Poole Forge volunteers meshed their cookbook ideas into one unifying theme, "Hearth & Heritage Along the Conestoga." This book shares the stories of past and present community members, samples exceptional home cooked recipes and documents history about Churchtown and the surrounding area with a special emphasis on Historic Poole Forge and the newly-developed park.

Our committee wishes to thank all the community members who shared their stories and tales, tested the many delicious recipes, sponsored sections of the book and purchased the book to share with family and friends. The Churchtown area is truly a special place with rich heritage, heart-warming cooking traditions and architecture seeped in history. This cookbook has been a labor of love.

Table of Contents

Paymaster Sponsors

BRESSLER'S INC.
2563 Valley View Road
Morgantown, PA 19543
(610) 286-6013

VILLAGE DOLL HOSPITAL
4312 Division Highway
Blue Ball, PA 17506
(717) 354-3055

BARBARA POSSESSKY
Narvon, PA

WINDSOR FORGE, CHURCHTOWN
Lloyd & Sondra Simmers and Family

Forgeman Sponsors

BRENDA'S DRESS DESIGN
4312 Division Highway
Blue Ball, PA 17506
(717) 355-0914

NORMAN &
ELIZABETH HAHN
East Earl, PA

SHADY MAPLE FARM
MARKET & SMORGASBORG
1324 Main Street
East Earl, PA 17519
(717) 354-4981

LYON'S AND HOHL
1315 Sheep Hill Road
East Earl, PA 17519
(717) 355-9219

THE MAKARA FAMILY
John, Shelly & Katelyn
Narvon, PA

RICK & JEANETTE KLUMPP
Narvon, PA

FEEDING THE MASSES INDEX

CAERNARVON FIRE COMPANY & LADIES' AUXILIARY

Baked Beans

Bean Soup

Beef Bar-B-Que

Chicken Corn Soup

Filling for Thousands

Fire Company Punch

Pepper Cabbage

Veggie Soup for a Crowd

CAERNARVON ELEMENTARY SCHOOL

Brown Gravy (Government Good Gravy)

Cracker Pudding

Hamburg Gravy

Ice-Cream Dessert

Peanut Butter Kisses

Sweet and Sour Dressing

Lasagna with Ground Beef

AMISH WEDDINGS

Amish "Roasts"

36 Roast Chickens

Mashed Potatoes

Gravy

Cooked Celery

ALONG THE CONESTOGA

FEEDING THE MASSES
Local Recipes for Large Crowds

CHAPTER SPONSORED BY

Caernarvon Fire Company built in 1923.
Photo credit: Recollections of Caernarvon Township by Mary T. Petrofske, published for Friends of Bangor by Phoenix Publishing

Caernarvon Fire Company in 2009.
Photo credit: Megan Bensinger.

Churchtown Automotive Repair Shop

D&L Bensinger Military Vehicle Parts & Restoration

WE DEDICATE THIS CHAPTER TO THE FIRE FIGHTERS, AUXILIARY MEMBERS, AND THEIR FAMILIES FOR THE MANY HOURS OF SERVICE, COMMITMENT, AND DEDICATION TO THE CAERNARVON COMMUNITY.

— TONY & DEB MARTIN   — DARYL & LIDA BENSINGER

A FIREMAN'S PLEDGE

I promise concern for others.
A willingness to help all those in need.
I promise courage—courage to face and conquer my fears.
Courage to share and endure the ordeal of those who need me.
I promise strength—strength of heart to bear
whatever burdens might be placed upon me.
Strength of body to deliver to safety all those placed within my care.
I promise the wisdom to lead, the compassion to comfort, and the
love to serve unselfishly whenever I am called.

Caernarvon Fire Company & Ladies' Auxiliary

The Caernarvon Fire Company was formed in September of 1918. It was chartered on July 24, 1920. Meetings were initially held in the home of Peter Foreman until 1921 when they were moved to the Churchtown High School building. Plans for constructing a fire hall began and less than one year from the time, the first meeting was held in it on February 1, 1923. The hall was dedicated on August 25, 1923. Throughout the years, improvements, additions and remodeling were done to the hall four times, with the most recent being completed in 2009.

Churchtown had two fire companies for about ten years when the Conestoga Valley Fire Company (also known as the "West End" company) was formed in January of 1922 as the result of a feud between members of the original company over where the firehouse should be established. This company housed its Reo truck in Minnie Irwin's barn at South Churchtown Road and Route 23. Membership in the Conestoga Valley Company began to decline in 1933 when Davis Yohn, the originator and financier, died. Stories are told about the two companies (East End and West End) competing to see who could get to the fires first.

Caernarvon Fire Company jacket.

The first piece of apparatus that the Caernarvon Fire Company purchased was a Model T Roadster with two 30-gallon tanks for $1,244.00 in 1919. Much more apparatus has been purchased since then with the most recent being a pumper/tanker in 2005 at the cost of $500,000 for the vehicle itself, plus $20,000 to $30,000 for the equipment needed to outfit it. In addition to construction, remodeling and apparatus expenses, each active firefighter is supplied with personal protective gear – boots, helmet, coat, etc. at the cost of over $1,000 per set, and the firemen take numerous classes to learn the proper procedures for fighting fires and assisting at traffic accidents.

The firehouse has been an important part of our community. Over the years it has hosted spelling bees for the schools to earn money for field trips, school recitals, church services, Boy Scout and Girl Scout meetings, Memorial Day concerts, quilting bees, farm safety demonstrations for the one-room school students and pork and sauerkraut dinners served by the Red Rose Alliance among other things.

Newest addition to the Churchtown Fire Company.

Besides fighting fires and assisting at automobile accident scenes, members of the fire company remove downed trees and debris from the roads during and after storms, rescue horses and cows from manure pits, rescue cats from trees and people from floods, and pump water out of basements. They direct traffic during bike races and park cars at Historic Poole Forge events. They also compete annually in the tug-of-war contest at the New Holland Fair. Members of the Ladies' Auxiliary competed in the women's tug-of-war and the Bucket Brigade at the fair, also, until these events were removed from the fair schedule.

The Caernarvon Fire Company is a completely volunteer company with an active membership of 55. This includes fire police, firefighters and administration. Members range in age from 14 to older than dirt! Even though the members are not paid, it takes a lot of money to run the company. From 1923 until 1992, there were 5 major fund drives: in 1948 for the purchase of a truck, 1968 for the purchase of a truck and construction of a second bay on the fire hall, 1980 for a truck, 1987 for improvements to the hall and addition of two new truck bays, and in 1991 for a new truck. The company applies for state and federal grants and depends on donations from residents and businesses within the township for funding. Currently about one third of the township residents make yearly donations solicited via mass-mailings but this is not enough money to keep the company going, therefore fund-raisers are vital to the daily operations of the company.

The Caernarvon Fire Company Ladies' Auxiliary was founded in 1921. The main goal of the Ladies' Auxiliary is to assist and support the fire department financially and socially in its many activities; be it serving food and drinks to the firefighters at the scene of a fire, helping them at a social function or donating money to the department for the purchase of safety equipment for the fire fighters or to help with renovations on the hall. The auxiliary raises money by catering banquets at the fire hall, selling concessions at the Memorial Day Parade and selling food at local public sales. Several times over the years members of the auxiliary were joined by other local women to make quilts, which were then sold, with the proceeds being donated to several civic organizations including the Fire Company.

Ladies' Auxiliary circa 1930.

Although the active membership of the Ladies' Auxiliary is now about 1/5 of the size it was in 1924, there are many "non-members" who can be counted on to help at the turkey suppers and to make food for various events. The beef barbecue, chicken corn soup, ham and bean soup and baked goods sold from the food wagon are all donated.

During the early years of the company, money was raised at chicken and waffle suppers, card parties and carnivals. In recent years, the men have had various raffles and today, the main fund-raisers are a pancake breakfast the first Saturday in August and the bi-annual turkey suppers on the third Saturday in March and the third Saturday in October. The company has been having these turkey suppers since 1935 when adults paid 60 cents and children 30 cents for a wonderful meal. Many of the local residents enjoy the convenience of purchasing "to go" meals in the basement but some also wait in the engine room with customers who come from as far away as New York, New Jersey, Delaware and Maryland to eat family-style in

Turkey Supper entry ticket.

the auditorium. At a typical supper, about 1700 people (including over 100 volunteers who make the whole thing possible) are fed. Many members of the community get involved to make the supper a success – Amish, Mennonite, and "Englishers" set their religious differences aside and enjoy a camaraderie as they work together toward a common goal.

With a menu of turkey, filling, mashed potatoes, gravy, corn, green beans (which recently replaced peas), pepper cabbage, peaches, celery, carrots, cranberry sauce, dinner rolls, cake and ice-cream, actual preparations for the supper begin several weeks in advance. Food and paper products are ordered well before that. The number of turkeys needed varies depending on their weight but in recent years, anywhere from 80 to 107 birds (approximately 2200 pounds!) have been cooked for this one-day feast. About half of that weight in potatoes is used, plus 32 gallons of milk, 7 cases of cabbage, 70 pounds of carrots, 180 stalks of celery, 75 pounds of onions, 60 dozen eggs, 144 dozen rolls, 80

Turkey supper place setting.

pounds of sugar and 80 pounds of flour, 66 gallons each of corn, beans and peaches, 50 jars of grape jelly, 54 gallons of cranberry sauce and 220 boxes of ice-cream squares. Every day during the week leading up to the supper, you will find any number of folks at the fire hall doing their jobs. Knives and can opener blades need sharpened, pepper cabbage and filling must be made, celery and carrots cut and potatoes peeled and halved. Tables and chairs must be put in place in the dining room and those tables must be set. Fire apparatus gets moved out of the engine room, which then gets scrubbed down and filled with chairs for eager, hungry people to sit in while waiting their turn in the dining room.

If you are a new resident in the area and one day in March or October you discover a big paper plate on your doorstep, you are about to find out why. Members of the company distribute empty plates to residents during the week before the supper with a note asking them if they would please bake a cake. The morning of the supper, these same people go back out on their "cake routes" and pick up the finished cakes. Most of these cakes are sliced and served as dessert with the meal, but some are available to be purchased at the bake sales in the waiting room and take out areas.

Virginia Weber recalls the first year her neighborhood was reassigned from Goodville to Churchtown. "The police were called when a young man in an older car was parked along the road. He was then going house to house asking [residents] to donate a cake for the fire company supper. People here were not sure about this and that is when the police were called. This is my first memory of the turkey supper. A chocolate cake with peanut butter icing has been donated ever since." She is thankful to the fire company members for their service.

In this chapter you will find some of the recipes used by the fire company to feed the masses. Remember to reduce the quantities if you just want to make enough to serve your family! Also included are recipes used by the Ladies' Auxiliary for foods served at banquets and sold from the food trailer.

Baked Beans

4 (40 oz.) cans Great Northern beans

8 (16 oz.) cans baked beans

8 cups tomato juice

3 cups ketchup

3 cups brown sugar

3 cups molasses or King syrup

3 to 4 lb. fried bacon

onion to taste

Combine all ingredients.

Bake at 350 degrees for 2 1/2 hours.

— Caernarvon Fire Company Ladies' Auxiliary

Bean Soup

8 lb. ham (cubed)

8 qt. Great Northern Beans

4 cup shredded carrots

8 cup shredded potatoes

8 beef bouillon cubes

4 tsp. ham base

onion to taste

salt and pepper to taste

Combine all ingredients and cook for several hours until vegetables and beans are soft.

"Add some tomato juice if desired."

— Caernarvon Fire Company Ladies' Auxiliary

Beef Bar-B-Que

5 lb. ground beef

1 large onion

1 pepper or 1/2 tsp. pepper

4 stems celery

3 1/2 tsp. salt

1 3/4 cup ketchup

1 1/4 cup water

1 1/4 cup brown sugar

1/4 cup vinegar

1/8 cup mustard

Brown ground beef, onion and pepper.

Mix remaining ingredients and simmer for 30 minutes. Serve on buns.

"This is the recipe I use when I make Bar-B-Que for the food trailer to sell at public sales and at the fire hall at Churchtown."

— Anna Mae Shirk
   Narvon

Chicken Corn Soup

3 qt. cooked, cubed chicken

6 to 7 gallon chicken broth

6 qt. uncooked noodles

1 gallon corn

3 cups chopped celery

3 Tbsp. parsley or to taste

2 cup shredded carrots

12 hard boiled eggs,
    chopped (optional)

salt and pepper to taste

Bring chicken broth to boil with carrots and celery. Then add noodles. Cook until soft. Add the rest of the ingredients. *Makes 10 gallons*

— CAERNARVON FIRE COMPANY
    LADIES' AUXILIARY

Filling for Thousands

72 (5 lb.) bags bread cubes

54 pt. dippers chopped
    onion

72 to 90 pt. chopped celery

54 lb. butter

54 doz. eggs

18 small handful pepper

18 handfuls salt

54 handfuls parsley
    (or more)

Put 1/18th of all ingredients in huge metal tub (thoroughly cleaned and sanitized). Mix well. Taste. Add more of whatever seasoning is needed. Have someone else taste, add some more. Continue until all are satisfied. Repeat until all bread cubes are used.

— CAERNARVON FIRE COMPANY
    LADIES' AUXILIARY

Fire Company Punch

2 pkgs. raspberry Kool-aid

2 pkgs. cherry Kool-aid

4 cups sugar

4 qt. water

2 (46 oz.) bottles pineapple
    juice

2 qt. ginger ale

Mix ingredients. Add ginger ale before serving.

— CAERNARVON FIRE COMPANY
    LADIES' AUXILIARY

Pepper Cabbage

2 gray tubs chopped celery

1 1/2 gray tubs shredded peppers

10 gray tubs shredded cabbage

9 (5 lb.) bags sugar

6 gallons vinegar

3 handfuls salt

Put 1 qt. chopped celery, 1 pt. shredded peppers, 4 qt. shredded cabbage, 1 pt. sugar, 3 pt. vinegar and 1 handful of salt in five-gallon bucket. Mix well. Taste. Add more of whatever seasoning is needed. Have someone else taste, add some more. Continue until all are satisfied. Then mix the next bucket. Continue until all of the cabbage is used.

— Caernarvon Fire Company
Ladies' Auxiliary

Veggie Soup for a Crowd

1 cup chopped onions

1 qt. cubed potatoes

1 qt. chopped carrots

1 qt. corn

1 qt. green beans

1 qt. chopped celery

1 qt. baked beans

6 to 8 qt. tomato juice

1 cup brown sugar

1/4 cup butter

2 Tbsp. chili powder

12 tsp. beef soup base or 12 beef bullion cubes

3 lb. ground beef

1 qt. cooked noodles or barley can also be added

Brown ground beef in oven, stir often.

Precook all vegetables until tender.

Mix rest of ingredients and add together. Simmer 30 minutes. Can eat or can cool and freeze.

— Anna Mae Shirk
Narvon

Caernarvon Elementary School

Caernarvon Elementary School was once an integral part of our tiny community. What began in 1854 as Caernarvon Academy as a building with 2 classrooms, eventually became an elementary school with 12 classrooms, a library, art/music room and all-purpose room in 1966.

In the 1990's, two auxiliary classrooms and a teachers' lounge were added. Stone from the original Academy building was incorporated into the elementary school. The school was

Caernarvon Elementary School.

a focal point of the community and many residents used the school grounds, playground and fields.

The annual Memorial Day parade would line up in the parking lot and for several years, the New Holland Band/ELANCO elementary school band concert was held on the front lawn of the school before the parade. There were indoor and outdoor student concerts and shows, track and field day, bicycle rodeos and Family Fun Nights. Sadly, the school was closed in 2007 and demolished in 2008.

The stone is being preserved for use if another school gets built in its place. Caernarvon Elementary School cafeteria managers have included Joan Freezeman, Sarah Weller, Audrey Bechtold and June Freidly. Workers included Dot Leininger, Lois Auker, Deb Martin, Kim Murray, Mrs. Overly, Pat Johnson, Gail Schnettler, Melissa Faber and Michelle Bell. Also included in this chapter are recipes submitted by some of the "cafeteria ladies" from the school.

Brown Gravy (Government Good Gravy)

1 cup butter or margarine

2 1/4 cup all-purpose flour

1 gallon and 1 cup beef stock

1 Tbsp. and 1 tsp. onion powder

1/2 tsp. black or white pepper

Melt butter or margarine in stockpot. Blend in flour and cook on medium heat, stirring frequently until golden brown, 8 to 10 minutes. Slowly stir in beef stock, onion powder, and pepper. Blend well and bring to boil. Reduce heat. Simmer on medium heat, stirring constantly until thickened, 6 to 8 minutes.

Serve over mashed potatoes, noodles, rice, meat or poultry.

"Audrey was the cafeteria manager at Caernarvon Elementary school from 1981 until the school closed in 2007. This recipe is from the 'Government Book'."

— AUDREY BECHTOLD
Talmage

Cracker Pudding

1 qt. milk

2 eggs, separated

2/3 cup granulated sugar

1 tsp. vanilla

2 cups broken saltine crackers

1 cup grated coconut (medium shred)

While warming the milk, beat egg yolks and sugar until frothy. Add to hot milk and stir in crackers and coconut. Cook until thick. Remove from heat and add stiffly beaten egg whites and vanilla. Cool. *Serves 8*

"Sara worked at Caernarvon Elementary school from 1966 to 1982."

— SARA WELLER
New Holland

Hamburg Gravy

5 lb. ground beef

1 cup chopped onion

2 Tbsp. beef base

cornstarch mixed in water

3 qt. water

Brown beef and onion in pan. Add water and beef base. When it comes to a boil, slowly add cornstarch and water mixture until you have the right consistency. Serve over mashed potatoes.

"Lois worked in the cafeteria for a few years."

— LOIS AUKER
Terre Hill

Ice-Cream Dessert

12-pack ice-cream sandwiches

12 oz. jar of peanut butter or caramel topping (use 1 cup)

12 oz. Cool Whip®, thawed

1/4 cup chocolate syrup

Hershey's Symphony® candy bar, chopped

Line a 13 X 9-inch pan with ice-cream sandwiches. Probably only 11 will fit (eat the other one!). Spread the peanut butter or caramel topping over sandwiches. Spread the Cool Whip over topping. Drizzle the chocolate syrup on top, then top with the candy bar.

Cover and freeze for at least 45 minutes. Cut into squares.

"Shirley worked at Caernarvon from 1981 till 1990 filling in for various positions over the years."

— SHIRLEY WEIDMAN
Narvon

Peanut Butter Kisses

KISSES

3 1/2 cups peanut butter

1/2 cup soft butter

2 cups confectioner's sugar

2 Tbsp. vanilla

TOPPING

1 1/2 cup chocolate chips

2 Tbsp. butter

2 Tbsp. water

Mix peanut butter, sugar and vanilla together thoroughly. Pat into greased 9 X 13-inch pan or roll into balls. Melt topping together and spread on bars or drizzle over balls. If making in pan, cut the same day you make them Refrigerate and serve.

"The kids loved these; they taste like peanut butter cups!"

"Kim worked at Caernarvon Elementary school from 1997 to 2006."

— KIM MURRAY
East Earl

Sweet and Sour Dressing

1 cup mayonnaise

1 cup sugar

2 Tbsp. milk

1/3 cup vinegar

Mix mayonnaise and sugar, add milk; add vinegar last.

"This is Audrey Bechtold's recipe. We used this dressing to dip chicken nuggets into. Deb worked at Caernarvon Elementary School from 1995 to 1999."

— DEB MARTIN
Churchtown

Lasagna with Ground Beef

6 lb. 8 oz. raw ground beef (no more than 24% fat)

3 1/2 cups dehydrated onions or 1 gallon fresh onions, chopped

1/4 cup garlic powder

2 tsp. black pepper

1/2 cup parsley flakes

8 lb. 8 oz. canned tomatoes, with liquid, chopped

3 lb. 8 oz. tomato paste

1 1/2 gallon water

1/4 cup 2 Tbsp. flaked basil

1/4 cup 2 Tbsp. flaked oregano

2 Tbsp. flaked marjoram

2 tsp. flaked thyme

4 lb. 4 oz. lasagna noodles, uncooked

3 lb. 2 oz. American cheese, shredded

4 lb. 12 oz. mozzarella cheese, shredded

Brown ground beef, drain. Add onions and garlic powder. Cook for 5 minutes.

Add pepper, parsley flakes, canned tomatoes, tomato paste, water and seasonings. Heat to boiling, uncovered. Remove from heat.

Assemble ingredients in 4 steam table pans (12 X 20 X 2 1/2-inch) as follows:

1st layer – 1 qt. 1/2 cup sauce
2nd layer – 10 uncooked noodles, lengthwise
3rd layer – 1 qt. 1/2 cup sauce
4th layer – 6 1/2 oz. American cheese (1 3/4 cups) and 10 oz. mozzarella cheese (2 1/2 cups)
5th layer – 10 uncooked noodles crosswise
6th layer – 1 qt. 3/4 cup sauce
7th layer – 6 oz. American cheese (1 1/2 cups 2 Tbsp.) and 9 oz. mozzarella cheese (2 1/4 cups)

Tightly cover pans. Bake in a conventional oven at 350 degrees for 1 1/4 to 1 1/2 hours or a convection oven for 325 degrees for 45 minutes

Remove pans from oven. Uncover. Let stand for 15 minutes before serving..

Cut each pan in 5 X 5-inch squares (25 pieces per pan).

Serves 100

— Audrey Bechtold, Caernarvon Elementary Cafeteria Manager
  Talmage

Amish Weddings

Amish weddings are traditionally held on Tuesdays and Thursdays in late October through December after the fall harvest. This keeps the weddings from interfering with the Sunday church services as it takes a day to prepare for the wedding and a day to clean up afterwards.

The wedding is an all day event held at the bride's home. Some time before the wedding, the portable walls in the house are all removed and the furniture is moved out to make room for the 300 to 350 guests who will be attending the service. Several church bench wagons bring the benches to the house to provide seating for the service.

Amish boy waiting at buggy.

The service begins at 8:00 AM and is similar to a regular Amish church service, with singing and sermons preached in German. The scriptures and sermons emphasize the seriousness of the union of man and woman. Because the Amish do not believe in divorce, after their engagement is announced, the Deacon counsels the couple before they take this serious step in their relationship. The couple is also counseled thoroughly the morning of their wedding while the guests are singing hymns.

During the ceremony, the women sit on one side of the room facing the men on the other side. The bride and groom sit facing each other in the center of the room with their attendants at their sides. The bride and her attendants wear new dresses (traditionally blue), white capes and aprons. The groom and his groomsmen wear white shirts, black vests, suit coats and bow ties. The attendants are called the "nevasitza" and are usually a brother and sister of the bride and a brother and sister of the groom. They follow the couple around all day attending to their needs. There are no flowers and no candles.

Toward the end of the service, the bride and groom come forward to take their vows, which are very similar to traditional "English" wedding vows. They acknowledge and confess their belief that God has ordained marriage to be between one man and one woman and that He provided them as marriage partners for one another. They promise to love and take care of each other for the rest of their lives. The minister offers them a blessing and pronounces them man and wife.

English / German Bible.

At this point, some of the benches are made into tables and the noon meal, lovingly prepared by the bride's family and friends, is served. Preparation for this meal actually begins months before the wedding with the planting of a large crop of celery, which is an important part of the meal. Leafy celery stalks in jars are placed on the tables as centerpieces. Tables are set up in a "U" shape around the large room and the bride and groom are seated in a corner called the "eck" with the bride to the left of the groom, and one pair from the nevasitza beside each of them. The guests are seated with the men on one side of the table and the women on the other side. It takes several seatings for all of the guests to eat. When one group is finished eating and the tables are cleared, the next group is seated. Both men and women help serve and clean up after the meal.

After the bride and groom have eaten, they open their gifts and the guests come to watch when they have finished their own meals. When everything from the noon meal is cleaned up, they have "afternoon table." The young girls stand in a group and the boys pick them to go in and sit with them for singing and snacks. These snacks vary widely but may include things such as soft pretzels, wraps and fruit. This is a fun time for the bride and groom and the youth.

Amish bride and groom hats.

Later in the evening, those remaining gather for supper. It is a task of the bride and groom to make sure that each unmarried person 16 years old or over has a partner to sit with. This is an important, traditional part of an Amish wedding. It is a time that the young people can talk and get to know each other. More singing follows the evening meal. Sometimes guests stay as late as 10 or 11:00 PM.

On their wedding night, the newlyweds spend the night at the home of the bride's family so they can get up bright and early to help clean up. During the first several months of their marriage, the couple will visit the homes of 5 or 6 relatives each weekend, having meals with them and spending the night at some of their houses, returning to the bride's house on Sunday night. During these visitations, they receive many of their wedding presents. Sometime in the spring, the couple will set up housekeeping at their own place.

THE AMISH WEDDING LUNCH MENU IS:

- ▸ "Roasts" (Roast chicken with bread stuffing)
- ▸ Cooked celery
- ▸ Mashed potatoes
- ▸ Gravy
- ▸ Cole slaw
- ▸ Doughnuts
- ▸ Pies
- ▸ Fruit salad
- ▸ There are many homemade wedding cakes and sometimes a bakery-made wedding cake.

SUPPER VARIES BUT A TYPICAL MENU WOULD INCLUDE:

- ▸ Meatloaf
- ▸ Butter potatoes
- ▸ Peas
- ▸ Macaroni and cheese or noodles
- ▸ Salad
- ▸ Desserts

Amish "Roasts"

32 chickens

14 lb. butter

5 Tbsp. salt

2 Tbsp. pepper

10 qt. fine cut celery

5 qt. bread cubes for each chicken

60 eggs

6 onions, sliced fine

Cook liver and hearts in big kettle on stove, then grind. Melt butter in big kettle. Mix ground liver and hearts with sliced celery; brown and cool this mixture. Beat eggs, add pepper, salt and seasoning and add this to bread cubes. Mix in the cooled celery and meat and stuff the chickens with this bread cube mixture.

36 Roast Chickens

36 chickens

36 gallons of bread cubes

72 eggs

7 lb. butter

1/2 gallon Crisco®

16 Tbsp. salt

3 scant Tbsp. pepper

1 1/2 gallon celery, chopped
very thin

Add the ingredients to 36 gallons of bread cubes and mix thoroughly. Add to this 6 dozen beaten eggs. This is done the day before.

Bake the chickens, finely chop the meat.

On the morning of the wedding, mix the meat and filling and heat.

Mashed Potatoes

potatoes

butter

milk

salt

Peel and dice potatoes the morning of the wedding, enough to fill about four 12 quart kettles. Cook until soft. Smash with lots of butter, milk and salt.

Gravy

chicken broth

seasoning (various)

flour

Use chicken broth, add water and seasoning, thicken with flour. *Makes two 8-quart kettles*

Cooked Celery

12 qt. kettle full of celery

1/2 cup water

1 stick butter

2 Tbsp. salt

2 1/2 cup sugar

3/4 cup vinegar

5 heaping Tbsp. flour

2 to 3 cups white vinegar

1 cup brown sugar

3 cans Carnation® milk

On the morning of the wedding, combine celery, water, and butter. Cook until soft.

When soft add salt, sugar, and vinegar. Cook on low heat until the couple has said their vows (a couple of hours).

Mix the flour, white vinegar, sugar, and milk separately and add to mixture. Beat together. Do not let it cook!

Add more sugar, salt and milk if necessary. You will need five or six kettles full for an Amish wedding.

BREAKFAST & BREADS INDEX

ALONG THE CONESTOGA

BREAKFAST & BREADS
The Bed & Breakfasts of Churchtown

Churchtown Inn

Address	2100 Main Street Narvon, PA 17555
Toll-free	(800) 637-4446
Phone	(717) 445-7794
Email	innkeepers@churchtowninn.com
Website	www.churchtowninn.com

"All the touches that make an inn special are here."
– *Bernice Chesler, 'Bed and Breakfast in the Mid-Atlantic States'*

Inn at Twin Linden

Address	2092 Main Street Churchtown, PA 17555
Toll-free	(866) 445-7614
Phone	(717) 445-7619
Email	info@innattwinlinden.com
Website	www.innattwinlinden.com

"A couple acres of bliss"
– *L.A. Times*

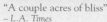

Washington Inn

Washington Inn

Address	2111 Main Street Churchtown, PA 17555
Email	info@historicwashingtoninn.com
Website	www.historicwashingtoninn.com

The Bed & Breakfasts of Churchtown

The Churchtown community is blessed with many historic homes and churches. A walk through the small hamlet reminds us of a time gone by. The community is surrounded by family owned farms and cottage businesses. In the 19th century, many wealthy families were drawn to this area because of the iron ore available in the surrounding land. Forges were established and mansions built. A few of these outstanding mansions still exist today and remain an intricate part of the community. Churchtown is fortunate to have four historic Bed & Breakfast establishments. Three of these historic Bed & Breakfasts are within walking distance of each other.

Starting from the east end of town, The Washington Inn stands on the corner of Water and Main Street. It is an impressive fieldstone structure with pillars and dormers. The west side of the Inn (closest to Bangor Church) was the original residence built sometime around 1750. The east side was added in 1812 by Cyrus Jacobs and included a large first floor room used throughout the years as a ballroom, a store, a saddler shop, a meeting room for the school board and the supervisors, the hose company and likely many other uses. The rear portion

Washington Inn 1966.

of the building was added sometime in the 1930's. It has been known as the Washington House, and the Washington Inn. There is a long told story that claims George Washington was a guest at the Inn. A 1968 Wall Street Journal article written about the Bangor Church and Churchtown stated, " George Washington, then a colonel,worshiped here in 1758: he was returning from the Battle of Fort Duquesne.

Sharon and Brad Krock purchased the Inn in 2008 from previous owners and long time residents Kathy and Robert Weaver and Venita and Kenneth Draude. The Krocks have begun an extensive renovation of the property and plan to reopen the Inn in a couple of years. They will host wedding receptions, teas, and quiet weekend escapes in their historic seven bedroom Inn. The Krocks have restored a small stone farmhouse a couple of miles outside of Churchtown that is now available for rental for the weekend or by the week. This charming stone farm house was built sometime between 1790 and 1830 and is nestled

Washington Inn aerial view.

on ten secluded acres of meadows, forests and fields. A perfect retreat for a weekend or week getaway. Visit the website for more details.

The Washington Inn has served the community for hundreds of years. The Innkeepers have heard numerous accounts from neighbors and friends about the time they had dinner, ate school lunches, celebrated anniversaries and even had wedding receptions at the Washington Inn. The Krocks hope to keep the Inn as a piece of Churchtown's living history and open it's doors to the community once again. A recommended recipe from the kitchen at the Washington Inn is Alan's Banana bread located in this chapter.

Across the street from the Washington Inn sits the Churchtown Inn. This outstanding Federal style mansion was built in 1735 and was known as the Edward Davies mansion. According to tradition, the original section of the Davies House was built in 1735 by David Jones, a miner. Some years later, in 1804, Eleanor Fausset sold the property to Senator Edward Davies, a member of the 25th Congress and a State Legislator. In 1806, Senator Davies expanded the home by adding the western section of the house, including the double parlors with raised ceilings.

Characteristically, the mansion is a Federal Style building, two-and-one-half stories in height. The recessed front entrance doorway has original side paneling and recessed six-panel door; above the door is a pointed arch fanlight and surrounding arch with keystone, both also original and intact. These features as an ensemble are an excellent example of a Federal or Adamesque doorway. The center hall is eight feet wide and runs through the main building to the "Old Kitchen" in the rear; the hall ceiling is over ten feet high as are the ceilings in the parlors. The ceilings in the easterly portion are slightly lower, which accounts for a number of step-up/step-down levels.

The Davies Mansion, with its Federal features intact, is indeed an outstanding example of an early eighteenth and nineteenth century property in the rural village of eastern Lancaster County. It has served many residents well, and has been used over the years as a tinsmith's shop, rectory, boarding house, and dormitory for children attending the Churchtown Presbyterian Academy.

Churchtown Inn front patio.

In 1987, Jim Kent and Stuart Smith, from north New Jersey, bought and converted the Edward Davies Mansion into a Victorian Bed and Breakfast. Being multitalented, they sang, played music and danced regularly in the parlors on many weekends. Concerts, teas, and Murder Mystery Weekends were some of the special event weekends they hosted. The Inn's special events and wonderful breakfasts continued when, in 2001, Diane Curry and Michael Franco bought the Inn. Diane updated the bedrooms with beautiful, local hand made Amish Quilts. A bright and regal Standard Poodle named Porter was added to the family and entertained guests with his charming personality. All the while Jim Kent and many of his friends and former guests continued to visit the Inn on a regular basis.

Diane and Mike jumped at an offer to work on a beautiful island close to Puerto Rico and put the Inn up for sale in June. Jim and Chris Farr, looking for a Bed and Breakfast in Lancaster County for over a year, found what they were looking for the very first day the Inn went on the market! Chris, with a background in ecology education, has had a large natural water feature, bird feeders, wildflower garden and bird boxes built outside the beautiful breakfast room, making the view even more interesting. The plan is for the Inn to be a National Wildlife Bird Sanctuary. While the gardens are quiet and peaceful, Jim and Chris enjoy hosting Wedding Vowel Renewal weekends, Thanksgiving Day weekend, Amish Dinner weekends, Teas, and of course, the Churchtown Inn's famous and wacky 'Who Dun It Mysteries'.

Churchtown Inn garden arbor view.

As early as 7:45, steaming hot coffee and a selection of teas is available in the parlors where guests may relax, try their hand at a jigsaw puzzle or lounge in a comfy chair with a book. At nine o'clock, the breakfast bell chimes and the gourmet breakfast begins, created from the finest local ingredients.

The glass-enclosed garden breakfast room was hand-crafted by a local Amish man. The 200 year-old stone wall, the view overlooking a koi pond with waterfall, and an 86-acre Mennonite farm in the background creates an enchanting breakfast experience. Beautifully dressed tables crowned with Royal Doulton china sparkle in sunlight or candlelight, and soft music plays in the background. Some of the Inn's favorite breakfast treats include frozen fruit creme cups, peach soup, and apple, honey and walnut compote. The moist and chewy homemade granola or creamy, Amish baked oatmeal are made fresh. A house specialty of scrambled Guten Morgen eggs is always available as well as cinnamon apple french toast, egg soufflé with sweet red pepper cream sauce, or Louisiana lemon creme crepes with Lancaster County wild strawberries. Plus, a selection of fresh muffins, pastries, and locally-made breakfast meats. Sweet treats made by local residents include butter pecan fudge, Iced carrot cake, raspberry toasted coconut bars or rich chocolate truffles. Check out their apple cinnamon french toast and fresh peach bread enclosed in this section and their delicious King cookie recipe located in the cookie section.

Just a short walk up the street from the Churchtown Inn, is the beautifully restored Inn at Twin Linden. During the 19th century the abundance of iron ore in the neighboring town of Morgantown drew wealthy families to the area. Many of these families started forges such as Windsor, Poole and Spring Grove. In 1849, Robert Jenkins, the Iron master for Windsor Forge, built this Italianate style home as a wedding gift for his daughter Sarah. Her husband was Rev. Alfred Nevin so the mansion became known as the Nevin Mansion. The property was later coined "Twin Linden" stemming from the two wedding trees that were planted on the property to signify the union of Sarah and Alfred Nevin. These gorgeous trees still stand today. In stylistic terms, the three-story height and nearly flat roof of the main or front block of this house may mark it as a very simplified version of the Italianate style. Some attributes of later Classical Revival influence may also be discerned in some features of the exterior. These include the use of some moldings of Grecian profiles, the large front porch or piazza with its Tuscan order columns, and the manner of the paneling seen in the first floor shutters. The overall external character of this large residence is somewhat evocative of some 1840-1870 period houses seen to this day in Chester County. Some rather similar houses in Chester County may still be seen between Honeybrook and Downingtown.

Since construction of Twin Linden, the recorded deeds have been from Robert Jenkins to Catherine Jenkins Jacobs - 1856, to Mary B. Hoskins - 1898, to Levi Dohn - 1918, to J.C. Henninger - 1933, to Francis Steuart - 1955, to Jerald L. and F. Elizabeth Martin - 1963, to Robert and Donna Leahy - 1987, to Norman and Susan Kuestner 2005. It appears that the mansion was primarily used as a personal residence until the ownership of Francis

Twin Linden front porch.

Steuart who purchased Twin Linden in 1955. This is evidenced by a copy of the "92nd Memorial Day Service" flyer dated Friday, May 30, 1958 which contains a sponsorship from the Twin Linden Home for Aged Men and Women. In the early 1960's, the Steuarts converted the building into several rental apartments, and in 1963 sold it to Jerald and Elizabeth Martin. The Martins, who still reside in Churchtown today, maintained the building as a rental property until it was sold to Robert and Donna Leahy in 1987. The Leahy's converted the building to the "Inn at Twin Linden", a six-room Bed and Breakfast that opened for business in 1990. The Inn at Twin Linden had now regained the look and feel of the original Nevin Mansion. The Leahy's later converted most of the third floor attic space into the Palladian Suite. In keeping with the Italianate style, grand Palladian windows in the suite provide spectacular views of the inn's garden and the neighboring farmland. Then when you least expect it, Tuscany meets Mennonite farmland on the lower lawn of the property where a pergola was constructed for a spot to enjoy a bottle of wine while savoring the almost surreal view of the adjacent farm valley. Subsequently, the Garden Gate Suite was constructed above the carriage house offering a deluxe retreat with ultimate privacy and an outdoor balcony with grand views. After 18 years of inn keeping, the Leahy's sold the inn to Norman and Susan Kuestner in the summer of 2005. The Kuestners continue to operate Twin Linden as an 8-room Country Inn, Bed and Breakfast.

Twin Linden garden loggia in the spring.

While many ghost stories have been circulated about Churchtown's haunted homes, there has been no evidence of any paranormal happenings at Twin Linden. It was rumored that the Leahy's witnessed a repeated yellowing of the sheets in the "Sarah Jenkins Room" regardless of how many times they were changed. Is this a convenient coincidence that Sarah died of yellow fever? The Kuestners have not experienced this phenomenon, and believe it is highly unlikely as the location of the Sarah Jenkins Room is actually in a part of the building that was added long after Sarah's death. While a haunting of this historical building would be a great selling point to some bed and breakfast travelers, it is not a story that can be told with any sincerity.

Here and now, in 2009, the Inn at Twin Linden offers the luxurious ambiance of a restored 1800's country estate – a gracious manor surrounded by beautiful gardens and stately trees – providing accommodations that marry modern comfort with a 19th century feeling. Oak and antique furnishings, refined décor and exquisite meals create a warm ambiance of country elegance. Located in the heart of the Amish and Mennonite community, farm-dotted valleys stretch as far as the eyes can see. The "clip-clop" of horse-drawn buggies can be heard echoing down the main street. Days at Twin Linden begin with a sumptuous three-course breakfast served in an elegant garden-view dining room. Guest rooms feature canopy beds, fireplaces, and private baths – most with whirlpool spa tubs. Guests can sip afternoon tea while enjoying a gentle swing on the porch that overlooks pastoral views, providing tranquility and rejuvenation to travelers who have come to enjoy the experience of Pennsylvania Dutch Country. A specialty of the Inn at Twin Linden is romantic candlelight dinners that are offered to in-house and community guests by reservation. Dining at Twin Linden has come to be recognized as the unique amenity that makes your stay here a memorable experience. The Innkeepers have enclosed three favorite recipes for your enjoyment. Look for their Mexican egg stack recipe in this section, the pasta and bean soup in the Soups, Salads, and Sandwiches section, and a scrumptious strawberry trifle located in the Pies and Pudding chapter.

A couple of miles outside of Churchtown sits the Lincoln Boone Bed & Breakfast. It is an 18th century restored farm and serves as a quiet retreat for travelers. The Lincoln Boone Bed & Breakfast has a history rich with character and even a few legends thrown in. There are more pieces of the puzzle to fit together, but a few interesting morsels have been discovered.

The original tract of land was purchased from the Penn family in 1741. By 1755 a house had been built at the present location. The most prominent owner of the farm was Mr. James Lincoln and his wife Elizabeth from 1810 to 1834. Mr. Lincoln was a great-uncle to our esteemed 16th president. In 2000, the James Lincoln deed was acquired at auction. It bears the signature of James' grandfather Abraham, who was named after the president. James' mother was Anne Boone, a first cousin to the legendary frontiersman Daniel Boone of nearby Reading, Pennsylvania. Thence the name, "Lincoln-Boone Bed and Breakfast."

Lincoln Boone Country Cottage.

One local historical book, The Annals of Conestoga Valley , mentions this farm numerous times and alludes to James Lincoln's role in the underground railroad in helping runaway slaves escape southern plantations and bounty hunters in the 18th and 19th centuries. There is also knowledge of a limestone cavern that runs under the property and some say runs under the town of Morgantown, though no one seems to know for sure if it factored into the harboring of fugitive slaves. Recent excavation has turned up an underground aqueduct that runs just south of the house which probably was used to bring running water into the basement in colonial times.

In 1834 the large bank barn that is nearest Red School Road was built by the new owner of the property, David Mast. About this same time a sizable addition was added onto the north side of the house, connecting the rear summer kitchen to the main house with two rooms on each floor. Local historians believe that the addition would have been added sometime before the barn was built, perhaps in 1832. The barn itself was reconstructed after being hit by a tornado in 1979.

There is a cemetery located on the northern edge of the farm. Buried there are Rozanna's grandfather, great grandfather and great great grandfather. The earliest marked grave dates from 1809, but there are numerous other unmarked graves that local legend holds date back to the 18th century.

The farm is currently owned by Steven and Rozanna Leever who purchased it from her father, Stephen S. Stotztfus in 2000. The farm has been in Rozanna's family since 1903. Her father, Stephen S., purchased it in 1965 from his father, Stephen R. Stoltzfus, who had owned the property since 1933. The Stoltzfus family was Amish and all of their children attended the local one room schoolhouse located on the southern edge of the farm along Route 23. This same "Little Red Schoolhouse" has been featured in National Geographic several times over the years and is currently a tourist information center.

Stephen's daughter Rozanna, her husband Steve, three daughters and one son have lived on the farm since 1995 and are attempting to restore its historical charm. Now they want visitors to Lancaster County to experience the beauty and serenity of the Conestoga Valley as guests of the Lincoln-Boone Bed and Breakfast.

The Lincoln Boone Bed & Breakfast offers a 1740 colonial country cottage nestled on 9.4 acres of woodlands. Enjoy a walk in the woods or sit on the patio and savor the views of the valley below. Bird watching, flower collecting, hiking the trails and dog walking are a few of the pleasures enjoyed by those who stay at this colonial cottage. Make your own breakfast in the charming cottage kitchen or order baked goods from Levi & Lydia for a delightful morning treat on the patio. Three recommended recipes from their kitchen include Rozanna's crustless quiche and breakfast pie found in this section and their baked apple appetizer in the appetizer chapter.

Churchtown is fortunate to have these wonderful historical destinations. Explore their websites and recipes, share their unique stories and tell your friends and fellow travelers about the truly special and delightful Churchtown Bed & Breakfasts.

Lisa's Baked Oatmeal

3/4 cup vegetable oil

1 1/2 cup brown sugar

1/4 cup honey

3 large eggs

3/4 tsp. salt

3 tsp. baking powder

4 1/2 cup quick oats

1 1/2 cup milk

Mix all ingredients in bowl and pour into a greased 9 X 13-inch pan and cook uncovered at 350 degrees for 35 to 40 minutes or until light brown.

— LISA SHIRK
Narvon

Eleanor's Baked Oatmeal

3 cups quick oats

1 cup packed brown sugar

2 tsp. baking powder

1 Tbsp. cinnamon

1 tsp. salt

1 cup milk

1/2 cup melted butter

1/2 cup applesauce

2 large eggs

Combine all ingredients in a bowl and spoon into a greased 9 X 9-inch pan. Bake at 350 degrees for 40 to 50 minutes. Nuts and fruit may be added for variety. Serve with milk.

— ELEANOR HIBSHMAN
Narvon

Whole Wheat Oatmeal Pancakes

2 large eggs

1 cup oatmeal

1 cup whole wheat flour

1 1/2 cup milk

4 Tbsp. vegetable oil

2 Tbsp. sugar or honey

1 1/2 Tbsp. baking powder

1/2 tsp. salt

Beat the eggs until fluffy. Add milk, oil and sugar. Stir in flour, baking powder, salt, and oats. Let set a few minutes before frying. If the mixture becomes too thick, add a little more milk. Pour batter by 1/4 cupfuls onto a greased hot griddle (400 degrees). Turn when bubbles form on the top of the pancakes. Cook until the second side is golden brown.

"These pancakes are very good and filling especially served with fruit, syrup and whipped cream."

— VERA JANE NEWSWANGER
Morgantown

Easy Delicious Granola

4 cups old-fashioned rolled oats

2 cups sweetened shredded coconut

2 cups sliced almonds

3/4 cup vegetable oil

1/2 cup good honey

1 1/2 cups small diced dried apricots

1 cup small diced dried figs

1 cup dried cherries

1 cup dried cranberries

1 cup roasted, unsalted cashews

Preheat the oven to 350 degrees.

Toss the oats, coconut, and almonds together in a large bowl. Whisk together the oil and honey in a small bowl. Pour the liquids over the oat mixture and stir with a wooden spoon until all the oats and nuts are coated.

Pour onto a 13 X 18 X 1-inch sheet pan. Bake, stirring occasionally with a spatula, until the mixture turns a nice, even, golden brown, about 45 minutes.

Remove the granola from the oven and allow to cool, stirring occasionally. Add the apricots, figs, cherries, cranberries, and cashews. Store the cooled granola in an airtight container.

Alternate vanilla yogurt and granola in parfait glasses and top with fresh fruit for a beautiful and delicious treat.

"The granola parfaits have become part of our traditional Christmas morning brunch."

"They look festive served in a wine glass served along with egg & sausage strata, fresh baked breads and pastries."

— KAY RAFFENSPERGER
Blue Ball

Light Wonderful Pancakes

1 cup flour

2 Tbsp. granulated sugar

2 Tbsp. baking powder

1 egg, beaten

2 Tbsp. vegetable oil

1 cup milk

Mix all ingredients together. Fry up.

— MARY ANN GOOD
Terre Hill

Apple Fritters & Rings

1 cup flour

1 1/2 tsp. baking powder

1/2 tsp. salt

2 Tbsp. sugar

1 large beaten egg

1/2 cup and 1 Tbsp. milk

1 1/2 cup chopped apples
(your choice)

Beat egg and milk. Add sifted flour, baking powder, salt and sugar. Add chopped apples. Drop by spoonfuls in to deep fat heated to 370-375 degrees and fry till golden brown. Drain on paper towels. Sprinkle with cinnamon and sugar.

Apple rings: pare and core apples leaving whole. Slice crosswise 1/4 inch thick. Dip in melted butter and fry. Serve hot sprinkled with sugar or syrup.

"A Lambert favorite. This recipe was found on a scrap of paper when the old farm house was cleaned out."

— DAISY LAMBERT
East Earl

Hoe Cakes for George Washington

9 cups white cornmeal

1 1/4 tsp. dry yeast

1 large egg

1 pitcher of warm water

1 Tbsp. butter

1 cup honey

Mix 4 cups white cornmeal, 1 1/4 tsp. dry yeast, and pour in warm water to mix (like a pancake batter). Cover and set on the stove overnight. Next morning pour in more cornmeal and add the egg and enough warm water to the consistency of pancake batter. Cover again and set aside for 20 minutes.

Prepare the griddle or skillet with melted butter until water sprinkled on it, beads up. Spoon batter on to the hot griddle and cook like a pancake.

Serve warm with butter and honey just like a modern day pancake.

— RAY & MEGAN SMECKER
Churchtown

Welshcakes

8 oz. self raising flour

a pinch of salt

1 tsp. mixed spice

1/4 cup butter or margarine

2 oz. lard

3 oz. caster sugar (white coarse sugar)

3 oz. mixed currants and sultanas (golden raisins)

1 large egg, beaten

Sieve the flour, salt and spice in to a mixing bowl. Rub in the fats until the mixture looks like fine breadcrumbs. Add the sugar and dried fruit. Pour in the beaten egg and stir to make a fairly firm dough.

On a floured board, roll or press the dough out to about 1/4 inch thick. Cut into discs with a 1 1/2 inch or 2 inch cutter.

Bake the Welshcakes on a medium hot griddle, turning once, until golden brown on both sides but still a little soft in the middle. *Makes 12 cakes*

"Melanie was born when the Greens lived in the East Tenant House."

— GAYNOR GREEN
Bowmansville

The backyard garden at the Inn at Twin Linden is the perfect place for guests to relax, read a book, and savor a morning cup of coffee. The garden hosts a water garden and a beautiful view of the surrounding landscape.

Apple Cinnamon French Toast

4 Tbsp. butter

4 large baking apples, peeled, cored and sliced

1 cup dark brown sugar, packed

2 Tbsp. dark corn syrup

1 tsp. cinnamon

6 slices homemade cinnamon swirl bread

3 large eggs

1 cup milk

1 tsp. vanilla

Melt butter over medium heat. Add apples slices and cook, stirring occasionally until tender. Add brown sugar, corn syrup and cinnamon to apples. Cook, stirring until brown sugar dissolves. Pour apples mixture into a greased 13 X 9-inch pyrex dish. Spread to an even layer.

Cut bread into 6 equal slices. Arrange bread slices in one layer on top of apples.

In medium bowl beat eggs, milk and vanilla extract until well mixed. Pour over bread slices. Cover with plastic wrap and refrigerate overnight.

Next day, preheat oven to 350 degrees. Remove plastic wrap and bake French toast 40 to 50 minutes until lightly browned and puffy. Check after 20 minutes. If browning too quickly, cover lightly with foil. Let stand at least 5 full minutes before cutting. *Serves 6*

If bread is too puffy, cut seam mid-way through cooking. This recipe freezes well after baking.

"What makes this recipe special for me is the fact that I get to visit with Rachel, Sadie's Bakery owner, and her beautiful garden while I'm buying her delicious cinnamon bread!"

"I serve this breakfast predominantly in the late summer and into early winter so that I can get the best local apples I can find! And Hoover's Farm Stand and Zimmerman's Orchards, both are right here in Churchtown/Goodville, are two of my stops for fruits and vegetables."

— CHRIS FARR
Churchtown Inn

Churchtown Inn Fresh Peach Bread

1 1/2 cups sugar

1/2 cup shortening (Crisco)

2 extra large eggs

2 1/4 cups fresh peach puree
(approx. 6 to 8 medium
sized peaches)

2 cups flour (unsifted)

1 tsp. cinnamon

1 tsp. baking soda

1 tsp. baking powder

1/4 tsp. salt

1 tsp. vanilla

1 cup toasted large chop
local black walnuts (can
use pecans or walnuts)

Cream sugar and shortening together. Add eggs and mix thoroughly. To make peach puree, quickly wash peaches, slice, leaving skin on, and puree in a food processor (leave some large peach chunks) Add peach puree and dry ingredients to batter. Add vanilla and chopped nuts and stir until blended. Pour into two regular size loaf pans (about 5 x 9 inches) that have been well greased and floured – don't skip this step.

Bake at 325 degrees for 55 minutes to one hour. Let bread cool a few minutes before removing from pan.

"Everyone has their favorite farm stands. I have five I like to visit regularly throughout the growing seasons. That way I get to catch up with what happened over the winter. I send my guests to their stands, our guests get to take home some of Lancaster County's best. Again, what makes the difference in this bread is the fresh, local ingredients."

— CHRIS FARR
Churchtown Inn

Fruit Stuffed French Toast for Two

4 slices of your favorite
bread

1/4 cup Neufchâtel cheese
or cream cheese

2 large eggs

2 Tbsp. milk

2 tsp. sugar

1/4 tsp. cinnamon

favorite pie filling

syrup

powdered sugar

Spread cream cheese on one side of each slice of bread. Spoon pie filling on two of the slices of bread. Put the other two slices on top. You can use extra cream cheese around the edges to keep the bread sticking together if needed.

Mix together milk, eggs, sugar and cinnamon in a bowl big enough to dip the bread. Fry on counter top grill or in a skillet sprayed with cooking spray for 2 minutes per side. Top with syrup and powdered sugar and serve.

— VERA JANE NEWSWANGER
Morgantown

Wonderful Baked French Toast

1 cup brown sugar

1/2 cup butter

2 Tbsp. light corn syrup

12 slices of bread

1/4 cup sugar

1 tsp. cinnamon

6 large eggs

1 1/2 cup milk

1 tsp. vanilla

walnuts or pecans

Place brown sugar, butter and corn syrup in a pan. Bring to boil and add a cup or more of nuts. Remove from heat and pour in to greased 9 X 13-inch cake pan. Place 6 slices of bread on the bottom of the pan covering the nut mixture.

Meanwhile, mix sugar and cinnamon and sprinkle 1/2 of this mixture on top of the bread. Then top with the rest of the bread slices and then the rest of the sugar mixture. Mix milk and eggs in a bowl and pour over the bread. Let stand overnight or for a few hours.

Bake at 350 degrees for about 1/2 hour.

— MARY ANN GOOD
Terre Hill

Auntie's Zucchini Pie

3 to 5 zucchini squash, sliced

1/2 cup sliced onion

1/2 cup butter

1 pkg. crescent rolls

2 tsp. mustard

2 large eggs, beaten

8 oz. grated swiss cheese

4 tsp. fresh chopped parsley

1/2 tsp. dill weed

1/2 tsp. salt

1/4 tsp. fresh ground pepper

1 tsp. garlic powder

Melt butter in a large fry pan. Add the zucchini and onion. Cook until soft and tender.

Spread the crescent rolls in a 10-inch pie plate like a crust with a large edge. Mix all of the other ingredients in a large bowl. Fold in the cooked vegetables. Pour into pie shell (it will be juicy).

Bake at 350 degrees for about 45 minutes or until center is firm.

"Great for buffet or Italian dinner. Easy presentation to take anywhere."

— SUSAN MARRIS
Marris Hill Farm

Breakfast Casserole

1/2 lb. chipped ham

3 medium potatoes, cooked
in skins and cooled,
peeled and grated

1 cup cream cheese or
Velveeta®

4 large eggs, scrambled and
slightly cooked

parsley flakes

In a 1 1/2 quart greased casserole dish, layer potatoes, slightly cooked eggs, ham and cheese. Top with parsley. Bake at 375 degrees for 15 minutes.

"This is a great recipe to make ahead for guests."

— VERA JANE NEWSWANGER
Morgantown

Breakfast Pie

8 slices bacon , cooked crisp
and crumbled

1/2 cup corn flake crumbs

1 Tbsp. bacon drippings

5 eggs

2 1/2 cups frozen hash
browns

1 1/2 cups shredded
Monterey Jack cheese

1/2 cup cottage cheese

1/3 cup milk

1 green onion, thinly sliced

Combine corn flake crumbs and bacon drippings; set a side. Beat eggs until foamy.

Stir in remainder of ingredients. Pour into greased 9-inch pie pan. Sprinkle with corn flake mixture. Cover and refrigerate overnight.

Bake uncovered at 325 degrees for 50 minutes. Recipe can be doubled and baked in a 13 X 9-inch pan. *Serves 6*

— LINCOLN BOONE BED & BREAKFAST
Narvon

Eggs & Sausage Casserole

1 lb. mild sausage

6 large eggs, beaten

1 1/2 cup milk

1 tsp. dry mustard

3 slices white bread, cubed

8 oz. mild cheddar cheese,
cubed

dash of salt

Brown the sausage and drain. Throw everything together in a buttered 9 X 13-inch pan.

Bake at 350 degrees for 45 to 60 minutes. This casserole may be prepared the night before and baked the next day. *Serves 6*

— MARYANN OESTREICH
Narvon

Ham & Egg Casserole

8 slices of white bread with crust removed

1 cup shredded mild mozzarella cheese

1 cup shredded sharp cheddar cheese

6 large beaten eggs

1 tsp. dry mustard

4 cups milk

1 cup cubed boiled ham

Butter a 9 X 13-inch pan. Place in layers the bread, cheese and ham.

Beat eggs. Combine the mustard and milk. Pour over all the layers. Refrigerate overnight.

Bake at 350 degrees for 1 hour.

— MARYANN OESTREICH
Narvon

Scrambled Eggs with Peppers, Leeks & Cockles

2 red and 2 green peppers, roasted and cut in strips

olive oil

4 slices bread

2 cloves garlic, halved

8 large eggs

1/4 pint double cream

salt and fresh ground pepper to taste

1 leek washed and cut in strips

4 oz. fresh cockles (tiny clams)

To roast and skin peppers: grill whole peppers, turning until skin blisters and blackens all over. Place charred peppers in a polyethylene bag for 5 minutes. Remove from bag and peel away skin, which will be quite loose. Halve peppers, seed and cut in strips.

Rub the slices of bread with cut garlic and fry in olive oil until crisp. Drain well. Whisk the eggs and cream together with some black pepper.

Cook the leek very gently in olive oil. Add half the prepared peppers, egg mixture, a little salt and the cockles and gently scramble. *Serves 4*

Serve the eggs on the garlic toast. Decorate with the reserved strips of pepper.

— GAYNOR GREEN
Bowmansville

Mexican Egg Stack

1 1/2 lb. fresh Chorizo sausage

4 oz. cream cheese

1/2 cup milk

8 eggs

1/4 cup red bell pepper, chopped

2 Tbsp. sliced green onions with tops

salt and pepper to taste

1 Tbsp. butter or margarine

8 (1/4 in. slices) fresh tomato

1 1/4 cups shredded sharp cheddar cheese or Mexican blend cheeses (without seasoning)

6 small (4-in. diameter x 2-in. deep) spring form pans (sides only)

Preheat oven to 400 degrees. Brown Chorizo in sauté skillet and drain.

Place cream cheese and milk in bowl. Microwave on high for 1 minute. Whisk until smooth. Let cool slightly. Add eggs, salt and pepper to bowl; whisk to combine. Wisk the cream cheese mixture, chopped bell pepper and onion into the egg mixture.

Melt butter in 10 to 12-inch skillet over medium-low heat, and scramble eggs until set, but still moist. Place eggs in a sieve or colander to cool. (Draining in a colander will prevent liquid from collecting on bottom of eggs from the steam) Place closed spring form pans on a parchment lined baking sheet. Divide sausage evenly among pans. Top with prepared eggs evenly in each pan, spreading and pressing down lightly to fill the pan. Top each with a slice of tomato. Sprinkle each with shredded cheese. Bake for 8 to 10 minutes or until heated through. Slide a thin spatula between parchment paper and spring pan and carefully lift onto a plate. Run a thin knife around inside of spring pan to loosen sides of pan from egg, release spring pan and remove. Serves 6.

Serve with a side of pan fried diced potatoes, a small dollop of each guacamole, sour cream, fresh tomato salsa and toasted tortilla triangles. Mix it up by using other sausages and cheeses.

— THE INN AT TWIN LINDEN
Churchtown

Breakfast Cake

CRUMBS

4 cups flour

2 cups sugar

1 cup creamed butter

1 tsp. baking soda

1 tsp. cream of tartar

FILLING

4 large eggs

1 cup sour milk (1 cup milk
with 1 tsp. vinegar)

1 tsp. vanilla

Combine ingredients to make crumbs. Save 1/2 cup for the top of cake.

Mix filling ingredients and add to crumb mixture. Pour into a greased 9 X 13-inch baking dish and bake at 350 degrees for 1 hour.

"Family recipe passed down from my Aunt Anastasia Ridilla, who was 92 years old in 2008."

— MARYANN OESTREICH
Narvon

Russian Coffee Cake

CAKE

3/4 cup butter

1 1/2 cups sugar

5 egg yolks

1 1/2 tsp. vanilla

3 cups cake flour

1 1/2 tsp. baking soda

1 1/2 tsp. baking powder

3/4 pint sour cream

5 egg whites

FILLING

3/4 cup finely chopped
pecans

1 tsp. cinnamon

3/4 cup light brown sugar

1 1/2 tsp. softened butter

Cream the butter and sugar. Beat in egg yolks and vanilla. Sift the dry ingredients together and mix into the batter. Add the sour cream. Whip egg whites to stiff peaks and gently fold into the batter. Pour half of batter into greased pan.

Mix filling ingredients by hand till combined. Sprinkle half of the filling on top. Add remaining batter and sprinkle rest of filling on top.

Bake one hour at 300 degrees.

"This is a family recipe from the Dumchock's of Hickory Ridge, (near Shamokin) PA."

— MARYANN OESTREICH
Narvon

Yiyetchnik

1 dozen large eggs, beaten

1 quart of milk

pinch of sugar

pinch of salt

Cook all ingredients in a double broiler until no milk is left. Mixture should become lumpy. Line a colander with cheesecloth and pour in egg mixture. Drain. Twist cloth to form a small cheese ball and tie. Hang in the refrigerator for 4 to 6 hours. Great served with red beet horseradish.

"Russian/Ukrainian recipe served mainly at Easter. I learned to make this as a girl with my mother, Susan Burka Dumchock."

— MARYANN OESTREICH
Narvon

Alan's Banana Bread

1 1/2 cups barley flour

2 tsp. baking powder

2 tsp. baking soda

1/4 tsp. ground cinnamon

1/8 tsp. salt

1 heaping tsp. soy flour + 1 Tbsp. water, mixed (for soy-free version, use 1 1/2 tsp. Ener-G® egg replacer + 2 Tbsp. water, mixed)

1 cup mashed ripe bananas (approximately 2 medium sized bananas)

3/4 cup sugar

1/4 cup cooking oil

1/2 tsp. vanilla

1/2 cup chopped walnuts (optional)

large-crystal sugar (natural demerara cane sugar, optional)

Grease bottom and halfway up the sides of an 8 X 4 X 2-inch loaf pan. In medium bowl, combine flour, baking powder, baking soda, cinnamon and 1/8 teaspoon salt. Make a large well in center of dry ingredients and set aside.

In a separate small bowl, mix soy flour and water (or Ener-G® egg replacer and water). Mash bananas directly in small bowl with the egg replacement mixture. Add sugar, oil and vanilla and mix well. Add wet banana mixture all at once to dry mixture and stir just until moistened. If desired, add chopped nuts, and fold in gently, being careful not to over-mix the batter. Spoon batter into pan. If desired, sprinkle cane sugar on top of batter for a sweet crunchy addition to the bread. Bake at 350 degrees for 45 to 55 minutes or until wooden toothpick inserted near center comes out clean.

Cool on wire rack for 10 minutes. Remove loaf from pan and cool completely on wire rack. Wrap and store overnight before slicing. This recipe works well as muffins, just reduce baking time to about 20 to 25 minutes.

— WASHINGTON INN
Churchtown

Bara Brith (Currant or Speckled Bread)

2 cups wheatmeal flour

1 tsp. yeast

4 oz. brown molasses sugar

4 oz. butter, melted in 1/4 pint milk

3 oz. seedless golden raisins (sultanas)

3 oz. currants

1 oz. candied peel

1 tsp. salt

1 tsp. mixed spice

Cream the yeast with some of the milk and add to the flour and salt. Work into a dough with the milk, leave to rise until doubled in bulk about 1 hour.

Add sugar, spices, fruit and mix well. Place in a buttered loaf tin and leave to rise about 45 minutes.

Bake in hot oven for 20 to 30 minutes and glaze with sugar syrup when cool.

Best eaten in thin slices with plenty of butter.

— GAYNOR GREEN
Bowmansville

Cornbread

1 1/2 cup sugar

3/4 cup shortening

2 cups sour milk

2 large eggs

1 tsp. baking soda

3 tsp. baking powder

1 tsp. salt

2 cups cornmeal

2 cups flour

Cream sugar and shortening. Add eggs and sour milk. Combine all the dry ingredients and then mix with the wet ingredients. Pour into a greased 9 X 13-inch pan and sprinkle with a little sugar on top. Bake uncovered at 350 degrees for 35 minutes or until golden brown.

— ROSE NEWSWANGER
Narvon

Sugarless Corn Bread

4 large eggs

1 1/3 cup milk

2/3 cup melted butter

2 2/3 cup flour

1 1/3 cup cornmeal

1 Tbsp. baking powder

1 tsp. salt

Beat the eggs and add milk and butter. Sift the flour, cornmeal, baking powder and salt. Make a well in the dry ingredients and add the liquid mixture. Stir together till moist. Pour into a greased pan or muffin tin. Bake at 375 degrees for 25 to 30 minutes.

— LINDA BOYER
Narvon

Grandma's Popovers

1 cup milk

2 large eggs

1 cup flour

1/2 tsp. salt

1 Tbsp. melted butter

Preheat oven to 450 degrees. Place 8 to 10 glass custard cups on a baking sheet with an edge. Spray the cups with oil. Place cups and tray in oven to warm. Whisk eggs one at a time into the milk. Mix the flour, salt and melted butter. Whisk the dry and wet ingredients together. Do not over mix.

Pour mixture into warmed custard dishes about 1/3 full. May also use one greased glass casserole baking dish.

Bake 35 to 40 minutes until golden brown. Do not open the oven more than once during baking. Keep an eye on time/temperature. Do not over bake.

This recipe doubles easily.

"These were first made in my family by my maternal grandmother, Bess Eggleston in the 1930's. These were always a wonderful, delicious treat served morning, noon and night for family and guests. Always good with butter and jam but also great with gravy dishes."

— SUSAN MARRIS
Churchtown Farm Inn

Funnel Cake

2 beaten eggs

1 1/2 cups milk

2 cups sifted flour

1 tsp. baking powder

1/2 tsp. salt

2 cups cooking oil

Deep fry fat at 360 degrees. Combine eggs and milk, set aside. Sift flour, baking powder and salt. Add to egg mixture. Beat until smooth. Test to see if it can flow through funnel. If too thick, add milk. If too thin, add flour. Heat the oil in an 8 inch skillet. Pour 1/2 cup batter into funnel holding finger over open end. Release and drizzle batter into hot oil. Fry until golden, then turn and fry other side. Drain. Serve with powdered sugar.

"Leah McClure passed this recipe along."

— LINDA BOYER
Narvon

Ol Susannah's Bread

2 cups flour

1 tsp. baking soda

1/2 cup butter

1 cup sugar

2 large eggs

1 to 2 apples peeled, cut up

2 bananas mashed

2 Tbsp. sliced almonds

1 tsp. cinnamon & sugar

Foil line 1 large bread pan or 2 small pans. Cream together butter and sugar until fluffy. Add eggs and beat together. Add flour and soda and blend. Mix in all of the fruit of your choice. Spread into pans. Top with almonds and cinnamon sugar topping.

Bake at 375 degrees for 20 minutes. Then turn oven to 350 degrees for 60 minutes or until firm in the middle.

"Always a quick and easy gift pleaser and never fail delicious!"

— SUSAN MARRIS
Churchtown Farm Inn

Orange Zucchini Bread

3 large eggs

1 cup vegetable oil

1 tsp. vanilla

1 orange pureed in blender

2 cups grated zucchini

2 cups sugar

3 cups flour

1/4 tsp. nutmeg

1 tsp. salt

3/4 tsp. cinnamon

1/2 tsp. baking powder

1/2 tsp. baking soda

Mix all the dry ingredients together. Separately mix all the wet ingredients together. Blend mixtures together. Bake in two greased loaf pans at 325 degrees for 1 hour.

— SHARON COLON
Narvon

French Bread

butter and cornmeal or
farina to dust baking
sheet

1 pkg. active dry yeast

1/4 cup warm water (110 to
115 degrees)

1 1/2 tsp. salt

3/4 cup hot water

1/2 cup sifted flour

3 1/4 cups sifted flour

1 egg white, slightly beaten

1 Tbsp. water

Lightly butter 15 1/2 X 12-inch baking sheet and
sprinkle with cornmeal or farina. Soften 1 package of
dry yeast in the 1/4 cup warm water. Let yeast stand 5
to 10 minutes. Meanwhile, put the salt into a large bowl.
Pour 3/4 cup hot water over the salt. When mixture is
lukewarm, blend in 1/2 cup sifted flour and beat until
smooth. Stir softened yeast and add, mixing well. Add
about half the 3 1/4 cups flour to yeast mixture and beat
until very smooth. Mix in enough remaining flour to
make a soft dough. Turn mixture onto a lightly floured
surface. Allow to rest 5 to 10 minutes.

Knead the dough by folding the opposite side toward
you. Using heels of hands gently push dough away.
Give dough a quarter turn. Repeat kneading process
rhythmically until dough is smooth and elastic, 5 to 8
minutes, using as little additional flour as possible.

Select a deep bowl just large enough to allow dough to
double. Warm it or rinse in hot water and dry; butter
lightly. Shape dough into a smooth ball and place in
bowl.

Grease surface lightly by turning ball in bottom of bowl.
Turn greased side up. Cover with waxed paper and a
towel. Let rise in a warm place, about 80 degrees until
doubled, about 1 1/2 to 2 hours.

Punch down with fist. Fold edge toward center and turn
dough over. Cover. Let rise again until almost doubled,
about 45 minutes. Punch down again; turn onto a lightly
floured surface.

Roll dough into a 14 X 8-inch oblong. Roll up tightly
into a long slender loaf. Pinch ends to seal. With palms
of hands, gently roll dough back and forth, pulling to
lengthen and taper the ends.

(continued on next page)

Place diagonally on prepared baking sheet. Make diagonal cuts with a sharp knife at 2 inch intervals, 1/4 inch deep. Brush with part of a mixture of the egg white slightly beaten and 1 tablespoon water. Cover loosely with a towel and set aside in a warm place until doubled.

Brush again with egg white mixture and bake at 425 degrees for 10 minutes. Brush again and reduce temperature to 375 degrees. Bake 15 minutes. Brush again. Continue baking about 20 minutes or until bread is golden brown. To increase crustiness, place a flat pan in bottom of oven and fill with boiling water at beginning of baking period.

"Freddy Rey makes this bread at the Shirktown Day in an original outdoor oven."

— FREDDY REY
   Elverson

Freddy Ray beside a brick oven at Shirktown days preparing ingredients to bake his french bread. The aroma of baking bread fills the surrounding area.

Pumpkin Bread

3 cups sugar

1 tsp. cinnamon

1/2 tsp. salt

1 tsp. baking soda

3 1/2 cups all purpose flour

1 cup vegetable oil

2/3 cup water

2 cups cooked pumpkin

4 large eggs, beaten

Mix together all of the dry ingredients. Add all of the liquid ingredients to the dry and mix with a wooden spoon (do not use a mixer). For variety add chopped nuts or raisins.

Bake at 350 degrees for 1 1/2 hours in 3 buttered loaf pans, 8 1/2 X 4 1/2-inch. This recipe makes 3 loaves of bread. Let set for about 10 minutes to cool covered with a cloth before serving.

— LORELLE WEAVER
Narvon

Pecan Pie Muffins

1 cup firmly packed light brown sugar

1/2 cup all purpose flour

1/2 cup coarsely chopped pecans

2 large beaten eggs

2/3 cup softened butter (almost melted)

Preheat oven to 350 degrees. Line muffin tins with paper muffin liners. In a bowl, stir together brown sugar, flour and pecans. In a separate bowl, beat the eggs and butter together until smooth. Stir into the dry ingredients till just combined.

Spoon batter into muffin cups and fill about two thirds full. Bake for 20 to 25 minutes. Cool on a wire rack. Before baking decorate the top of each muffin with a half pecan. *Makes 12 muffins*

— MARY A. PARMER
Narvon

Quick Muffins

2 cups flour

4 tsp. baking powder

1/3 cup brown or white sugar

1 cup milk

1 large egg

1/3 cup oil

1/3 cup granola

1/3 cup sliced almonds

1 tsp. cinnamon & sugar

fruit of your choice: 2 apples peeled and cut up, handful of craisins, 1/2 cup blueberries or black raspberries or cut up one peach to replace one apple.

Put flour, baking powder and sugar into bowl. Combine milk, egg and oil in another bowl. Pour wet ingredients into the dry and mix. Fold in the fresh fruit.

Spoon mixture into greased muffin tins. Divide the almonds and granola evenly over the top. Sprinkle with cinnamon and sugar. Bake at 400 degrees for about 25 minutes. Do not over bake. *Makes 12 large muffins*

"Easy, never fail treat!"

— SUSAN MARRIS
Marris Hill Farm

Roasted Corn Muffins

1/4 cup softened butter

1/3 cup sugar

1 large egg

2 tsp. honey

1/4 tsp. salt

3/4 cup flour

1/2 cup yellow cornmeal

1/4 tsp. baking powder

1/4 cup milk

1/2 cup frozen corn

In a small mixing bowl, cream the butter and sugar. Beat in the egg, honey and salt. Combine the flour, cornmeal and baking powder. Add to the creamed mixture alternately with the milk. Fold in the frozen corn. Fill greased or paper lined muffin cups two thirds full. Bake at 400 degrees for 20 to 25 minutes or until toothpick comes out clean.

— SONDRA SIMMERS
Narvon

Cinnamon Twists

TWISTS

1 cup sour cream

2 Tbsp. vegetable oil

3 Tbsp. sugar

1/8 tsp. baking soda

1 tsp. salt

1 large egg, unbeaten

1 pkg. yeast

1/4 cup warm water

3 cups flour

2 Tbsp. soft butter

1/3 cup brown sugar

2 tsp. cinnamon

ICING

3/4 cup confectioner's sugar

1 Tbsp. milk

pinch of salt

1/2 tsp. vanilla

Dissolve yeast in warm water. Bring sour cream to a boil in a large saucepan. Remove from heat. Add vegetable oil, sugar, baking soda and salt. Stir until blended, cool to lukewarm. Add egg and yeast. Stir until well blended. Mix in flour and knead lightly. Cover and let rise for 1/2 to 1 hour.

Roll dough 1/4 inch thick in a rectangle 6 X 24 inches. Spread the entire surface with the soft butter. Sprinkle half the dough lengthwise, with the mixture of brown sugar and cinnamon.

Bring unused half of dough over and press firmly. Cut dough into 24 (1 ") strips. Take each strip of dough at both ends and twist in opposite directions, forming spiral sticks.

Place on greased baking sheet about 2 inches apart. Pressing both ends firmly and flatten to sheet, cover with a clean cloth and let rise until very light, about 1 hour.

Bake 12 to 15 minutes at 350 degrees. Glaze with icing while warm.

— A.M.RINGLER
Narvon

Sweet Dough (Futch-keys)

12 cups flour

1 scant cup sugar

4 large beaten eggs

1 cup shortening

3 cups lukewarm milk

1 large quick yeast cake

Place yeast in 1/2 cup lukewarm water with 1 teaspoon sugar for 5 minutes. Sift flour into a large bowl and add sugar and salt. Make a well and add the beaten eggs, shortening, milk and yeast in water. Mix well until a very soft dough forms. Let rise 1 hour, then cut in to four portions and let stand for 10 minutes. Flatten with your hand and cut 1" thick slices. Let rise until thick again.

Fry in deep, hot fat until golden brown. Serve after rolling in powdered sugar.

"Ukrainian recipe: The word futch-keys means 'cheaters' since these are doughnuts without holes. I can remember making these with my Dad, John Dumchock, growing up in Singac, NJ."

— MARYANN OESTREICH
Narvon

Harvest Potato Doughnuts

1 cup potatoes

1 1/2 Tbsp. shortening

2 large eggs

1/2 cup sweet milk

2 1/2 cup flour

3/4 cup sugar

1 Tbsp. baking powder, cinnamon and/or vanilla

Peel and cook the potatoes until soft. Then mash in potato water. To 1 cup of mashed potatoes add shortening, eggs and milk. Set aside. Sift all dry ingredients and add to the potato mixture. Add vanilla. Dough will be soft. Roll out to about 3/4 inch thick and cut with doughnut cutter. Fry in deep fat at 365 degrees until brown. Drain the doughnuts on paper towels. Dust with powdered sugar and cinnamon.

Hint: Some potatoes are more watery than others. Add flour to mix until the dough starts to leave the sides of the bowl like bread dough.

"Mammy Mint's haying midmorning treat. Great anytime!"

— LINDA BOYER
Narvon

Ruth's Sticky Buns

BUNS

1 pkg. of yeast

1/4 cup lukewarm water

1 cup scalded milk (cool)

1/4 cup shortening

1/4 cup sugar

1 tsp. salt

3 1/4 to 3 1/2 cups flour

GOO

1 cup brown sugar

1/2 cup butter

2 Tbsp. molasses

nuts

Soften yeast in lukewarm water. Mix milk, shortening, sugar, salt and 1 cup of flour. Beat with spoon. Then add yeast, egg and remaining flour. Knead till smooth and elastic. Let rise till double in size. Punch down. Roll out and spread with 2 Tbsp. soft butter and 1/2 cup brown sugar and a little cinnamon, if desired.

Roll as a jelly roll and slice in to 1 inch thick rolls.

Heat brown sugar, butter and molasses. Add nuts and a little water to thin. Do not boil. Just enough to dissolve and blend. Pour cooled goo in greased 9 X 13-inch pan. Place sticky buns on top and let rise till double. Bake at 350 degrees for 20 minutes.

— RUTH GOOD
East Earl

Judy's Sticky Buns

1 loaf of frozen white bread dough

1/4 cup butter

3 Tbsp. vanilla pudding (not instant)

1 tsp. cinnamon

1/2 cup brown sugar

1 cup chopped pecans

1 cup raisins

Spray a 9 X 9-inch pan with oil. Sprinkle nuts and raisins in the bottom of the pan. Cut dough into 9 pieces and place evenly in pan.

Heat the remaining ingredients till combined and pour over the dough. Cover with plastic wrap and let rise in refrigerator overnight. Bake at 350 degrees for 30 minutes. Cool slightly. Invert to serve.

— JUDY SINCLAIR
Narvon

Judy's sticky bun recipe won the 'Best of the Sticky Bun' contest at Historic Poole Forge Heritage Day 2008.

Shrewsbury Biscuits

3/4 cup butter

3/4 cup sugar

1 large egg

2 cups self raising flour

1 Tbsp. water

1 tsp. vanilla

1 tsp. grated lemon rind

Cream butter and sugar until soft and white. Gradually add egg and flavoring. Work in the water to form a soft dough. Roll the dough out 1/8 inch thick and cut into shapes. Bake 15 to 20 minutes or until light brown at 350 degrees. *Makes 16 biscuits*

— EDNA SWEITZER
East Earl

Biscuits & Chocolate Gravy

BISCUITS

1 cup milk

2 cups self rising flour

3 Tbsp. miracle whip or mayonaise

GRAVY

1/2 cup flour

3/4 cup sugar

6 Tbsp. cocoa

1/4 cup butter

4 cups milk

1 tsp. vanilla

Mix biscuit ingredients together and let rise for 1/2 hour. Form into biscuits. Bake at 350 degrees for the first 10 minutes and then 400 degrees for 20 minutes or until golden brown.

For gravy, mix the dry ingredients together. Melt butter in a sauce pan and add the dry ingredients. Stir till smooth. Add the milk and vanilla slowly. Cook until thickened like pudding. Spoon over biscuits and serve.

"When my husband was in the service he met a man from Oklahoma whose wife was an excellent cook. She shared this recipe with us."

— SHIRLEY WEIDMAN
Narvon

APPETIZERS & BEVERAGES INDEX

APPETIZERS & BEVERAGES
Farming Along the Conestoga

HOME GROWN
BEANS
TOMATOES
ASPARAGUS
STRAWBERRIES
SUGAR PEAS
CAULIFLOWER
BAKED
636

CHAPTER SPONSORED BY

Churchtown Veterinary Clinic

This chapter is dedicated to the many generations of farm families who have lived and toiled in the Eastern Conestoga Valley. Their stewardship through the centuries has yielded some of the most efficiently and reliably productive agricultural land in the world. May divine providence continue to bless this bountiful land and its caretakers in perpetuity.

Farming Along the Conestoga

Mother Nature blessed us with the mighty Susquehanna river and all the streams and tributaries that supply its source. She blessed us with rich tillable soil and gentle rolling hills. The Susquehanna is rich in history as it is in breathtaking scenery, spectacular wildlife and year round recreational activities. From the earliest Native Americans to the Industrial Revolution, so much of America can be traced to this waterway.

The Little Conestoga Creek is a tributary of the Conestoga River and part of the Lower Susquehanna river system in Pennsylvania. This stream system flows northeast to southwest for approximately 50 miles beginning in southern Berks county, meandering through Lancaster County and finally spilling into the Susquehanna river at Safe Harbor just sixteen miles north of the Pennsylvania-Maryland border. The principal tributaries of the Conestoga river are Cocalico Creek, Mill Creek and Little Conestoga Creek. They all drain into the Conestoga River watershed in this order. The Conestoga watershed is comprised of 114 stream miles and they drain a watershed area of approximately 217 square miles.

The name of the creek comes from the Susquehannock "Kanestoge", meaning "at the place of the immersed pole". This was the name of the principal Susquehannock Indian settlement, now Conestoga, Pennsylvania. During the 1600's nearly 2000 inhabitants occupied the area around the village of Conestoga, but by 1763 the Susquehannocks were compelled to move to the Ohio area or be killed by anti-Indian vigilantes.

The first steamboat in America floated on the Conestoga River in 1763. In the 19th century the popularity of the Conestoga wagon enhanced the recognition of the stream and Lancaster County. The wagon assisted the transportation of settlers and goods throughout the east and later transported a generation of Americans to the western frontier. The word Conestoga was also used for naming a cigar. So many cigars were made in this watershed during the late 1800s that a local cigar was named the Conestoga and later called the "stogie" throughout the United States.

Many parts of the Conestoga hardly seem the size generally designated to be called a river but because of lobbying in the late 19th century insisting that any stream holding scheduled commercial transport should be called a river, and so steamboat service to a local amusement park (probably Rocky Springs) along its banks qualified. So the designation of Conestoga river caught on and has remained to this day.

A large part of the land along the Conestoga has traditionally been used for agriculture. Much of this pastural land was originally farmed by Pennsylvania German farmers. They built a host of covered bridges to span the Conestoga. They include Hunsecker's Mill Covered Bridge, Pinetown Bushong's Mill Covered Bridge, Zook's Mill Covered Bridge, and Poole Forge Covered Bridge. Another bridge, Kurtz's Mill Covered Bridge was removed to a new location.

During the 1800s many grist mills were built along the Conestoga in order to power the large water wheels and take advantage of the waterway for transporting goods and services. Many dams were built to control the water and increase productivity at the mills. Some dams were built to control wildlife. In Caernarvon township, one large dam was

Fishing in the Conestoga, near Churchtown.

constructed near Windsor Forge. It was 4-5 feet deep and held many fish. Local fishermen visited the dam area on a regular basis and took home many catfish, eels and trout to supplement their tables.

A great sport during this time was the catching of eels. When the dams were drained the community would come and fill their baskets with catfish, suckers and eels. The catching of the eels was a great sport and fun to watch by the community. The eels were so plentiful that in the Fall, when they headed down stream to breed, fishermen would place blownets across the Conestoga to catch them. In the Spring, the blownets were positioned up stream to catch the suckers as they headed up river to spawn. Because of the many dams the communities along the stream were well supplied with fish, eels, snappers and frogs. Frogs were very plentiful and an even greater sport than catching fish and eels. Between catching them at night by the light of a torch or tying red flannel to hooks and dangling them, the sport was always successful and fun. The brave souls who liked snappers could hunt them in the mud along the shores of the river.

Today, there still exists many dams along the Conestoga that impound its waters. Most of these dams are in disrepair and have been abandoned. There is active movement to remove more of these dams so the river may once again flow its course and encourage the abundance of fish and wildlife in and around its shores. Over the years with ungoverned fishing and the introduction of predatory fish like the German carp, the natural habitat of the native breeds was decimated. Another impairment to the Conestoga in the last century has been the excessive use of fertilizers and the increased quantity of animal and human waste causing the runoff to contaminate the stream. In recent years, great strides have been made to restore the watershed but time and education are needed to change the problem.

Rescuing Maggie McDowell.

During the 1972 Agnes hurricane that devastated this part of Lancaster county, the Conestoga overflowed its banks causing massive flooding and erosion. One story centers around Historic Poole Forge and a resident in the West Tenant house. Eighty plus year old, Maggie McDowell was forced to take shelter in the second floor because of rising water. After three unsuccessful boat rescues, she had to be rescued by climbing out the small second floor window on a plank suspended from the window to a large combine driven by Frank Weaver. George Martin (then Fire Chief) and John David Martin helped her across the plank and remembers her saying "never had so many men paid attention to me." The large combine was the only suitable piece of machinery able to tackle the job.

The vast areas running along both sides of the Conestoga include upland woods, mature forests, wooded wetlands, overgrown meadows and manicured agricultural fields. In mid-April to mid-May a diversity of native woodland wildflowers dots the landscape, including unusual species such as nodding trillium, bloodroot, and per foliate bellwort. Wildlife in and around the Conestoga has

George Miller in his cornfield early nineteen hundreds.

always been a rich source of food. Some 23 species of ducks, five species of geese, as well as loons, cormorants, and grebes can be observed in and around the creek. Herons, egrets, bitterns, rails, plovers, and sandpipers are also found. Nesting Bald Eagle, Osprey, hawks, red fox, and white-tailed deer are also present, as well as warblers during migration. Grassland birds, such as Bobolink and Eastern Meadow lark, are also common. The area supports game and non-game mammals, birds of prey, songbirds, waterfowl, snakes, turtles, frogs, toads, salamanders, newts, snakes, possums, skunks, shrews, moles, voles, raccoons, foxes, turkeys, pheasants, chipmunks, eagles, falcons, hawks, and bats.

What is it that makes our land so special? First is the climate. With few extremes and reliable rainfall, the long growing season gives us a great start. But the bottom line is the soil, and in order for it to continue to be productive, it requires hardworking knowledgeable farmers. Generations of farm families have dedicated their lives as caretakers of the land. Crop rotation, when, where, and how much fertilizer, control of water run off by contour plowing, cover crops, and no-till planting are methods of protecting and enriching the soil. When to plant, when to cut your hay and harvest the corn, are skills handed down from father to son. Add hard work and a love of what you do, and you have the keys to the success of farming in Lancaster County.

When Caernarvon Township decided to purchase the Poole Forge property, it was accomplishing several goals. One was finding a suitable property for a public park, but we also saw an opportunity to preserve a beautiful local historical landmark. Preserving our very

Twentieth century Lancaster County farm.

special township is a priority for our residents. As the eastern Gateway to Lancaster County, Caernarvon Township gives most visitors their first view of the beautiful, productive farmland in the county. Widely recognized as the most productive, non-irrigated land in the nation, the county is home to more than 5,000 farms. Blessed with an almost perfect climate for growing, and a respect for the land, generations of hardworking farmers have consistently produced higher yields per acre than almost anywhere in the world.

Caernarvon Township mirrors the rest of the county in that our farms are primarily dairy, but with a diversity that includes poultry, swine, beef, crops and vegetables. With produce stands at our doorsteps, greenhouses around the corner, and an ever-changing patchwork of crops, the township more than holds up its part of the "Garden Spot." Lancaster County is proud of its farming heritage and the optimistic outlook for farming in the future. One in five jobs are created through agriculture. The average Lancaster County farm boasts 85 acres and they rank first in the number of laying eggs, third in the number of horses, fourth in total number of farms and eighth in the number of cows. Lancaster County is number one in farm preservation. This last point is one which should give us all a great deal of satisfaction. Organizations such as The Agricultural Preserve Board, Lancaster Farmland Trust, and the Lancaster County Conservancy, all work tirelessly to keep farmlands, woodlands, and open space here forever in Lancaster County. These groups use public and private funds to do their work, and all have waiting lists. Our Township supports these organizations to preserve land in our township. The people of Lancaster County and the farmers themselves have worked very hard to keep the county doing what it does best - feeding people.

Caernarvon Township has 14,000 acres of land with 7,000 of those in an Agriculture Security Zone. With the majority of our farmers belonging to the Amish and Mennonite communities, we have the whole spectrum of farming technology. Strong and steady mules, powerful Belgian draft horses, or the latest tractor can all be seen in our fields. Caernarvon Township is committed to preserving our farmland, which in turn preserves the way of life we enjoy. Those of us who live in this area feel very blessed by the abundance that surrounds us. Not only do we benefit from a steady source of fresh food for ourselves, our production adds to the general economy in so many ways. Our farming community and its culture is the primary reason for the tourist economy of Lancaster County.

The Conestoga creek tributary that runs behind Churchtown has many tales and stories to share. Louis Trego of Churchtown remembers cutting ice blocks from the frozen dam across Boot Jack road and carrying them by sleds to the undertakers in town for use in their business. A few long time residents remember cutting blocks of ice from the creek to make homemade ice cream too. George Martin confesses his boyhood prank of hiding in the rafters of the Poole Forge covered bridge and dropping things down on people and trying to scare the horses as they came through the bridge. George and his friends liked to play under the bridge too. Ruthie Good and her friends vividly remember spending many summer afternoons swimming in the creek at the Boot Jack bridge and playing along its shore. Cathy Shirk shared a story she remembered about spending Memorial Day weekend along the shores of the creek. Her family and relatives would carry chairs and tables down to the creek along Boot Jack road. They would picnic and watch the guys shoot snakes.

When we read the stories and listen to the tales about the abundance of fish and wildlife that once occupied this beautiful stream, and view the beautiful and productive farms that surround the Conestoga, it seems only right to nurture the Conestoga and protect the farms of this wonderful community. This beautiful "Eastern Gateway to Lancaster County" must remain a place of beauty, bounty and enjoyment for all.

Barbara's Popcorn

2 cups light brown sugar

1/2 cup molasses (Ole Barrel Syrup®)

2 Tbsp. butter

1 gallon popped corn

Boil together the sugar, molasses and butter for about 2 1/2 to 3 minutes. Pour popcorn into hot syrup while on the stove. Coat the corn and spread on cookie sheet. Break apart after the corn is cooled.

"A favorite treat of Lorraine's."

— LORRAINE RAFFENSPERGER
BARBARA F. ZOOK
Blue Ball

Cracker Jacks

1/2 cup butter

1 cup granulated sugar

1/2 cup white corn syrup

1 tsp. vanilla

1 tsp. baking soda

2 (10 oz.) Ritz® peanut butter bits

16 oz. roasted peanuts

Mix 2 boxes Ritz bits and roasted peanuts in a large bowl. Boil butter, sugar and corn syrup for 5 min. Take off stove and add vanilla and the baking soda. Pour over the Ritz bits and peanuts and coat thoroughly. Spread on a non-stick sheet (can spray lightly). Bake 1 hour at 250 degrees.

— SHIRLEY WEIDMAN
Narvon

Delicious Graham Snacks

1/2 cup butter

1/2 cup margarine

1/2 cup granulated sugar

1 pack of graham crackers

crushed nuts (pecans, almonds, or walnuts)

Break graham crackers into fourths and put on cookie sheet. Melt butter, margarine, and sugar and boil for 3 minutes. Pour over crackers, sprinkle nuts over top and bake at 350 degrees for 9 minutes. Place on wax paper to cool.

— KELLY SIEDHOF
Narvon

Seasoned Pretzels

18 oz. small pretzels

1 pkg. Hidden Valley Dry Ranch Dressing® mix

1 tsp. lemon pepper

1 tsp. garlic powder

1 tsp. dill weed

1 cup vegetable oil

Spread pretzels on cookie sheet and pour oil over. Mix the dry ingredients and sprinkle over the oiled pretzels. Mix thoroughly. Heat oven to 325 degrees and bake for 15 minutes, stirring every 5 minutes. (The pretzels can be put into a zip lock bag, pour in the oil and mix till coated, then add the dry ingredients and shake. It makes it easier and less messy to mix.)

— Vera Jane Newsanger
Morgantown

Spiced Pecans

2 cups pecan halves

1/2 cup light brown sugar

4 Tbsp. heavy cream

Blend sugar and heavy cream until smooth. Add pecans and mix till coated. Spread on greased cookie sheet and bake at 350 degrees for about 20 minutes. Stir at 10 minutes. Remove from cookie sheet to cool.

"Great for gifts and after dinner treat!"

— Lorraine Raffensperger
Blue Ball

Artichoke Dip

2 (14 oz.) cans artichokes

1 1/2 cup Hellman's® mayonnaise

3/4 cup parmesan cheese

1 cup grated mozzarella cheese

1 small onion chopped fine (or 2 – 3 scallions chopped with part of greens also)

1/2 tsp. dill weed

2 1/2 Tbsp. butter

1/2 cup bread crumbs

Drain artichokes and squeeze out juice. Mash artichokes fine or use a processor to mince coarsely. Add mayo to artichokes in bowl and mix thoroughly adding remainder of ingredients. Stir together completely. Spread mixture in attractive flat casserole unbuttered. Melt butter; add bread crumbs and dill weed. Pour over top. Bake uncovered at 350 degrees for 30 to 40 minutes until bubbly hot. Serve immediately with favorite cracker.

"Still a popular request for showers, parties, and catering since the 1970's. Can make day ahead, bake when needed."

— Marris Hill Farm
Goodville

Breadsticks & Pepperoni Pizza Dip

BREADSTICKS

1 1/2 cups warm water

1 Tbsp. yeast

1 Tbsp. oil

1 Tbsp. sugar

1 1/2 tsp. salt

4 cups occident flour

shredded cheese (optional)

BUTTER MIXTURE

1/2 cup melted butter

3 Tbsp. oil

3 Tbsp. parmesan cheese, grated

1 tsp. garlic powder

2 Tbsp. parsley flakes

PIZZA DIP

1 (8 oz.) pkg. cream cheese

1/2 cup sour cream

1 tsp. oregano

1/8 tsp. garlic powder

1/2 cup pizza sauce

1/2 cup pepperoni sliced and quartered

1/4 cup onion, chopped (optional)

1/4 cup pepper chopped (optional)

1/2 cup shredded mozzarella cheese

Mix water and yeast. Add oil, sugar and salt. Add flour. Knead, let rise approximately 1 hour. Roll to fit jelly roll pan. Top with butter mixture and sprinkle with desired amount of shredded cheese (optional).

Bake at 350 degrees for 15 to 20 minutes or till edges are a little brown. Cut into strips and serve with warm pizza sauce or pepperoni pizza dip.

Beat together cream cheese, sour cream, garlic powder and oregano. Spread into 9 inch pie pan and bake for 10 minutes at 350 degrees. Remove and add sauce, pepperoni, peppers and onion and top with cheese.

Bake another 5 minutes or till hot.

Great with breadsticks or tortilla chips.

— FARM FAVORITES
East Earl

Bean Salsa

1 (15 oz.) can black eyed peas, drained

1 (15 oz.) can black beans, drained

1 (15 oz.) can whole kernel corn, drained

1/2 cup onion, diced

1/2 cup green pepper, diced

1 (14 oz.) can diced tomatoes, undrained

1 (8 oz.) bottle Italian salad dressing

Mix ingredients. Refrigerate 24 hrs. Serve with tortilla chips.

— JEANETTE KLUMPP
Narvon

Chip Dip

1 (8 oz.) pkg. of cream cheese

1/2 onion or substitute maraschino cherries (amount to your liking)

orange juice

1 tsp. orange rind

Place cream cheese in bowl. Chop onion or maraschino cherries very fine and mix thoroughly. Pour in orange juice and stir until mixture thins to dipping consistency. Add orange rind.

— MARYANN OESTREICH
Narvon

Fianna's Cheese Spread

4 Tbsp. butter

1 pound sharp cheddar cheese

2 eggs beaten

3/4 cup milk

chopped green & red pepper

Melt the butter in a double boiler. Add cheese, cut in thin slices and melt with the butter. Beat the eggs and then add milk. Beat again to blend. Add this to the cheese mixture in the double boiler. Cook until thickens. Remove from the heat and add the chopped peppers. Chill. Use as a cracker spread or with raw vegetables.

"This recipe came from Fianna Weaver who worked for Betty's parents, Dr & Mrs Duttenhofer in Churchtown. She lived to be almost 101 years old."

— BETTY STURLA
A lifelong resident of Churchtown now living in Lancaster

Butter Dips

2 1/4 cup flour

1 Tbsp. sugar

3 1/2 tsp. baking powder

1 1/2 tsp. salt

1 cup milk

1/2 cup margarine or butter

1/2 tsp. seasoned salt

1/2 tsp. garlic powder

Sift dry ingredients, then add milk and turn with fork, just until dough clings together. Put on well floured board and knead lightly, then roll to 1/2 inch thick rectangle; cut into strips about 3/4 inch X 4 inches. In a 9 X 13-inch pan melt butter and add seasonings. Roll strips in butter, and then lay side by side in pan. Bake at 450 degrees for 15 to 20 minutes.

Can use different spices or add grated cheese, herbs, and spices to dough.

— SALLY KELLERMAN
South Coventry

Herb Cheese Spread

2 (8 oz.) pkgs. cream cheese
(regular or low fat)

1/2 cup butter, softened

2 large garlic cloves, pressed

1 tsp. oregano (dry)

1/4 tsp. of each: thyme,
dill weed, ground
course pepper, basil and
marjoram

Soften cheese and butter. Beat together and add all herbs. Beat again. Form into a ball or log. Refrigerate 24 hours. Roll in chopped parsley and serve with crackers.

"From the Village Herb Shop in Blue Ball."

— KAY RAFFENSPERGER
New Holland

Hot Dip

8 oz. Velveeta® cheese

1/2 cup butter
(no substitutes)

1 (6 oz.) can drained
crabmeat or 1 pkg. fresh
crabmeat cut into pieces

Combine in small saucepan, melting all together on stove burner. Stirring slowly as heating. Do not burn. Serve immediately in heated dish or small fondue pot with hard crackers to dip. Dill weed may be sprinkled on top.

"Delicious, easy, quick – used many years for catering and parties."

— MARRIS HILL FARM
Goodville

Rye Bread Dip

1 1/2 to 2 pts. sour cream

2 Tbsp. chopped fresh parsley

2 tsp. dill weed

2-3 tsp. Beau Monde® seasoning (1000 Spice® brand)

1 1/2 pts. mayonnaise

2 Tbsp. chopped scallions

3 pkgs. dried corned beef, chopped

1 to 2 loaves round rye or dark pumpernickel bread

fresh parsley

fresh strawberries or kumquats if desired

Combine all ingredients together in bowl. Cover and refrigerate overnight or 2 days. Cut out center of round loaf of rye or dark pumpernickel bread. (I cut out a star design in large loaf). Using chunks of bread or cut another loaf into pieces of your liking to serve with it. Serve on a large platter filling hollowed out loaf last minute. Put dipping chunks of bread surrounding loaf. Garnish with fresh sprigs of parsley and fresh strawberries.

"Several times I put this platter full on a sleigh that we used as a coffee table and for catering on tables I used a box or smaller sleighs."

— MARRIS HILL FARM
 Goodville

Shrimp Dip

1 (8 oz.) pkg. cream cheese

1 pt. sour cream

1 can drained shrimp or 6 to 8 fresh cooked shrimp broken into pieces

1 Italian dressing mix (Good Seasons®)

2 tsp. lemon juice

Combine all together after cream cheese is softened. Make 2 days ahead of desired need. Refrigerate and fold together once or twice during that time. I always sprinkle dill weed on top to garnish. Serve with your favorite cracker.

"A very popular easy recipe still using since the 1950's. Popular with parties and gatherings."

— CHURCH HOLM FARM INN

Cream Cheese & Veggie Pinwheels

2 cans crescent rolls

1 (8 oz.) pkg. cream cheese

small amounts of vegetables (grated carrots, finely chopped onion, green or red peppers, broccoli)

bacon bits or crumbled bacon

Mix cream cheese with a fork. You may separate cream cheese mixture into several bowls and add a mixture of vegetables to bowls. Add bacon bits to some bowls. Take crescent rolls and divide into squares. Spread cream cheese mixture on square and roll up and cut into pinwheels. Place on lightly greased baking sheet. Bake at 375 degrees for 10 to 15 minutes.

— MARY A. (BUNNY) PARMER
Narvon

Cream Cheese Roll-Ups

1 cup confectioner's sugar

2 (8 oz.) pkgs. cream cheese

1 egg

2 loaves sliced Italian bread

1 cup sugar

1 Tbsp. cinnamon

1 1/4 cups butter

Trim crust from bread and press to flatten. Mix cream cheese, confectioner's sugar, and egg. Spread on bread and roll up. Dip in melted butter and then in cinnamon-sugar mixture. Place on greased cookie sheet, cover and freeze. Uncover and bake frozen at 350 degrees for 12 to 15 minutes until slightly toasted.

"We used this recipe as an appetizer for our daughter's wedding. We often make it for special occasions. They are very good."

— JANICE MARTIN
East Earl

Frosted Ham Balls

1 lb. ground cooked ham

onion powder to taste

1/2 cup mayonnaise

2 (3 oz.) pkgs. cream cheese

1 Tbsp. milk

chopped parsley (optional)

Mix all ingredients except parsley. Shape into balls. Roll in chopped parsley if you want. Chill. Serve with crackers.

— ROSE NEWSWANGER
Narvon

Deviled Eggs

6 eggs

1 Tbsp. mayonnaise

2 tsp. yellow mustard

2 tsp. pickle relish

splash of Worcestershire sauce

salt and pepper to taste

Place eggs in single layer in saucepan. Cover with water, at least 2 inches over tops of eggs. Put lid on pot and bring water to a boil. As soon as water comes to a full boil, remove pan from heat.

Wait for 20 minutes and then drain hot water from eggs and fill with cold water. When eggs are cool, peel them. (Tip – use older eggs, they peel easier than fresh ones.) Slice eggs in half lengthwise.

Remove yolks, set whites aside. Mash yolks with fork. Add remaining ingredients and mix well.

Spoon mixture into egg white halves. Sprinkle with paprika or season-all.

— Lida Bensinger
Narvon

Red Beet Deviled Eggs

2 dozen red beet eggs (see canning chapter to make red beets)

3/4 cup mayonnaise

4 Tbsp. mustard

4 tsp. vinegar

1/8 tsp. salt

paprika

black or green olives (optional)

Cut eggs in half lengthwise. Scrape out yolk with spoon. Chop yolks with fork. Combine yolks, mustard, vinegar, and salt. Mix with mixer until smooth. Fill red egg halves with filling. A cake decorator bag and tip may be used. Top with paprika and sliced olives.

"This is typically requested for me to make for family gatherings!"

— Cindy Diem
Narvon

Party Fondue

4 pints of hot fudge sauce

several cut up chunks of strawberries, pineapple, banana slices, seedless grapes, nectarine slices, melon balls, etc.

Pour hot fudge into any size fondue pot or chafing dish. Keep over heat so fudge sauce gets very hot and stays at an even temperature.

Arrange fresh greens and/or flowers around serving area with prepared and cut up fruits. Have another container filled with dipping skewers.

Make sure there is plenty of room as people will eat and socialize. Offer a discard container also.

"An all over favorite – no matter where or how long --- parties, gatherings and weddings."

— SUSAN MARRIS
Goodville

Baked Apple Appetizer

PER APPLE

1 apple (gala apples preferred)

1 Tbsp. brown sugar

1 tsp. softened butter

1/4 tsp. cinnamon

maple syrup

fresh mint leaves (optional)

Heat oven to 375 degrees. Core apples and remove 1 inch of skin around the middle of each apple to prevent them from splitting. Place apples upright in baking dish.

Fill center of each apple with above mixture. Pour water (1/4 inch deep) into baking dish. Bake about 30 to 40 minutes or until apples are tender when pierced with a fork. You may spoon pan juices over apples during baking.

For presentation, place each apple in a serving dish. Pour equal portions of pan juices in the center of each apple. Drizzle a teaspoon of warm maple syrup over apples and place a sprig of fresh mint leaves in the middle of the apple to resemble the apple leaves. Delicious served with homemade granola as well.

— LINCOLN BOONE BED & BREAKFAST
Narvon

Crab A-La-Greenbank

1 lb. lump crabmeat

1/2 lb. shrimp cooked, peeled and chopped

1/2 large green pepper, chopped

1 cup mayonnaise

1 tsp. Worchestershire sauce

Old Bay® seasoning to taste

sprinkle of cracked pepper and salt

bread crumbs

Mix all ingredients. Place in a well buttered 7 X 11-inch shallow baking pan. Top lightly with wet bread crumbs. Garnish with old bay seasoning. Bake uncovered at 360 degrees until lightly browned on top, about 35 minutes.

This recipe was developed to serve in place of crab cakes as it can be baked and reheated for serving at a later time if desired.

"When this dish is served I often get requests for the recipe!"

— JACK HILLARD
New Holland

Mushrooms Parmesan

1 lb. mushrooms with 1 to 2 inch caps

2 Tbsp. olive oil

1/4 cup chopped onion

1/2 clove finely chopped garlic

1/3 cup fine dry bread crumbs (1 slice)

3 Tbsp. grated parmesan cheese

1 tsp. chopped parsley

1/2 tsp. salt

1/8 tsp. oregano

2 Tbsp. olive oil

Grease shallow 1 1/2 qt. casserole. Clean mushrooms. Cut stems from caps. Place caps open side up in casserole. Set aside.

Finely chop mushroom stems. Heat olive oil in skillet. Add stems and chopped onion and garlic. Cook slowly until onion and garlic are lightly browned.

Combine bread crumbs, parmesan cheese, parsley, salt, and pepper. Mix in onion, garlic and stems. Pile mixture lightly into inverted caps. Pour 2 tablespoons olive oil into casserole.

Bake at 400 degrees for 15 to 20 minutes or until mushrooms are tender and tops are browned. *Serves 6*

— MARYANN OESTREICH
Narvon

Pepper Poppers

1 (8 oz.) pkg. cream cheese, softened

1 cup shredded sharp cheddar cheese

1 cup shredded Monterey jack cheese

6 bacon strips, cooked and crumbled

1/4 tsp. salt

1/4 tsp. chili powder

1/4 tsp. garlic powder

1 lb. fresh jalapenos, halved lengthwise and seeded

1/2 cup dry bread crumbs

In a mixing bowl, combine cheese, bacon, and seasonings, mix well. Spoon about two tablespoonfuls into each pepper half. Roll in bread crumbs, place on a greased 15 X 10 X 1-inch baking pan. Bake uncovered at 300 degrees for 20 minutes for spicy flavor or 30 minutes for medium flavor and 40 minutes for mild flavor. Serve with sour cream, ranch dip or dressing. *Makes 2 dozen*

— SHIRLEY K HOSTLER
  Mifflintown

Spinach Balls

4 (10 oz.) pkgs. frozen chopped spinach

4 cups stuffing mix

1 cup parmesan cheese

1 tsp. thyme

2 garlic cloves, minced

2 large onions, chopped

8 eggs

1 1/2 cups melted butter

salt and pepper

Cook spinach and drain. Squeeze out liquid. Add remaining ingredients and mix well. Chill for 2 hours or more. Roll into 1 inch balls. Bake on greased cookie sheet at 300 degrees for 30 minutes.

— MARYANN OESTREICH
  Narvon

Stuffed Mushrooms

2 (8 to 10 oz.) pkgs. button mushrooms (the regular kind)

2 (8 oz.) pkgs. cream cheese

1/2 lb. chipped ham (chip in fine pieces)

splash of lime or lemon juice

1 to 2 tsp. garlic powder

Clean and hollow out mushrooms. Mix everything else and stuff to overflowing in the mushrooms. Bake uncovered at 375 degrees for 25 minutes or until mushrooms are cooked.

— BRENDA MARTIN
Narvon

Sweet & Sour Cocktail Balls

COCKTAIL BALLS

4 lb. bulk pork sausage

1 1/2 cups soft bread crumbs

4 eggs, slightly beaten

SAUCE

3 cups catsup

1/2 cup white vinegar

1/2 cup soy sauce

3/4 cup brown sugar

Mix together first 3 ingredients and form into small balls (makes about 150). Brown the balls. Mix the remaining ingredients for the sauce. Simmer and add the cooked sausage balls for about 30 minutes. Okay to freeze.

"This is an absolute requirement for our holiday season. Fantastic, delicious and perfect!"

— MARTA RAFFENSPERGER
New Holland

Golden Punch

6 cups water

2 1/2 cups sugar

1 (46 oz.) can pineapple juice

1 (12 oz.) can frozen orange juice

1 (6 oz.) can frozen lemonade

1/2 tsp. almond extract

1 (2-liter) bottle ginger ale

In a large saucepan bring the water and sugar to a boil. Cook and stir for 2 minutes. Pour into a large container. Add the pineapple juice, concentrates and extract. Cover and freeze. Remove from freezer 3 hours before serving. Just before serving mash the mixture with a potato masher and stir in the ginger ale.

— KATHY MARTIN
Narvon

Lime Tomato Sipper

1 tsp. instant chicken
   bouillon granules

1 cup boiling water

3 cups tomato juice

2 Tbsp. lime juice

1 tsp. sugar

1 tsp. Worchestershire sauce

1 tsp. celery salt

1/4 tsp. basil

celery stalk

Dissolve bouillon in boiling water, mix with all other ingredients and chill. Garnish each glass with a stalk of celery.

— MAURINE VAN DYKE
Narvon

Lorraine's Tea

1 cup sugar

tea leaves

1 (12 oz.) can frozen
   lemonade

1 (6 oz.) can of orange juice

Boil sugar and 2 1/2 cups water for 5 minutes. Add 2 generous cup of tea leaves (Lorraine used peppermint tea leaves) Steep 1 hour, strain. Add frozen lemonade with 3 cups water and a 6 ounce can of orange juice with 3 cans water.

— LORRAINE RAFFENSPERGER
Blue Ball

Meadow Tea Concentrate

4 cup fresh peppermint
   leaves, packed

1 cup fresh spearmint leaves,
   packed

2 cups sugar

4 cups water

Take leaves off stems and rinse. Bring water and sugar syrup to boil. Boil 5 minutes. Pour over leaves. Let stand 5 to 6 hours. Strain. Ratio: 2 cups concentrate to 2 quarts water. Concentrate freezes well.

— JANESSA FISHER
Narvon

Hot Cider

4 to 6 mulling tea bags
(hot mulled cider)

1/2 gallon cider

4 to 5 cinnamon sticks

Heat beverage in crock pot or on stove top until steamy hot (not boiling), approximately 30 minutes to 1 hour. Add 4 to 6 mulling tea bags and simmer to taste. Put cinnamon sticks in and simmer on low.

— SHIRLEY WEIDMAN
Narvon

Rhubarb Punch Concentrate

2 qt. chopped rhubarb

2 cups sugar

2 cups hot water

2 Tbsp. cherry Jell-O®

1 cup pineapple juice

1/2 cup lemon juice

Chop rhubarb. Put in kettle and cover with water, cook until soft. Drain with nylon or sieve. Add sugar. Dissolve jello in hot water. Add other ingredients. Freeze. When ready to serve add water to taste (1 part concentrate to 2 to 3 parts water) and 1 qt. ginger ale (optional).

"Refreshing on a hot summer day!"

— LISA W. SHIRK
Narvon

Old Fashioned Lemonade

9 to 12 large lemons
(approximately)

2 cups sugar

water

Combine two cups water and 2 cups sugar in a saucepan. Simmer until sugar is melted. Squeeze enough lemons to make 2 cups juice. Combine sugar mixture and lemon juice in a one gallon container. Add water to make one gallon. Chill and serve.

— BARBARA DIEM
Narvon

SOUPS, SALADS, & SANDWICHES INDEX

SOUPS, SALADS, & SANDWICHES
Memorial Day Parade & Historical Society

CHAPTER SPONSORED BY

Armed Forces Memorial in Churchtown cemetery.

Caernarvon Memorial Society

1866 - 2009

143 years celebrating the citizens of
Caernarvon Township who served in the
Armed Forces in both war and peace.

Address   2118 Main Street
           Narvon Pa. 17555

Email   jlbct@comcast.net

Phone   (717) 445-4926

Memorial Day Parade & Historical Society

On Monday, May 25, 2009 Churchtown held its annual Memorial Day Parade for the 143rd year. It is believed to be one of the oldest parades in the country, having begun in May of 1866 when a group of Civil War soldiers and some others who returned from the war gathered in the Churchtown Cemetery with leading citizens of Caernarvon Township to pay tribute to the fallen soldiers. They took their hunting rifles and fired over the grave of the last soldier buried, which is how this tradition began.

In 1868 the honoring of Union Civil War veterans became formally known as Decoration Day to be celebrated on May 30. After World War I it was expanded to include all American veterans of military action. In Caernarvon Township the parade and celebration was an informal affair until about 1900 when the Churchtown Memorial Society was organized, known today as the Caernarvon Memorial Society. The tradition of placing flowers on the graves started with the first gathering in 1866 and today includes flowers and American Flags on over 165 gravestones. To this day we honor the veterans from the Revolutionary War to present, who are buried in our local cemeteries, for their service in war and peace.

Memorial Day Ceremony 2007 with Veteran Ed Beck bowing in prayer behind the podium.

Preparations for Memorial Day begin five months before the event. A week before the ceremony many volunteers place American flags on the graves of veterans in the three local cemeteries and on the telephone poles on both sides of the street throughout this quaint little village. Local residents also decorate their porches with flags. Very early on the morning on Memorial Day, volunteers from the Memorial Society drape a large flag across Main Street in front of the fire hall.

Many folks in attendance recall the day when they were a child and carried flowers to the graves of those who served our country. Now they watch their children or grandchildren follow in their footsteps. It has become an annual tradition for many local families returning each year to honor those who served our country. One such person is Army veteran Joe

Gordon of Churchtown. He recalls carrying flowers as a child and now watches his son and grandchildren participate in the parade. He is also linked to the original parade and service dating back to 1866. His grandfather was one of the Civil War soldiers who participated in the very first tribute held in Churchtown.

By early afternoon, the Ladies' Auxiliary is serving food in the fire hall. Many local favorites like barbeque sandwiches, ham and bean soup, chicken corn soup, and a

Veteran children and grandchildren carrying flowers in parade.

variety of pies including shoo-fly pie are available to satisfy ones hunger.

During the day, you can also stop by the Caernarvon Historical Society and see the pictorial display of the local veterans who served our country. The Caernarvon Historical Society was established in 1975 to restore the Caernarvon Presybertian Chapel for the bicentennial in 1976. The restoration was done with federal grant money and finished

Veteran Mike McClure riding in antique jeep.

in 1976. In 1979 following the restoration work, the building was dedicated as the Society Headquarters. In 2004, the Donegal Presbytery donated the property to the Society and presented the keys in a dedication ceremony. Robert Jenkins, Ironmaster of Windsor Forge and his wife were the founders of the church. The couple and most of their children are buried in the cemetery adjoining the church. The Society's permanent location is in the Caernarvon Historical Society Church building. The Society sponsors a variety of events including regular meetings in the Caernarvon Historical Society building the second Wednesday of the month at 9:00 a.m. They also feature guest speakers and have started a new program called "Let's Talk History", which is held the fourth Wednesday of each month at 7:00 p.m. The Society routinely takes part in community traditions such

New Holland band.

as Memorial Day and Churchtown Days in August.

The Memorial Day festivities begin at 6:00 p.m. with a concert by the New Holland Band and the Eastern Lancaster County Elementary Band performing together, beginning with the National Anthem and followed by many favorite patriotic tunes. At 7:00 p.m. the parade commences from the site of the former Caernarvon Elementary School. It includes the New Holland Band, the Honor Guard provided by the New Holland VFW, antique military jeeps transporting veterans, antique cars, a tractor with a large American flag and fire equipment. The highlight is the children - some carrying flowers, while others are riding their bicycles or being pulled in wagons decorated in red, white and blue. The parade heads west to the end of town, then turns around and goes back. On the way back, the procession stops at the Bangor Episcopal Church cemetery and the Caernarvon Presbyterian Church cemetery. The honor guard performs a brief ceremony at the grave site, consisting of a 21-gun salute and "Taps" being played on a bugle while the children place flowers on the graves. The parade ends at the Churchtown United Methodist Church cemetery where the honor guard performs and is followed by a service with a guest pastor and guest speaker for the evening. As the service continues the sun begins to set in this quaint town with its rolling fields dotted with farms. This year marked the first without a local favorite Ed Beck who passionately supported the event as a speaker for many years.

Woman and children on parade.

Bacon Soup

3 oz. lean bacon

1 oz. bacon fat

1 medium-sized potato

2 leeks

1 stick celery

1 egg

1 pint bacon or ham stock

1/4 pint milk

2 tsp. chopped parsley

salt and pepper

Cook and dice the bacon. Peel and slice the potato and leeks. Slice the celery.

Add the vegetables to the fat and cook for a few minutes. Stir in the stock and simmer for 30 minutes. Season to taste.

Separate the egg yolk from the white and blend the yolk with the milk. Remove the pan from the heat and add the milk and egg yolk.

Cook for 2 to 3 minutes but do not boil. Sprinkle with parsley and serve hot.

— GAYNOR GREEN
  Bowmansville

Cheddar Chowder

2 cups diced potatoes

2 cups sliced carrots

3/4 cup chopped onion

1/2 cup diced celery

1/2 cup water

1/4 cup butter

1/4 cup flour

1 tsp. salt

1/4 tsp. dry mustard

1 Tbsp. Worcestershire
  sauce

2 cups milk

3/4 cup grated cheddar
  cheese

1 tsp. parsley flakes

Combine first 5 ingredients in 2 quart microwave casserole. Cook on high 8 to 10 minutes. Melt butter; add flour, seasonings and milk. Cook 4 to 5 minutes on high until thick. Add cheese, stir until smooth. Add veggies and parsley. Cook 3 minutes on 80 percent power.

A microwave recipe that also works well on stovetop.

— JEANETTE KLUMPP
  Narvon

Chili Soup

2 lb. ground beef with onion

1 qt. tomato juice

1 qt. pizza sauce

1 cup ketchup

1 can chili beans

1 can baked beans

1 tsp. oregano

1/2 tsp. basil

2 tsp. chili powder

1/4 tsp. Italian seasoning

1 tsp. salt

1/4 tsp. garlic powder

Cook ground beef with onion. Mix together all ingredients and simmer for 20 minutes.

— LORELLE NEWSWANGER
Narvon

Crab Bisque

2 cups onion, chopped

1 cup celery, chopped

1 cup green pepper, chopped

4 cloves minced garlic

1/4 cup butter or margarine

4 cups diced peeled potatoes

2 cups milk

4 cups half and half

10 oz. Velveeta® cheese cubed

1 can (1 lb.) crab meat flakes

1/4 tsp. pepper

In soup kettle sauté onion, green pepper, celery and garlic in butter until tender. Reduce heat to medium and add potatoes and milk. Cook uncovered 20 minutes or until potatoes are tender, stirring occasionally. Remove ½ cup potatoes and mash. Return to kettle. Reduce heat to low. Stir in half and half and cubed cheese. Stir occasionally until cheese is melted. Add crab meat and pepper. Cook 10 minutes or until heated through.

— MARY A. (BUNNY) PARMER
Narvon

Hearty French Onion Soup

3 lb. onions, diced

1 1/2 Tbsp. butter

3 cups beef broth

3 cups chicken broth

1 Tbsp. instant coffee

salt and pepper

croutons

mozzarella cheese, sliced

Sauté onions in butter. Transfer onions to large saucepan. Add beef and chicken broths, coffee, and salt and pepper, to taste. Simmer for several hours. Then pour soup into individual oven-proof bowls. Top each bowl with croutons, then mozzarella cheese.

Bake at 350 degrees for 25 minutes. Note: To make croutons, slice day-old French bread and broil for 3 to 4 minutes or until golden brown, turning each minute.

— JANESSA FISHER
Narvon

Italian Chicken Garden Vegetable Soup

2 (14 1/2 oz.) cans chicken broth

1 (14 1/2 oz.) can diced tomatoes with basil, garlic and oregano

1 (15 1/4 oz.) can whole kernel yellow corn, drained

1 (14 1/2 oz.) can peas and carrots, drained

1 (14 1/2 oz.) can French style green beans, drained

1 to 2 cups cooked chicken cut into bite size pieces

Combine broth, un-drained tomatoes and remaining vegetables in a large pan. Bring to a boil, reduce heat. Simmer uncovered for 30 minutes or until heated through. Put chicken in last. Parsley, oregano or Italian seasoning may be added for more flavor.

Can double and freeze for a cold day.

— SHIRLEY WEIDMAN
Narvon

Mediterranean Seafood Chowder

1 1/2 cups green, red and yellow peppers

1 large onion quartered and sliced thinly

3 cloves of garlic or 1 1/2 tsp. garlic powder

1 (28 oz.) can crushed tomatoes

1 (14 1/2 oz.) can chicken broth

1 cup rice

1/2 cup white cooking wine or extra chicken broth

1/2 tsp. parsley flakes

8 oz. uncooked medium shrimp

8 oz. cod fillet, cut into pieces

In a large saucepan sauté garlic, onion, and peppers until tender. Add crushed tomatoes, chicken broth, rice, cooking wine or extra chicken broth and parsley flakes and bring to a boil. Cover and simmer 15 to 20 minutes or until rice is tender. Add shrimp and fish pieces and cook for about 5 to 8 minutes.

— MARY A. (BUNNY) PARMER
Narvon

Circa 1950's photo of children carrying flowers to place on graves at the United Methodist Cemetery.

Pasta & Bean Soup

1 Tbsp. olive oil

6 slices bacon, diced

2 carrots, diced

2 celery ribs, diced

1 medium onion, chopped

1 Tbsp. minced garlic

1 (48 oz.) can low sodium
chicken broth

2 cups water

1/4 tsp. Italian seasoning

1/4 tsp. ground black pepper

1 cup uncooked elbow-
shaped pasta or ditalini

1 (19 oz.) can chickpeas,
rinsed

4 cups packed fresh spinach
leaves coarsely torn

grated Parmesan cheese for
serving

Heat oil in a large pot over medium-high heat. Add bacon and sauté 5 minutes or until browned. Remove with a slotted spoon and set aside. Remove about 2/3 of the bacon fat and discard. Add carrots, celery, onion and garlic to fat in pot. Cook, stirring often, until vegetables are tender, about 7 to 8 minutes. Add bacon, chicken broth, 2 cups of water, Italian seasoning and pepper.

Bring to a boil, reduce heat, cover and simmer 10 minutes. Add pasta and cook 8 minutes or until pasta is slightly underdone. Stir in chickpeas and spinach. Return to a simmer and cook 2 minutes or until hot. Serve with Parmesan cheese and crusty Italian bread. *Serves 6*

— THE INN AT TWIN LINDEN
Churchtown

Potato Soup

1 1/2 qt. water

6 medium potatoes, cubed

1 onion, chopped

2 carrots grated

6 pieces celery, sliced thin

1 cup milk

3 Tbsp. margarine

1 tsp. salt

1/4 tsp. pepper

2 Tbsp. flour

Cook potatoes, onion, carrots, and celery in water until tender. Drain and reserve liquid. In a kettle combine milk, margarine, salt and pepper. Stir in flour until thickened. Stir in cooked vegetables. Add reserved liquid until soup is of desired consistency.

— KATHY MARTIN
Narvon

Santa Sausage Soup

1 lb. sweet Italian sausage (casings removed)

1 cup thinly sliced onion

2 cloves garlic, minced

6 cups chicken broth

2 carrots, peeled and thinly sliced

1 (8 3/4 oz.) pkg. small dried cheese-filled tortellini

4 cups fresh spinach leaves, coarsely chopped

1 (15 1/2 oz.) can red kidney beans, drained

1/4 tsp. ground pepper

1 tsp. dried basil

salt to taste

Cut sausage into 1/2" pieces and sauté until cooked through. Transfer to a large stockpot. Sauté onions and garlic in same pan for about 2 minutes then add to stock pot. Add chicken broth and sliced carrots to stockpot and bring to a boil. Reduce heat and simmer for 10 minutes. Add tortellini and simmer for 10 more minutes. Stir in spinach leaves and kidney beans. Season with pepper, basil and salt to taste.

"Great for a family/friends get-together. A very colorful and appetizing soup."

— Darlene May Emery Stauffer
  Narvon

Sausage Clam Soup

8 to 10 oz. bulk hot Italian sausage

1 medium onion, chopped

1 large garlic clove, chopped

1/2 lb. sliced mushrooms

3 cups tomato sauce

1 (15 oz.) can chopped tomatoes

1 bottle clam juice

2 cans minced clams

1 Tbsp minced parsley

1 tsp. basil

Sauté sausage in a little olive oil, drain. Add onion, garlic and sauté. Add mushrooms. Then tomato sauce, chopped tomatoes and clam juice. Simmer 15 to 20 minutes. Add minced clams, parsley and basil. *Serves 6*

"Hearty soup. Great with a crusty dipping bread. Also freezes well."

— Kay Raffensperger
  New Holland

Slovakian Christmas Mushroom & Sauerkraut Soup

1 cup dried mushrooms (any kind) or fresh mushrooms

1 lb. pack of sauerkraut w/ juice

1 small onion, chopped

2 cloves of garlic

1 quart of water or more if needed

1 tsp. salt

1/2 tsp. pepper

2 Tbsp. flour

2 Tbsp. butter

Chop mushrooms and soak overnight in warm water, then drain. If using fresh mushrooms, this step is not necessary.

Heat the water with sauerkraut, onion, garlic, salt, pepper and mushrooms in a soup pot. Simmer for 2 to 3 hours.

Prior to serving, make zaprashka (roux). Mix 2 tablespoons of flour and 2 tablespoons of browned butter in a small sauce pan. After it bubbles, add it to soup and mix well. Simmer for 15 more minutes and then serve. *Serves 4*

"Every Christmas Eve we would participate in a Holy Supper. My grandmothers would make this soup (along with others). We would start the meal with a blessed wafer with honey. The meal would consist of many soups, pierogies and bobalki (little quarter-sized loaves of bread in sauerkraut and potato pierogy water)."

— Maryann Oestreich
Narvon

Spicy Crab Soup

1 (32 oz.) frozen vegetables

4 cups water

2 cups tomato juice

1 can (15oz.) chopped tomatoes

2 Tbsp. beef bouillon granules

1 to 1 1/2 Tbsp. seafood seasoning (Old Bay®)

1 lb. crab meat

1/2 tsp. black pepper

hot sauce to taste

Add vegetables to water and bring to a boil. Simmer for 10 minutes. Add the remaining ingredients and simmer for an additional 25 to 30 minutes before serving.

— Betty Sturla
A life long resident of Churchtown now living in Lancaster

Stuffed Pepper Soup

1 1/2 lb. ground beef

water

1 large green pepper

1 yellow or orange pepper

1 large red pepper

1/4 cup sugar (or Splenda®)

1 (14 oz.) can stewed
tomatoes

1 (29 oz.) can tomato sauce

1/2 cup to 3/4 cup minute
rice (more rice for thicker
soup)

1 can tomato soup

Cook ground beef covered with 2 to 3 inches water in a sauce pan. Cook until burger is cooked and breaks into pieces. Put burger and water in a crock pot. Chop peppers. Add in crockpot. Sprinkle sugar. Add stewed tomatoes, tomato sauce, tomato soup and minute rice. Stir. Cook in crockpot 4 to 5 hours on high. Stir often.

"My friend Sandy got this recipe at the mountains and shared with me, which I've shared with friends at Poole Forge."

— SHIRLEY WEIDMAN
Narvon

Taco Soup

1 lb. hamburger

1/2 chopped onion

2 to 3 qt. tomato juice

1 pkg. taco seasoning

1 can kidney beans

1 pint corn

1/4 to 1/2 cup sugar

1 tsp. salt

1/4 tsp. pepper

1/2 cup Sure-Jell®

corn chips

sour cream

grated cheese

Cook hamburger and onion. Drain. Add next 7 ingredients, heat until hot. Add water to clear-jell to make a smooth paste.

Add paste to soup when near to boiling point. Serve over corn chips, sprinkle cheese on top. Add a spoon full of sour cream.

— LISA SHIRK
Narvon

Two Bean Soup with Dried Tomatoes

2 Tbsp. olive oil

1 cup chopped onion

1 cup chopped sweet red pepper

1 carrot, thinly sliced

1 jalapeño pepper, stemmed and seeded, finely chopped

1 garlic clove, finely chopped

1 tsp. ground cumin

1/2 tsp. dried oregano

2 cup reduced sodium chicken broth or part broth and part water

1 (15 or 19 oz.) can black beans, rinsed, drained.

1 (15 or 19 oz.) can red kidney beans, rinsed and drained.

1 (28 oz.) can whole tomatoes in juice, cut up

1/2 cup cut up dried tomatoes

salt and freshly ground black pepper to taste.

Heat oil in large broad saucepan. Stir in onion, sweet red pepper, carrot, and jalapeño. Cook, stirring, until golden, about 10 minutes.

Add garlic and cook 1 minute. Add cumin and oregano and cook 1 minute. Add chicken broth, black beans, red kidney beans, tomatoes and dried tomatoes.

Bring to a boil, breaking up tomatoes with side of spoon. Cover and cook over low heat 20 minutes to blend flavors.

Season with salt and pepper. *Serves 5*

— LORRAINE RAFFENSPERGER
Blue Ball

Jell-O® Mold

1 large box or 2/3 cup Jell-O® of any flavor

1 (8 oz.) pkg. cream cheese

1 small container of Cool Whip®

11 oz. of any fruit

Mix dry gelatin and cream cheese, then add 1 1/2 cups boiling water, and 3/4 cup cold water. Stir until dissolved, and refrigerate until set. Then beat with a fork until mushy. Add the Cool Whip and fruit. Put in a mold and chill 1 1/2 hours.

"Our family favorite is orange gelatin with mandarin oranges."

— SUSIE SMUCKER
Narvon

Pinwheels

1 pkg. (4 oz.) or 1/2 to 2/3 cup of gelatin, any flavor

1/2 cup warm water

1 1/2 cups mini-marshmallows

Spray 8 or 9-inch square pan with cooking spray. Spread on bottom and sides with paper towel.

Mix gelatin and water in 2 qt. microwaveable bowl. Microwave on high for 1 1/2 minutes. Stir mixture until completely dissolved.

Add marshmallows and microwave for 1 minute or until marshmallows are puffed and almost melted. Stir mixture slowly until marshmallows are completely melted and mixture is smooth. Creamy layer will float on top.

Pour into prepared pan. Refrigerate for 45 minutes or until set. Loosen edges with a sharp knife dipped in water for easy rolling. Starting at one edge, roll up tightly with seam side down, and cut into 1/2 inch slices. Serve immediately or refrigerate until ready to serve. *Makes 10 pieces*

— Sharon Colon
Narvon

Mary's Cranberry Salad

4 cups water

4 cups fresh cranberries

2 cups sugar

1 (16 oz.) pkg. mini marshmallows

1 (6 oz.) pkg. strawberry or cherry jello

6 cups grated tart apples

Cook water, cranberries, and sugar together until cranberries pop – several minutes. Add mini marshmallows, melt, then take off burner and add jello. Add apples.

— Mary Jane Newswanger
Morgantown

Susan's Cranberry Salad

1 bag frozen cranberries

2 fresh oranges

2 cups sugar

1 small box of Strawberry or Raspberry Jello

1 small can Mandarin oranges

1 cup cut up celery

2 cups cranberry relish

1/2 cup chopped nuts

1 cup halved grapes

For the relish, grind or process minced frozen (thaw 15 minutes) cranberries, 2 whole fresh oranges that have been cut up first before grinding. Add 2 cups sugar 1 day ahead before using.

Make Jello as directed. After adding the boiling water, let cool. Then in desired dish or mold add 1 cup cold water, and can of Mandarin oranges, making enough liquid. Add remaining ingredients. Stir well. Refrigerate until firm. Cover and always make 1 day ahead before needed. Serve individually on Boston lettuce or just spoon from bowl.

"Our favorite anytime of year. Always have frozen cranberries to use year round. Make a relish to use for this salad and or have the plain relish anytime also."

— SUSAN MARRIS
   Goodville

Pineapple Coleslaw

4 cups shredded cabbage

1 cup diced, unpeeled red apples

1 can pineapple chunks or tidbits, drained

1 cup mini marshmallows

1/2 cup chopped celery

Miracle Whip for salad dressing

lettuce

Combine cabbage, apples, pineapple, celery, marshmallows, and enough salad dressing to moisten. Toss lightly. Serve on lettuce lined bowls.

"Use low calorie Miracle Whip or dressings and it makes a great salad for diabetics. Add cooked, diced chicken and you have lunch."

— LINDA BOYER
   Narvon

Coleslaw Cabbage Salad

LAYERS

1 quart shredded cabbage

3/4 cup fried, crumbled bacon

1 cup shredded cheddar cheese

1/4 cup salad toppings such as cucumbers, tomatoes or other favorites

DRESSING

3/4 cup mayonnaise

1/4 tsp. mustard

1/2 tsp. celery seed

1/2 cup vinegar

1/2 cup vegetable oil

1 tsp. onion salt

1 1/2 cups sugar

1 (8 oz.) pkg. cream cheese

2/3 cup milk

Mix together dressing ingredients except cream cheese and milk. Then add cream cheese and milk. Mix well. This recipe makes 4 cups of dressing.

Layer on a plate 12 inches in diameter:

1st layer – cabbage
2nd layer – 1 cup dressing
3rd layer – bacon
4th layer – shredded cheese
5th layer – salad toppings

— VERA JANE NEWSWANGER
Morgantown

Pepper Cabbage

1 medium head of cabbage

1 carrot, grated

1 green pepper, chopped

1 tsp. salt

Syrup:

2 cups sugar

1 cup vinegar

1/2 cup water

1 tsp. celery seed

1 tsp. mustard seed

Shred the cabbage, and then add the salt and let stand for one hour. Next, add the carrot and green pepper. Finally add the syrup.

For the syrup, mix all ingredients and boil 1 minute. Cool until lukewarm. Pour over cabbage mixture. This can be frozen.

— KATHY MARTIN
Narvon

Susan's Coleslaw

1/2 head of cabbage

2 Tbsp. chopped, fresh parsley

1 tsp. dill weed

1 tsp. salt

2 Tbsp. sugar

1/2 tsp. black pepper

1 tsp. red vinegar

1/2 cup chopped celery

1 cut up apple

1 small can crushed pineapple or cut up chunks

1 tsp. celery seed

1 can mandarin oranges

1/2 cup mayonnaise or more

1/3 cup Miracle Whip®

Chop or slice cabbage coarsely to your liking. Add all ingredients into bowl. Stir together well so it all becomes smooth and wet. Make 1 to 2 hours before needed, folding together twice during that time. Serve in individual, small dishes.

"My mother always added cut up tomato, onion, and celery to her cabbage coleslaw made fresh before serving. She used Hellman's Mayo for everything."

— SUSAN MARRIS
  East Earl

Las Vegas Salad

3/4 cup Miracle Whip

1 1/2 cup cottage cheese

1 1/4 cup finely chopped celery

1/4 cup finely chopped green pepper

1/4 cup finely chopped onion

2 small boxes of lime gelatin

2 cups water

Mix first 5 ingredients together, set aside. Heat 2 cups of water until boiling. Add 2 small boxes of lime gelatin. Mix until dissolved.

Fold into the cottage cheese mixture. Refrigerate until firm. Can mold or refrigerate in bowl or single serving dishes.

— DORIS HAMILTON
  Willow Street

Macaroni Salad

Salad

1 lb. macaroni, cooked (still tender)

18 hard-boiled eggs cut up

1/2 to 2/3 cup chopped celery

1/2 to 2/3 cup grated carrots

1 Tbsp. finely chopped onion

1 pt. Miracle Whip®

3 tsp. yellow mustard

Dressing

2 cup sugar

1/2 to 3/4 cup vinegar

4 eggs, beaten

1/2 tsp. salt

1 tsp. butter

Mix salad ingredients together in bowl.

Cook sugar, vinegar, salt, and butter on medium-low heat until bubbling. Add eggs until thickened. Add to macaroni mixture. Cool. *Serves 20*

— Janessa Fisher
Narvon

Wonderful Macaroni Salad

Salad

2 cups cooked macaroni

2 hard boiled eggs, chopped

1 cup chopped celery

1 small onion, diced

1 cup shredded carrot

Dressing

2 eggs

1 cup granulated sugar

1/2 cup vinegar

1/2 tsp. mustard

1/2 tsp. butter

2/3 cup mayonnaise

Mix salad ingredients together in bowl.

Beat eggs well. Mix with other dressing ingredients except mayonnaise. Then cook dressing mixture until it boils for only 1 minute. Take off heat, adding salt to taste, add to the macaroni. Cool completely, and then add mayonnaise.

— Mary Ann Good
Terre Hill

Pellichelli Salad

iceberg lettuce, torn in small pieces

6 fresh ripe tomatoes skinned and cut in 3/4 inch pieces

3 cups green beans, cooked and cut in 1 inch pieces

1 medium onion, sliced very thin

celery seed

olive oil and vinegar

Combine ingredients in a large salad bowl. Pour olive oil and vinegar into mixture until moist. Sprinkle celery seed generously. Serve promptly.

"A true Windsor Forge Mansion Recipe."

— MARGARET HUNT LANDIS
   Columbia

Pellichelli Salad is a simple Italian-style salad that my mother served every summer when I was growing up. Years later, I learned that it was named for the young Italian, Angelo Pellichelli, who lived for a time at Windsor Forge Mansion with Blanche Nevin. My mother and her (second) cousin, Mary Jacobs (later married to J. Walter Harward), ate it when they spent summers at Churchtown while they were growing up. Cousin Mary told me that she "hated that oily salad".

My mother was Margaret Lincoln Hunt who was married to my father, Clarkson Toms Hunt, II, at the mansion on June 29, 1922.

Susan's Holiday Salad

1 bunch broccoli cut into florets

1 cup cauliflower

2 cans large, green salad olives and black olives

1 pint cherry or grape tomatoes

1 can artichoke hearts that have been marinated

1 cup small whole mushrooms

1 pkg. chunks of bite sized cheddar cheese or other cheeses

2 cups celery, cut up

3 Tbsp. chopped, fresh parsley

1 tsp. dill weed

fresh, ground black pepper

1 yellow pepper, sliced lengthwise

1/2 cup baby carrots

1/2 red onion, sliced

2 scallions/greens, sliced

2 shakes of sea salt

1 whole bottle of Italian dressing

Alter ingredients with vegetables of choice. Put all ingredients into a large pan or bowl. Pour 1 bottle of Italian dressing over all of the salad ingredients. Fold together, cover, and refrigerate over night. Stir salad occasionally.

— Susan Marris
  East Earl

Lettuce Salad Dressing

1 cup sugar

1/4 cup vinegar

1 cup milk

2 cups mayonnaise

1 small onion

1 Tbsp. mustard

1 tsp. salt

Mix everything together in blender.

"This is excellent with fresh loose-leaf lettuce from the garden."

— Vera Jane Newswanger
  Morgantown

Sauerkraut Slaw A-La-Greenbank

1 qt. sauerkraut

1 cup onion, chopped

1 cup celery, chopped

1 small green pepper, chopped

1/2 cup sugar

1 cup vinegar

Mix all ingredients and marinate for a day or two. Mix occasionally while marinating. This makes a very nice side dish.

"The base for this recipe came from my grandson's household. The name Greenbank is for the community in which I live."

— JACK HILLARD
New Holland

Secret Sauce A-La-Greenbank

2/3 cup sugar

1 cup olive oil

1 1/2 cups vinegar

1 cup water

1 cup ketchup

1/4 cup mustard

1/4 cup blackstrap molasses

1/8 cup salt

1/8 cup black pepper

1/8 cup crushed garlic

1/8 cup liquid smoke

Mix all these ingredients together.

"I use this to marinate mushrooms and also for salad dressing. My niece asked for this recipe and then said 'or is that a secret?' hence the name secret sauce!"

— JACK HILLARD
New Holland

Beef Barbeque

1 lb. hamburger

1/2 cup onion, chopped

1/4 cup ketchup

1 Tbsp. brown sugar

1 Tbsp. vinegar

1 tsp. mustard

1/2 tsp. Worcestershire sauce

1/2 tsp. salt

Sprinkle salt over hamburger. Brown hamburger and onion. Add remaining ingredients. Simmer for 10 minutes. Serve on hamburger rolls.

— JANESSA FISHER
Narvon

Chicken Pita Sandwich

1 can chicken

1 tsp. mayonnaise

1 tsp. mustard

pinch of pepper

pita bread

lettuce

Strain chicken. Stir in mayonnaise, mustard, and pepper. Cut opening in pita bread. Add lettuce to shell. Fill with 3 Tbsp. of chicken mixture.

— LISA MARIE SIMMERS
Narvon

Christi's Stromboli

DOUGH

1 1/3 cup warm water

1 tsp. salt

1 pkg. dry yeast

2 oz. oil

4 cups flour

FILLING

12 slices provolone cheese

12 slices boiled ham

12 slices soft salami

1 1/2 lb. sweet Italian sausage

24 slices of pepperoni

1 1/2 cups shredded mozzarella cheese.

Mix together the warm water and yeast. Add the salt and oil. Gradually add 4 cups of flour and knead until blended. Divide into 3 parts. Brush with oil and cover with a clean cloth. Let sit until filling is ready.

Crumble and brown the sausage in oil. Drain. Roll dough to form 3 large rectangles. Lay 4 slices of cheese and some pepperoni down the middle of the dough overlapping the pieces.

Next add the ham, then salami brushed with mustard. Add 1/3 of cooked sausage and 1/2 cup mozzarella cheese. Fold over sides and ends and seal. Brush the top with butter. Sprinkle with salt, pepper and oregano.

Bake at 500 degrees for about 15 minutes.

— ALEX DIEM
Narvon

Grilled Reuben

8 slices Jewish rye bread

1 lb. corned beef or turkey

4 slices Swiss cheese

1 cup sauerkraut

8 Tbsp. Thousand Island
  dressing

butter

Top four slices of bread with corned beef, 1/4 cup sauerkraut, a slice of cheese and a slice of bread. Butter outer sides of sandwich.

Grill both sides of sandwich on a griddle or in a heavy skillet until cheese begins to melt and bread is lightly toasted, about 4 minutes on each side. *Serves 4*

— KATHERINE SMUCKER
Elverson

Hot Ham Sandwiches

3 lb. thinly sliced deli ham

2 cups apple juice

2/3 cup packed brown sugar

1/2 cup sweet pickle relish

2 tsp. mustard

Separate ham slices as you put them in to a 6 qt. slow cooker. In a bowl combine the apple juice, brown sugar, relish and mustard. Pour over ham. Cover and cook on low 4 to 5 hours until heated through. Serve on hamburger or Kaiser rolls.

"I use this recipe often for groups as it makes 20 to 25 sandwiches, and am always asked for the recipe!"

— KATHY MARTIN
Narvon

Veggie Melt Sandwich

1 medium zucchini sliced

6 to 8 slices sweet pepper

4 to 6 slices onion

1/2 cup sliced mushroom

2 to 4 slices provolone
  cheese

2 Tbsp. dijon mustard

2 ciabatta rolls (or 4 slices
  bread)

Sauté vegetables in butter or olive oil until tender-crisp. Season with salt and pepper to taste. Spread 1 Tbsp. mustard on each roll.

Divide vegetables between rolls; top with a slice of provolone cheese. Place sandwiches in panini press (or grill in skillet) until bread is toasted and cheese is melting. *Serves 4*

— KAREN ZIMMERMAN
Narvon

Nana's Cape Cod Chicken Salad

SALAD

4 cups cooked boneless
    skinless chicken breasts

1 cup celery, diced

1/2 cup dried cranberries

1/2 cup pecans, chopped

DRESSING

3 Tbsp. sugar

2 Tbsp. honey

2 Tbsp. clear corn syrup

1 Tbsp. cider vinegar

4 Tbsp. water

1 Tbsp. canola oil

1 1/2 cups Miracle Whip
    salad dressing

1/4 tsp. paprika

1/2 tsp. poppy seeds

Cut chicken into small bite-sized chunks. Mix in celery, dried cranberries, and pecans.

For dressing, mix rest of ingredients in a separate bowl. Pour over chicken and mix well. Add salt and pepper to your taste.

— BARBARA DIEM
   Narvon

Poppy Seed Party Sandwiches

10 to 12 pkg. party rolls

1 lb. chipped ham

1/2 lb. sliced Swiss cheese

1/2 cup butter

1 1/2 tsp. dry mustard

1 1/2 tsp. poppy seeds

2 tsp. onion flakes

1 1/2 tsp. Worchestershire
    sauce

Leave rolls together and with a long bread knife slice through horizontally and lift tops off. Put the intact bottoms into a 9 X 13-inch pan.

Put cheese slices and then ham on the rolls. Put the roll tops on. Then brush the tops and sides with the sauce you make by mixing the remaining ingredients over low heat.

Bake uncovered at 350 degrees for 20 minutes. Cut apart and serve.

— AMANDA SAUDER
   Lititz

MEAT & MAIN DISHES INDEX

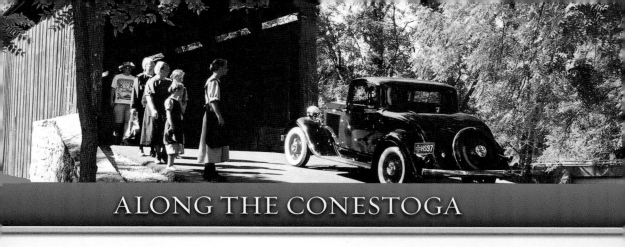

ALONG THE CONESTOGA

MEAT & MAIN DISHES
Poole Forge Covered Bridge

 Owens Optometrics

Sensenig's Jewelry store with optometrist.

Doctor	Robert L. Owens, OD, FAAO
Address	654 East Main Street
	New Holland, PA 17557
Phone	(717) 354-2251
Website	www.owensoptometrics.com
Email	eyeline8@hotmail.com

Our practice is the oldest continual ophthalmic practice in Lancaster County. It started as an extension to Jonathan Sensenig's Jewelry store. He set up an optical shop prior to the establishment of the Pennsylvania College of Optometry in 1919; to the best of our knowledge this was in about 1907. He later took the necessary course work to become an optometrist. In the mid-forties, Dr. Albert (Buddy) Wascou assumed his practice and continued providing eye care to our community until his untimely death in 1981, at the age of 59. Dr. Robert Owens joined his practice in 1980 to support Dr. Wascou during his final year of practice; Dr. Owens subsequently purchased the practice in 1981. In 1989, the practice was moved from its original downtown location to its present site in Garden Spot Centre, across from the high school.

Read Dr. Owen's Covered Bridge story on page 177.

Poole Forge Covered Bridge

Poole Forge is a Lancaster County gem. Far from the County's population centers, but not too far off the beaten track, the park is a splendid place for a picnic, a family reunion, or just a lazy summer afternoon. There is something for everyone: peace and quiet; unspoiled land; the beginnings of the Conestoga River; a modern pavilion; and history galore: the ironmaster's mansion and outbuildings; the iron kilns; and to top it off, an authentic covered bridge.

Poole Forge Bridge, built in 1859, just celebrated its 150th birthday. Levi Fink signed the contract to build the bridge for $1219. Mr. Fink also built three other Lancaster County covered bridges, none of which still stand. Poole Forge Bridge is 99 feet long, average for the County's bridges. The bridge is the traditional "barn red," and was included on the National Register of Historic Places on 11 December 1980.

North entrance of Poole Forge covered bridge.

Why a bridge at Poole Forge? Bridges were expensive propositions, which is why governments ordinarily paid for them (the other common method being lotteries conducted among interested citizens). Because of the expense, before a government agreed to pay, it needed assurance that the bridge was needed. The easiest way to establish that was to show the bridge's importance to commerce (something governments are fond of taxing), and the simplest way of demonstrating that was physical proximity. Goods have to be able to get to market for commerce to happen, which is why covered bridges were so often built next to a mill — the mill's product needed to cross the waterway that powered the mill to get to market. Poole Forge was an important iron forge, hence the need to cross the Conestoga.

Many explanations have been suggested for why a bridge would need a roof: so that cattle would not be frightened to cross through what looks to be a barn. Or so that a farmer's hay, conveniently stashed, could be kept dry from the pop-up thunderstorm. That suggestion is closer to the truth, which is decidedly practical. An uncovered wooden bridge will rot within ten to twenty years. By roofing the structure, builders protect what

Interior timber structure of Poole Forge covered bridge.

supports the bridge: the trusses, the arrangement of timbers. With reasonable maintenance of the roof, sides, and deck, and with luck (meaning no destruction from man or Mother Nature), the bridge could last indefinitely.

Poole Forge Bridge's truss is a Burr arch. A truss is the bridge's framework, timbers arranged in a triangle, the only two-dimensional figure that stress cannot deform. Theodore Burr, one of the 19th century's preeminent covered bridge builders, invented and patented the Burr arch. Builders place two arches on each side of a covered bridge to sandwich the truss. The ends of the arch are embedded in the bridge's abutments, its stone and/or

"Elias McMellen" engraving.

concrete ends that rest on either side of the waterway and support the bridge's approach. By using arches, builders can construct a stronger and longer bridge than is possible without them.

On one of Poole Forge's arches is carved: "Elias McMellen A.D. 1859." Mr. McMellen is the champion of Lancaster County covered bridge builders, known to have built at least 29 bridges, and to have rebuilt or repaired another 16. Of the 28 bridges presently standing in the County, Mr. McMellen built or worked on half of them. Poole Forge is the earliest known of Mr. McMellen's work, and has raised a number of questions just by the inscription, because we know nothing else of his work on that bridge. Was Mr. McMellen an apprentice to Mr. Fink? If so, why does Mr. McMellen's name appear, but not Mr. Fink's? Why does Mr. McMellen's name appear at Poole Forge, but not on any other of his County bridges? Was Poole Forge Mr. McMellen's masterpiece (classic definition), so that Mr. Fink, finding it satisfactory, directed Mr. McMellen to "sign" it? That we will likely never know the answers keeps the questions interesting. (Incidentally, Elias McMellen was also a captain in the Union Army, and fought in the Civil War.)

A century after Messrs. Fink and McMellen built Poole Forge Bridge; the Commonwealth of Pennsylvania took it off the transportation grid and transferred it, ultimately, to private ownership. It stayed in private ownership, without maintenance, until 2005. Then, Caernarvon Township bought the entire Poole Forge property to offer to the community as a park. Today, after restoration by Historic Poole Forge, Inc., the grounds and the bridge have never looked better. The community has a wonderful park, peaceful and tranquil, and at its center still stands the old covered bridge. On 16 May 2009, Historic Poole Forge threw a party to celebrate the bridge's 150th birthday. At the same time, Historic Poole Forge generously shared its stage to help celebrate the 50th anniversary of another organization.

In 1959, with Poole Forge Bridge turning 100 years old, a group of concerned Pennsylvanians formed The Theodore Burr Covered Bridge Society of Pennsylvania, Inc. These citizens were concerned because of what they saw happening. Covered bridges were widely seen as a thing of the past, a hindrance to modern transportation needs, and the bridges were viewed with worse than indifference. The Pennsylvania Department of Transportation saw no need to save the remaining bridges, and, in fact, was replacing them with concrete and steel.

The Burr Society's twin aims are preservation and restoration of Pennsylvania's covered bridges. Over the last 50 years through the efforts of countless volunteers (such as those of Historic Poole Forge) these two aims are met now more

Restoration of Poole Forge covered bridge in 2008.

than ever before. But the challenges are ongoing and never ending. Full details, including a membership application, are available on the website, www.tbcbspa.com.

Chicken & Vegetable Lasagna

12 lasagna noodles

1 2/3 cup milk

2/3 cup parmesan cheese

1/2 large onion chopped

1/4 tsp. pepper

1/8 tsp. ground nutmeg

12 oz. sliced mushrooms

16 oz. frozen broccoli, thawed and chopped

(other vegetables can be mixed in or used in place of the broccoli)

1/4 cup butter or margarine

6 Tbsp. flour

1 (14 1/2 oz.) can chicken broth

16 oz. shredded cheese- Swiss, cheddar, mozzarella your choice (recommend a mixture)

2 cups chopped cooked chicken, turkey or ham

Preheat oven to 350 degrees.

Cook noodles to package directions, drain, set aside. In a large skillet, sauté onions and mushrooms in butter until soft. Stir in flour, and then gradually add broth and milk, stirring until smooth.

Add the parmesan cheese, pepper and nutmeg. Bring to a boil and cook until the sauce just thickens.

In a greased 9x13 pan, spread a little sauce on the bottom of the pan, and then layer the noodles, chicken, vegetables, sauce and cheese. Repeat this layering until all noodles have been used.

Spread a little remaining sauce and cheese on the top (vegetables and chicken can also be placed on top). Cover loosely with foil and bake for 30 minutes. Remove foil and bake 5 minutes more. Remove from the oven and let stand 10 minutes before serving.

"My grandmother, Dorothy Wimer lived at Poole Forge when I was a little girl."

— WENDY HUGHES
Oakdale

Chicken Casserole

2 cups cooked chicken, turkey or fish

2 cups stuffing mix

2 cans cream of mushroom soup

1/2 cup milk

1/4 cup slivered almonds

2 Tbsp. butter melted in 1/4 cup hot water

1 pkg. of frozen string beans

cranberry sauce

Place 2/3 cup of dry stuffing mix in the bottom of a buttered casserole dish.

Prepare frozen string beans so they are not quite finished cooking. Place on top of the stuffing mix. Sprinkle the almonds on top of the beans. Spread the meat on top. Dilute the soup with milk and pour over the meat. Mix the remaining bread cubes with hot water and butter and arrange on top of casserole.

Bake at 400 degrees for 25 minutes or until golden brown. Serve with cranberry sauce.

— MARYANN OESTREICH
Narvon

Chicken Cordon Bleu

4 large chicken breasts deboned and skinned

8 slices of boiled ham, thinly sliced

8 slices swiss cheese, thinly sliced

2 large eggs beaten

1 can Italian flavored bread crumbs

1/8 lb. melted butter

garlic salt to taste

Place chicken breasts between plastic wrap and pound thin. Rub melted butter on flattened chicken and sprinkle with garlic salt. Then place ham and cheese slices on top.

Roll up each chicken breast and dip in bread crumbs, then beaten eggs, then bread crumbs again. Put toothpicks in chicken to hold together while baking.

Bake in a greased casserole uncovered at 350 degrees for about 1 hour or until tender.

— BRENDA MARTIN
Narvon

Chicken Ettie

1 (8 oz.) box of spaghetti cooked and drained

3 to 4 cups chopped cooked chicken

1/4 cup chopped green pepper

1 cup chicken broth

1/4 tsp. celery salt

1/4 tsp. black pepper

3/4 lb. Velveeta® cheese

2 cans cream of chicken soup

Mix all the above ingredients together. Bake in a greased casserole.

Bake uncovered at 350 degrees for 1 hour. This recipe is also very good with leftover turkey.

— Betsy Perry
Terre Hill

Chicken Noodle Au Gratin

3 cups cooked noodles

2 cups cooked diced chicken

1 cup cooked peas

1 1/2 cups cooked carrots

2 Tbsp. bread crumbs

1/4 cup butter or margarine

1/4 cup flour

1/2 tsp. salt

2 cups milk

1 chicken bouillon cube

1/2 cup Velveeta® cheese

pinch of pepper

Melt the butter and blend in flour and seasoning. Add the milk and cook until thickened. Add the cheese, chicken, peas, carrots and noodles.

Pour into greased casserole dish. Sprinkle with bread crumbs.

Bake at 400 degrees for 15 to 20 minutes.

— Vera Jane Newswanger
Morgantown

Chicken Stir Fry

1 lb. boneless, skinless chicken breasts, cut into pieces

1 large green pepper cut into strips

2-3 carrots cut into thin slices

8 oz. bag of frozen snow peas

Sauce

1 cup chicken broth (1 cup water + 1 tsp. chicken bouillion)

1 Tbsp. soy sauce

2 Tbsp. corn starch

1 Tbsp. brown sugar

1/2 tsp. ground ginger

2 Tbsp. cooking oil for cooking

Prepare chicken and vegetables. In a separate bowl, mix broth, soy sauce, corn starch, brown sugar and ginger. Heat oil in a skillet and stir fry the chicken. Cook until meat is no longer pink.

Add the carrots and pepper and cook just until tender yet crispy. Add snow peas. Stir in broth mixture until thickens. Serve over cooked rice. Add salt & pepper to taste. Other vegetables may be added for more flavor.

— KATHY MARTIN
Narvon

Easy Oven Chicken

8 boneless chicken breast halves

1 pint sour cream

2 cans cream of mushroom soup

1 cup dry white wine

paprika to taste

Place chicken in a greased 9 X13-inch shallow baking dish. Combine sour cream, soup and wine. Pour over the chicken and sprinkle generously with paprika. Bake uncovered at 350 degrees for 1 1/2 hours. *Serves 6*

"A recipe used many times for Lenten dinners at Bangor Episcopal Church, Churchtown"

— MARGE DAILEY
New Holland

Jackie Mac

cooked chicken cut in bite size pieces (amount for your family size)

1 box elbow noodles or shells, cooked and drained

2 cans yellow corn, drained

2 cans cream of chicken soup

2 cups shredded cheddar cheese

1 cup milk

hard boiled eggs (optional)

bread crumbs on top (optional)

Combine all the ingredients and bake in a greased casserole dish at 350 degrees for about 30 minutes. May be cooked in the microwave oven for 10 minutes.

"Jackie made this for the Girl Scouts."

— RON FINK, IN MEMORY OF JACKIE M. FINK
Narvon

Mamie's Pheasant or Chicken Pie

1 pheasant or chicken

3 cups cubed carrots

3 cups potato cubes

4 cups corn

1 cup celery

2 Tbsp. parsley

saffron and salt to taste

6 hard boiled eggs

2 pie shells with tops

Cook pheasant in 2 quarts of water until soft. Remove meat from bones. save the broth. To the broth add carrots, potatoes, corn, celery, parsley and seasonings.

Cook until tender. Add the chopped meat and chunked hard boiled eggs. Pour into pie shell and top with crust.

Makes 2- 9-inch pies or 1- 9 X 13-inch pan. Bake at 425 degrees for 15 minutes, then 350 degrees for 30 minutes.

"During small game season, we would anxiously wait for my brothers and cousins to return from the quarry with a fresh killed pheasant so our Grandmother could make this delicious pie."

— CINDY DIEM
Narvon

Orange Cashew Chicken

CHICKEN

1 lb. skinless, boneless chicken breast cut into pieces

2 to 3 medium sliced carrots

1/2 cup chopped celery

2 Tbsp. oil

SAUCE

2 Tbsp. corn starch

1/4 tsp. ground ginger

3/4 cup orange juice

1/4 cup honey

1 1/2 Tbsp. soy sauce

1/2 cup salted cashews

In a large skillet (electric fry pan works great), stir fry chicken, carrots and celery in oil until juices run clear. Reduce heat.

In a bowl, combine sauce ingredients until well blended. Stir into the chicken mixture. Cook and stir for 2 minutes or until thickened. Stir in cashews. Serve over rice.

— KATHY MARTIN
Narvon

Oven Barbequed Chicken

Cooking oil

3 to 4 lb. chicken pieces

1/3 cup chopped onion

3 Tbsp. butter

3/4 cup ketchup

1/3 cup vinegar

3 Tbsp. brown sugar

1/2 cup water

2 tsp. prepared mustard

1 Tbsp. Worchestershire sauce

1/4 tsp. salt

1/8 tsp. pepper

Heat a small amount of oil in a large skillet. Fry the chicken pieces until browned. Drain. Place the chicken in a greased 9 X 13-inch baking dish.

In a saucepan, sauté onion in butter until tender. Stir in remaining ingredients. Simmer uncovered for about 15 minutes. Pour over the chicken.

Bake at 350 degrees for about 1 hour or until chicken is done, basting occasionally. *Serves 6*

— MARY JANE NEWSWANGER
Morgantown

Poppy Seed Chicken

2 cups cooked chicken, cut into bite sized pieces

8 oz. sour cream

1 can cream of mushroom, celery or chicken soup

1 1/2 cup crushed crackers

1 tsp. poppy seeds

1/4 lb. melted butter

Spread chicken on the bottom of a greased baking dish. Combine sour cream and soup and spread over the chicken.

Combine the cracker crumbs, poppy seeds and melted butter. Spread on top of the soup mixture. Bake uncovered at 350 degrees for 30 minutes.

— LIDA BENSINGER
Narvon

Scalloped Chicken Casserole

CHICKEN

1 (5 to 6 lb.) chicken

1 cup chicken broth

1 1/8 cup flour

1 Tbsp. salt

1/4 tsp. pepper

4 1/2 cups chicken broth

2 cups milk

FILLING

4 cups bread cubes

1/4 cup chopped onions

1 cup chopped celery

1 tsp. salt

1/4 tsp. sage

1/3 cup butter or margarine

Cook chicken and when cool remove the meat from the bones. Cut meat into bite size pieces and set aside. Meanwhile, in a large skillet, cook 1 cup of broth and blend in flour, salt, and pepper. Cook until bubbling. Stir in 4 1/2 cups broth and milk. Boil 3 minutes stirring constantly. Remove from heat.

Combine the filling ingredients together and toss lightly to blend. Divide the filling mixture evenly between two 9 X 13-inch greased baking dishes. Place the cut up chicken on top and cover with the white sauce. Mix altogether so the filling is moistened. Bake covered at 350 degrees for 1 hour.

"This is a favorite recipe to make for guests. Delicious with creamy mashed potatoes or rice."

— SHARON COLON
Narvon

Turkey Croquettes

3 cups chopped turkey 1/2 inch pieces

2 cups stuffing already prepared or 2 cups cooked rice

1 1/2 sticks of butter

1 small onion chopped finely

1/4 cup flour

pinch of pepper

1/4 tsp. sage seasoning

bread crumbs

1 large egg beaten

1/2 to 1 cup milk

Melt the butter in a skillet and add the onion and sage. Mix flour and milk in a bowl until smooth and then pour in to skillet until it thickens. Combine turkey, stuffing or rice into a large bowl and mix all together. Add the white sauce and make sure it is well mixed.

Cover and refrigerate for 3 hours. Form the turkey mixture into 2 inch croquettes. Then dip into egg mixture and roll in bread crumbs. Chill for 30 minutes.

Place on a greased baking sheet and bake at 375 degrees for about 8 minutes on each side or until golden brown.

— JoAnn Cress

Bacon Cheeseburger Meatloaf

1 lb. lean ground beef

10 slices of bacon cooked and crumbled

8 oz. grated cheddar cheese

2 eggs lightly beaten

1/4 cup bread crumbs

1/4 cup mayonnaise

1 tsp. Worchestershire sauce

1/4 tsp. salt

1/4 tsp. pepper

1/3 cup ketchup

2 Tbsp. mustard

1 (3oz.) can French fried onions

Combine meat and next 8 ingredients. Mix well. In a small bowl, combine ketchup and mustard. Add 1/4 cup of ketchup mixture to the meat and reserve remaining for the top.

Press meat mixture into a greased 9 X 3 X 5-inch loaf pan. Spread remaining ketchup mixture over loaf.

Bake uncovered at 350 degrees for 40 minutes. Then top with onions and bake another 10 to15 minutes or until loaf is no longer pink.

— Rick Klumpp
Narvon

Cabbage Casserole

4 cups shredded cabbage

1 lb. lean hamburger

1 medium chopped onion

1/2 cup cooked rice

1 can tomato soup

salt and pepper to taste

1 cup shredded Colby Jack cheese

In a skillet, brown the meat and onion. Add cooked rice and blend. In the bottom of a greased 2 quart casserole dish layer half the shredded cabbage. Add meat mixture and the remainder of the cabbage.

Pour undiluted soup over the top. Cover and bake at 350 degrees for 1 hour. Uncover the last few minutes to brown the top. Shredded cheddar cheese may be sprinkled over the top to melt. *Serves 4*

— CINDY DIEM
Narvon

Chinese Hash

1 1/2 lb. lean ground beef

1 cup finely chopped onion

1 cup celery

1 cup rice cooked until tender (makes about 2 1/2 cups)

1 can mushroom soup

1 can cream of chicken soup

1 cup water

1 small can of chopped mushrooms

1 can bean sprouts

2 Tbsp. soy sauce

chow mein noodles

Brown the ground meat. Then add onion and celery and sauté until slightly tender.

Cook the rice per package directions.

Then mix all ingredients together except the chow mein noodles and spread in a greased casserole dish. Bake uncovered at 350 degrees for 45 minutes. Then spread the chow mein noodles over the top and bake an additional 5 minutes.

— SHIRLEY SIEDHOF
Narvon

Favorite Lasagna

2 lb. lean ground beef

1 large onion

2 quarts of spaghetti sauce

1 lb. cottage cheese

2 large eggs, beaten

2 Tbsp. parsley

1 tsp. salt

1/4 tsp. pepper

12 lasagna noodles

1 lb. mozzarella cheese

Brown the meat with the onion. Drain and add 2 quarts of spaghetti sauce. Simmer for 20 minutes. Set aside.

In another bowl, combine cottage cheese, eggs, and seasonings and mix together.

Cook lasagna noodles according to package instructions. Using a 9 X 13-inch greased baking dish, spread a little sauce on the bottom and top with a layer of 4 noodles, then 1/3 of the cheese mixture. Repeat the sauce, cheese, and noodles until finished. Cover the top with mozzarella cheese. Bake at 375 degrees for 30 minutes. Let set 10 minutes before serving. *Serves 8*

— Mary Jane Newswanger
  Morgantown

Ground Beef Supreme

2 lb. lean ground beef

1 pkg. onion soup mix

10 oz. pkg. of frozen peas

2 1/2 cups cooked noodles

1 can cream of mushroom soup

1/4 cup milk

6 slices white American cheese

1 can tomato soup

1/4 cup milk

1/2 cup melted butter

1 1/2 cup crushed Ritz crackers

1/2 cup shredded cheddar cheese

Brown the meat, onion and soup mix. Stir in the cooked noodles, peas, mushroom soup and 1/4 cup milk. Pour into a greased 9"x13" casserole and place slices of cheese on the top. Cover with tomato soup and 1/4 cup milk. Melt the butter and cracker crumbs together and spread over the top. Sprinkle with cheddar cheese. Bake uncovered at 300 degrees for one hour.

— Vera Jane Newswanger
  Morgantown

Hamburg Stew

1 1/2 lb. lean ground beef

1 medium onion, chopped

2 to 3 carrots, chopped

5 potatoes, diced

2 celery stalks, sliced

1 can tomato juice

Brown the ground beef and onions in a large pot. Add juice. Then add the carrots, potatoes, celery and any other vegetables you may enjoy. Season to taste.

— GERTRUDE OESTREICH
 Ashland

Instant Filled Cabbage

3 slices of bacon

1 small chopped onion

1/4 cup chopped celery

1 lb. lean ground beef

1 large egg

3/4 cup uncooked minute rice

salt, pepper and parsley to taste

1 can tomato soup

1 (16 oz.) can chopped tomatoes

1 cup water

1 head of cabbage

Fry bacon until crisp. Drain and crumble into small pieces. Add bacon, onion and celery to the ground beef. Add egg, rice and seasonings. Mix everything together. In another bowl, blend the soup, tomatoes and water. Set aside.

Slice the cabbage into thin slices. Arrange 1/2 of cabbage in a greased 9 X 13-inch casserole dish. Then layer half the tomato and beef mixture. Repeat the layers. Bake at 350 degrees for 1 1/2 hours.

— MARY A PARMER
 Narvon

Lasagna Rolls

6 lasagna noodles

1 lb. lean ground beef

1 (15 1/2 oz.) can spaghetti sauce

1 tsp. fennel seeds

1 (8oz.) pkg. shredded mozzarella cheese

Cook lasagna noodles according to package instructions. Meanwhile, brown the ground beef, and drain excess fat, then stir in spaghetti sauce and fennel seeds. Simmer 5 minutes. Drain noodles. Spread 1/4 cup of meat sauce on each noodle and top with a sprinkling of cheese.

Carefully roll up each noodle and place seam side down in a greased 9 X 9-inch baking dish. Spoon remaining sauce over each roll and sprinkle with remaining cheese. Bake covered at 400 degrees for 10-15 minutes or until heated through.

— SHARON COLON
Narvon

Li'L Cheddar Meat Loaves

1 large egg

3/4 cup milk

3/4 cup shredded cheddar cheese

1/2 cup quick oats

1/2 cup chopped onion

1 tsp. salt

1 lb. lean ground beef

2/3 cup ketchup

1 1/2 tsp. mustard

1/2 cup brown sugar

In a bowl, beat the egg and milk. Stir in cheese, oats, onion and salt. Add ground beef and mix well. Shape into 8 loaves and place them in a greased 9 X13-inch baking dish. Combine ketchup, brown sugar and mustard and spoon over loaves.

Bake uncovered at 350 degrees for 45 minutes.

— MARY JANE NEWSWANGER
Morgantown

Meatloaf Pie

1 lb. lean ground beef

2 slices of stale bread crumbled or bread crumbs

2/3 cup milk

1 slightly beaten egg

1/4 cup chopped onion

1 Tbsp. Worchestershire sauce

1 1/4 tsp. salt

mashed potatoes

1/4 cup grated cheese of your choice

Lightly combine first 7 ingredients and spread into a 9-inch greased casserole pan. Bake at 350 degrees for 35 minutes. Drain off the fat.

Pile the mashed potatoes on the meat as if a meringue on a pie. Sprinkle with cheese and bake an additional 10 minutes.

— EVA BRUBAKER
East Earl

Popover Pizza Casserole

1 lb. lean ground beef

1 cup chopped onion

1/2 of a 3 1/2 oz. pkg. of sliced pepperoni, halved

1 (15oz) can of pizza sauce

1/2 tsp. crushed dried oregano

2 large eggs

1 cup milk

1 Tbsp. cooking oil

1 cup all-purpose flour

1 (6oz.) pkg. of thinly sliced mozzarella cheese

In a large skillet, cook the meat and onion until browned. Drain fat. Cut pepperoni slices in half. Stir pepperoni, pizza sauce and spices into the meat mixture. Bring everything to a boil and simmer for 10 minutes stirring occasionally.

Meanwhile for the topping, mix the eggs, milk and oil in a small bowl. Add the flour and stir until blended and smooth.

Grease a 9 X 13-inch baking dish. Spoon the meat mixture into the bottom. Arrange the cheese slices over the meat. Pour topping over the cheese covering completely. Sprinkle with parmesan cheese.

Bake at 400 degrees for 25 to 30 minutes or until topping is puffed and golden brown. Serve immediately. *Serves 8*

— ALEX DIEM
Narvon

Potato Patch Casserole

CASSEROLE

1 lb. lean ground beef

1/2 cup chopped onion

1 large egg

1/4 cup milk

1/4 cup dry bread crumbs

1 tsp. salt

4 cups potato slices

1 (10 oz.) pkg. frozen peas & carrots, thawed

1/4 tsp. pepper

1/4 tsp. celery salt

WHITE SAUCE

2 Tbsp. butter

2 Tbsp. flour

1 cup milk

1 1/4 tsp. salt

dash of pepper

1/2 lb. Velveeta® cheese

Combine the meat, onion, egg, milk, bread crumbs and seasonings. Shape into 18 meatballs and brown in cooking oil.

Make the white sauce with butter, flour, milk, salt and pepper. Add cheese and stir until melted. Combine the potatoes, peas and carrots.

Place in a greased roaster pan. Arrange the meatballs around the edge of pan and cover with sauce.

Bake covered at 350 degrees for 1 hour and then uncovered for an additional 30 minutes.

— A. M. RINGLER
Narvon

The Krock family dressed up as Ironmaster Old, his wife, and children during the 150th Year Anniversary of the Historic Poole Forge covered bridge. The Old's owned the property when the bridge was constructed.

Spaghetti Pie

6 oz. spaghetti

2 Tbsp. butter

1/3 cup parmesan cheese

2 well beaten eggs

1 lb. lean hamburger

1/2 cup chopped onion

1/2 cup diced green pepper

1 small jar of your favorite
spaghetti sauce

To make the crust cook the spaghetti noodles as directions state and drain. Add the butter, cheese and beaten eggs. Form into a buttered 8-inch baking dish.

Cook the meat, onion and pepper together. Add the sauce and pour into crust. Top with mozzarella cheese. Bake uncovered at 350 degrees for 45 minutes.

— MARY ANN GOOD
Terre Hill

Haystacks

2 lb. lean ground beef

1 large onion, chopped

1 cup ketchup or tomato
juice

2 Tbsp. brown sugar

2 Tbsp. mustard

1 tsp. Worchestershire sauce

1 tsp. salt

1/2 cup salad dressing

1 cup cheese spread

tortilla chips

Fry ground beef and onion until brown. Add the remaining ingredients and simmer 20 minutes more.

For cheese sauce melt 1/4 cup butter and gradually add 1/4 cup flour. Add 2 cups of milk and stir until thickened. Add 1/2 cup salad dressing and 1 cup cheese spread.

Serve with tortilla chips. Top with the meat mixture and cheese sauce. Can also be topped with mashed potatoes, baked beans, lettuce, onion, and tomatoes

— SUSIE NEWSWANGER
Narvon

Beef or Venison in Onion Gravy

1 can (10-3/4 oz.) cream of
mushroom soup

2 Tbsp. onion soup mix

2 Tbsp. beef broth

1 Tbsp. quick cooking
tapioca

1 lb. beef or venison cut into
1 inch cubes

hot cooked noodles or
mashed potatoes

In a slow cooker, combine the soup, soup mix, broth and tapioca. Let stand for 15 minutes. Stir in the meat. Cover and cook on low for 6 to 8 hours or until meat is tender. Serve over noodles or mashed potatoes.

— VERA JANE NEWSWANGER
Morgantown

Skillet Tamale Pie (Dutch Oven Recipe)

1 lb. lean hamburger

1 (6 oz.) can tomato paste

1 (15 oz.) black beans

1 Tbsp. chili powder

1 tsp. cumin

3/4 cup water

8 1/2 oz. corn muffin mix

1 (8 1/2 oz.) can cream corn

1 (4 1/2 oz.) can green chilis-undrained

1/4 cup milk

1 egg

Combine the first six ingredients in a large cast iron pan. Simmer for 10 minutes. Combine the remaining ingredients and spoon on top of the meat/bean mixture (corn muffin mixture will be soupy). Cover pan and simmer for 15 minutes.

"A famous Boy Scout recipe made in a Dutch oven. While Rick was a Boy Scout leader, this was a favorite recipe on camping trips."

— JEANETTE KLUMPP
Narvon

Theodore Burr Covered Bridge Society of Pennsylvania celebrating the Historic Poole Forge Bridge Anniversary. They aid in preserving and restoring covered bridges throughout the state.

Beef Roast with Coke

4 lb. beef roast

1 (12 oz.) can of coke

1 (10 3/4 oz.) can of
mushroom soup

1 pkg. dry onion soup mix

Blend coke, soup and dry onion soup mix together. Pour over roast and bake in a greased roasting pan. Cover the meat and bake at 300 degrees for 4 1/2 to 5 hours. This recipe makes its own gravy.

— LOUELLA J. HORNING
Narvon

Beef Stew

2 lb. beef cubes

2 cups diced carrots

1 medium onion, sliced

2 tsp. quick tapioca

1/2 tsp. pepper

1 cup water

2 cups frozen peas

2 cups diced potatoes

1 cup chopped celery

1 Tbsp. salt

2 cups tomato juice

1 Tbsp. brown sugar

Place the beef cubes in a greased roasting pan. Add the vegetables except the peas. Sprinkle tapioca, salt and pepper over the vegetables and meat. Add the tomato juice and water. Sprinkle brown sugar over everything.

Cover and bake at 350 degrees for about 3 hours. Add the peas near the end of the baking time.

— SHIRLEY WEIDMAN
Narvon

Chuck Roast Dinner

1 1/2 lb. boneless beef chuck roast cut into pieces

2 medium potatoes, peeled and cut into chunks

2 to 3 carrots cut into chunks

1 pt. tomato juice

1/8 cup Worchestershire sauce

2 Tbsp. quick cooking tapioca

1 tsp. beef bouillon granules

In a slow cooker put potatoes, carrots and beef. Add remaining ingredients. Cook on high for 6 hours.

Turn back to low for 1 1/2 to 2 hours more or until meat is tender.

— Kathy Martin
Narvon

Grandmother's Sauerbraten

4 to 6 lb. eye round beef roast

2 large sliced onions

3 to 4 scallions cut in pieces

2 Tbsp. whole peppercorns

12 whole allspice

12 fresh whole cloves

6 bay leaves

1 (14 oz.) bottle of ketchup

1 1/4 cup red wine vinegar

1/2 cup raisins

1 cup brown sugar (save until the end to add with cookies)

12 or more ginger snap cookies

Place meat into large greased sauce pan. Add all other ingredients except the cookies and sugar. Cover with water to cover the meat. Place a lid on pan and refrigerate for 3 days.

Stir and turn meat each day. Day before serving, transfer to a clean pan and simmer for 3 to 4 hours or until meat is tender. Remove meat and cool. Simmer the juices, adding the brown sugar and cookies. Cook until thickened. If too sour add some water and a little more sugar if desired. Slice the roast and gently add to gravy. Serve with buttered noodles.

— Churchtown Farm Inn
Narvon

Grandma's Noodles for Sauerbraten

1 bag of desired width egg noodles

2 tsp. salt

1 stick of butter

10 to 12 crackers

sprinkle of dill weed and black pepper

Melt butter in small fry pan. Add the crushed crackers, dill weed and pepper. Keep warm while noodles are cooking per package directions. Drain the noodles when tender and blend with the cracker mixture. Place buttered noodles into a serving dish. Keep warm until ready to serve with the sauerbraten.

— SUSAN MARRIS
Goodville

Korean Bul-Kogi "Korean Barbecue"

2 lb. beef flank steak

1 Tbsp. sesame seeds

3 spring onions finely chopped

4 cloves minced garlic

1/4 cup plus 1 Tbsp. soy sauce

2 Tbsp. sesame oil

1/4 cup sugar

2 Tbsp. sherry or beef stock

1/8 tsp. black pepper

Slice the meat very thin diagonally across the grain. Place the sesame seeds in a pan and brown lightly over low heat. Grind in a mortar. Combine the sesame seeds and remaining ingredients in a bowl and mix well. Add the meat and stir until well coated. Let stand 20 minutes or longer. Grill over charcoal, electric grill or under a broiler. Cook briefly on both sides.

"In honor of the land of my children's birth and a favorite in our family."

— MAURINE VAN DYKE
Narvon

Sweet Pot Roast

3 to 4 lb. beef roast

1 large onion

1 (10 1/2 oz.) can golden mushroom soup

1/2 cup water

1/4 cup brown sugar

1/4 cup apple cider vinegar

2 tsp. salt

1 tsp. mustard

1 tsp. Worchestershire sauce

Mix sauce together and pour over the roast. Bake for 3 to 4 hours at 275 degrees.

— MARY JANE NEWSWANGER
Morgantown

Eleanor's Swiss Steak

3 to 4 Tbsp. flour

1/2 tsp. salt

1/4 tsp. pepper

1 1/2 tsp. dry mustard

2 lb. round steak

frying oil

1 cup sliced onion

1 lb. sliced carrots

1 (14 1/2 oz.) can whole tomatoes

1 Tbsp. brown sugar

1 1/2 Tbsp. Worchestershire sauce

Combine the flour, salt, mustard and pepper. Cut the steak into serving slices and dredge in flour mix. Brown the meat on both sides in oil.

Place in a slow cooker and add the onions and carrots. Combine the tomatoes, brown sugar and Worchestershire sauce and pour into a slow cooker. Cook at low for 8-10 hours or on high for 3 to 5 hours.

— ELEANOR HIBSHMAN
Narvon

Brenda's Swiss Steak

4 Tbsp. flour

1 tsp. salt

1/8 tsp pepper

1 1/2 lb. round steak

2 Tbsp. oil

2 cups tomato juice

2 medium sliced onions

1 cup chopped celery

1 Tbsp. Worchestershire sauce

dash or two of tabasco sauce

1 tsp. sugar

1 tsp. salt for sauce.

Combine the flour, salt and pepper. Sprinkle half of mixture over the steak. Pound meat with a heavy mallet until flour mixture disappears. Turn steak over and repeat with remaining flour mixture. In a heavy skillet, heat oil over low heat and place steak in hot oil. Brown on both sides. Add remaining ingredients. Cover tightly and simmer over low heat for about 1 hour or until meat is tender.

— BRENDA MARTIN
Narvon

Ukrainian Goulash

1/4 cup salad oil

3 lb. beef chuck

4 medium finely chopped onions

1/4 cup tomato paste

1/4 cup chopped parsley

2 tsp. salt

1 tsp. dried thyme leaves

1/4 tsp. pepper

2 small bay leaves

Heat oil in a Dutch oven. Cut beef into 1 1/2 inch cubes. Add to the oil 1/3 at a time and brown on all sides, removing the cubes as browned. Preheat oven to 300 degrees. Add onion to pan drippings and sauté till golden brown, about 10 minutes. Return the meat to the skillet. Stir in 1 1/2 cups water, tomato paste, parsley, salt, thyme, pepper and bay leaves. Bring to boil. Bake covered for 2 hours or until beef is tender. Nice to serve with buttered noodles. *Serves 8*

— MARYANN OESTREICH
Narvon

Eggs & Potatoes

1 tsp. butter

3 cups mashed potatoes

8 large eggs

2 Tbsp. grated cheddar cheese

1/2 tsp. paprika

1/2 tsp. salt

1/4 tsp. pepper

Coat a 9-inch square baking dish with butter. Spread mashed potatoes in the dish. Make 8 evenly spaced holes in the potatoes. Carefully break an egg into each hole. Sprinkle with cheese and seasonings.

Bake uncovered at 400 degrees for about 10 minutes or until eggs are set and cheese is melted. *Serves 8*

— MAE MARTIN
Lititz

Historic Poole Forge volunteers Gary and Sarah enjoy a break under a shaded picnic table during the 150th Anniversary of the Covered Bridge.

Pad Thai

6 oz. Thai noodles

2 Tbsp. brown sugar

2 Tbsp. ketchup

1 tsp. soy sauce

1 tsp. salt

1/4 tsp. rice vinegar

2 Tbsp. canola oil

1 large egg

1 tsp. minced garlic

1 cup sliced cabbage

1/4 cup sliced carrots

1/4 cup green beans cut in 1 inch pieces

1/4 cup green onions cut in 1 inch pieces

1/4 cup snow peas

1/4 cup broccoli florets, halved

2 Tbsp. ground peanuts

1/4 cup bean sprouts

Break noodles in half and soak in warm water for 1 hour. Drain and set aside. Combine brown sugar, ketchup, vinegar, salt and soy sauce in a bowl and mix well to make the Pad Thai sauce.

Add oil to pan on medium heat. Add egg and stir lightly until almost firm. Add vegetables (except sprouts) to pan and stir fry with the egg.

Add noodles, garlic and Pad Thai sauce and stir until noodles are soft and sauce is mixed throughout. Add sprouts and peanuts. Toss lightly, remove from heat and serve.

"A delicious recipe from Thailand!"

— RICK KLUMPP
Narvon

Rozanna's Crustless Quiche

1 1/2 cup milk

3 eggs

1/2 cup Bisquick®

1/2 stick butter, softened

1/2 tsp. salt

1/4 tsp. pepper

1 cup shredded cheese

1 cup diced meat or vegetables

Grease 2 quart casserole dish. Blend milk, eggs, Bisquick, butter, salt, and pepper in blender. Pour into greased dish. Add cheese, meat, or vegetables of your choice and push down with a spoon.

Bake at 350 for 45 to 60 minutes.

— LINCOLN BOONE BED & BREAKFAST
Narvon

City Chicken

1 lb. veal, cut into 1 inch
cubes

1 lb. pork, cut into 1 inch
cubes

1 lb. beef, cut into 1 inch
cubes

salt

pepper

garlic powder

1 medium onion, grated
over meat

3/4 cup flour

1 or 2 eggs, well beaten

cracker or bread crumbs
with parsley

1 cup oil

wooden skewers

Cut the veal, pork & beef into 1 inch cubes and season with grated onion, salt, pepper and garlic powder. Refrigerate for 2 to 4 hours.

Place meat on pointed wooden sticks. Dip in flour, and then in beaten eggs and then bread crumbs, making sure each is completely coated.

Brown in a large skillet with 1 cup oil at low to medium heat. Cook until brown on all sides.

When browned, place on cookie sheet and bake at 300 to 325 degrees for 1 to 1 1/2 hours.

"This recipe is great served hot or cold. Great to take along on a picnic. All of the "kids" in our family loved eating city chicken!"

— MARYANN OESTREICH
Narvon

Baked Pig Stomach

1 pig stomach

2 lb. sliced raw potatoes

1 small chopped onion

3 lb. loose pork sausage

salt and pepper to taste

Mix together the potatoes, onion, sausage and seasoning and stuff the stomach. Place the stomach in a greased roasting pan. Add a small amount of water to the bottom of the pan. Bake covered at 350 degrees for about 3 hours or until golden brown.

— BRENDA MARTIN
Narvon

Baked Pork Chops

6 pork chops, cut 1/2 to 3/4-inch thick

2 Tbsp. shortening

1 can cream of chicken soup

1 medium onion, sliced

3 Tbsp. ketchup

2 tsp. Worchestershire sauce

Brown the pork chops in shortening and arrange in a greased baking dish. Slice the onion and place a slice on top of each chop. Mix together soup, ketchup and Worchestershire sauce and spoon over chops. Bake uncovered at 350 degrees for 1 hour. These chops are wonderful served with rice.

— Susie Smucker
Narvon

Kielbasa, Cabbage, & Dumplings

kielbasa links

1 large head of shredded cabbage

2 sticks of butter

1 large chopped onion

salt and pepper to taste

1 medium potato

1 cup flour

1 large egg

1 tsp. salt

Sauté cabbage and onion in melted butter till tender

Grate the potato. Mix all the ingredients together until blended well. Drop by 1/2 tsp. into boiling water. Cook over low heat for 20 minutes. Drain and rinse with cold water.

Cook your favorite kielbasa link and slice into bite size pieces. Add cabbage mixture, kielbasa and dumplings all together and serve.

— Betsy Perry
Terre Hill

Penny Saver Casserole

6 hot dogs, thinly sliced

4 medium diced and cooked potatoes

1 cup of peas

1/4 cup butter

2 tsp. minced onion

1 tsp. mustard

1 (10 1/2 oz.) can cream of mushroom soup

Combine potatoes, onion and butter in a greased casserole. Add remaining ingredients and mix. Dot with the sliced hot dogs.

Cover and bake at 350 degrees for 25 minutes.

— Mary Jane Newswanger
Morgantown

Oyster Stuffing

5 to 6 loaves of bread cubed

2 (8 oz.) cans of oysters

6 large eggs

2 cans of evaporated milk

black pepper to taste

Mix all the ingredients together and stuff a turkey or chicken or spread into a greased 9 X 13-inch casserole. Add some chicken broth to the stuffing if you cook it in a casserole. Bake at 350 degrees for 1 1/2 hours.

— BETSY PERRY
Terre Hill

Queen Scallops

SCALLOPS

4 scallops

1 Tbsp. lemon juice

2 oz. bread crumbs

2 oz. grated cheese

1/2 oz. butter

salt

SAUCE

1 oz. butter

1 oz. flour

2 oz. grated white sharp cheddar cheese

1/2 pint milk

Scrub the scallops and place in a warm oven (325 degrees) until the shells open. Remove the black part and gristly fibre leaving the red coral intact. Boil in salted water with the lemon juice for 10 minutes. Drain.

To make the sauce: Melt the butter in a saucepan and stir in the flour using a wooden spoon. Stir in the milk and heat gently for 2-3 minutes. Stir in the grated cheese.

To serve: Clean the scallop shells. Place a little sauce in each shell and sprinkle with bread crumbs. Place a scallop on top, cover with a little more sauce and sprinkle with bread crumbs and cheese. Dot with butter and bake at the top of a fairly hot oven (375 degrees) for 20 minutes. Garnish with parsley and serve with salad.

— GAYNOR GREEN
Bowmansville

Scalloped Oysters

1 quart fresh oysters (about 48)

4 cups premium oyster crackers

1 tsp. salt

1/2 tsp. pepper

1 tsp. Old Bay® seasoning

1/2 lb. butter

1 1/2 cups whole milk

3 cups oyster juice

Heat in pot milk, oyster broth, butter and seasoning but do not boil. Crumble a layer of crackers in the bottom of a greased casserole, then a layer of oysters and broth. Repeat the layers until finished.

Cover the casserole and place in refrigerator for 1 hour. Add more liquid if you can not see the juice in the casserole. Bake covered at 375 degrees for 30 minutes.

— GEORGE MARTIN
Narvon

Rabbit Fricassee

1 1/2 to 2 lb. fresh rabbit, cut up

1/2 cup flour

3 tsp. salt

1/4 tsp. pepper

6 Tbsp. bacon drippings or fat

2 cups minced onion

3 cups boiling water

1 bay leaf

1/2 tsp. salt

pinch of curry powder

Wash and dry cleaned rabbit after soaking over night in a pickling solution of: 1 cup vinegar, 1 bay leaf, 1 tsp. pickling spice and 3 cups water. Dredge and combine flour, 3 tsp. salt and pepper.

Heat the fat in a skillet. Add the floured rabbit pieces to the pan and sauté until golden brown on all sides. Remove the rabbit from the pan. Add the remaining ingredients to the drippings and stir.

Then add the rabbit pieces again and simmer covered for 2 hours or until meat is tender and the gravy has thickened. Serve the gravy over the rabbit.

— SHIRLEY WEIDMAN
Narvon

Braised Rabbit in Wine Sauce

1 1/2 to 2 lb. rabbit

2 slices bacon

1 cup sliced celery

1 medium onion, sliced

2 cloves garlic, minced

1/2 cup dry white wine

1/2 cup chicken broth

1 tsp. dried oregano, crushed

1/4 tsp. dried marjoram, crushed

1 bay leaf

1/2 cup whipping cream

2 Tbsp. snipped parsley

Cut across rabbit just below the front legs. Cut across rabbit just above the back legs. Cut through back-bone to halve the pieces with front and back legs attached. You should have 5 pieces. Rinse rabbit; pat dry.

In a 10-inch skillet cook the bacon till crisp and brown. Remove; drain on paper towels, reserving pan drippings in skillet. Crumble the bacon; set aside.

Cook the rabbit in pan drippings for 10 minutes, turning after 5 minutes to brown evenly. Remove rabbit, reserving drippings.

Cook celery, onion and garlic in pan drippings until tender. Slowly add the wine, chicken broth, oregano, marjoram, and bay leaf. Bring to boiling, scraping up the brown bits. Add the rabbit. Reduce heat; simmer, covered, 45 minutes or until rabbit is tender and easily pierced with a fork. Turn rabbit once during cooking.

Measure pan juices; reserve 3/4 cup. Return to skillet. Add cream. Bring to boiling. Reduce heat to medium; cook and stir about 6 minutes or until the cream thickens slightly. Pour thickened sauce over the braised rabbit. Sprinkle rabbit with the crumbled bacon and parsley. *Serves 4*

— FREDDY REY
Elverson

Salt Duck

one 4 to 5 lb duck

4 oz. sea salt

2 medium onions, chopped

2 oz. water

1 level Tbsp. plain flour

1/2 pint milk

Rub the salt well into the flesh of the duck, turning and recoating every day for 3 days. Keep the duck in a cool place throughout the salting process.

Thoroughly rinse the salt off the duck and put it into a large pan or casserole. Pour over cold water to cover, bring to a boil and simmer very gently for 1 1/2 hours, turning over halfway through.

Stew the chopped onion in the measured water very, very gently for about 15 minutes until tender. (It may be necessary to press some greaseproof paper down on top of the onions to retain the moisture.) Strain off the liquid, blend it with the flour using a whisk, and add the milk. Return to the onions, and bring this onion sauce to a boil. Simmer for a minute or two to cook the flour and thicken the sauce. Either liquidize or sieve the sauce, and taste for seasoning.

Serve the duck sliced, accompanied by the sauce. Fruity chutney tastes great with this dish.

— GAYNOR GREEN
Bowmansville

Hunter Style Venison Chops

6 venison chops about 3/4 inch thick

2 Tbsp. butter

3 Tbsp. red currant jelly

1/2 cup tomato sauce

1 1/2 cup chestnut puree, from scratch or bought

Season both sides of the chops with salt and pepper. Melt butter in frying pan large enough to hold all the chops. Brown the chops 5 minutes on each side and then remove from pan. Pour off all but two Tbsp. of the drippings. Add the jelly and stir until blended. Add the tomato sauce and incorporate well. Place the chestnut puree into a large platter and arrange the chops around. Pour the sauce over the chops.

— HENRY MARCONI
Narvon

Chestnut Purée

1/2 onion slice

1 Tbsp. unsalted butter

1 1/2 cups (10 oz.) roasted chestnuts

1 1/2 cups chicken broth

Cook onion and butter on low heat for about 7 minutes until softened. Add chicken broth and chestnuts and simmer another 10 minutes. Then puree the mixture in a blender until smooth. Reheat, add salt and pepper to taste.

— SANDY & HENRY MARCONI
Narvon

After hunting season each year in Lexington, New York, (if my hunting buddies were lucky enough to bring meat to the table), we would all gather at my cousin's home and he would cook these venison chops and chestnut purée up for us. Most of my buddies are gone but the recipe remains.

— HENRY MARCONI

Venison Meat Balls

MEAT BALLS

1 medium onion, finely chopped

1/2 cup uncooked instant rice

1 tsp. salt

1 tsp. ground pepper

1 lb. ground venison

SAUCE

3/4 cup water

1/3 cup brown sugar

1/3 cup ketchup

1/3 cup tomato soup

1 Tbsp. ground mustard

2 tsp. paprika

Combine the ingredients and form into 1 inch meatballs. Put in a greased baking dish.

Mix the sauce ingredients together until blended. Pour over the meatballs.

Bake uncovered at 375 degrees for 45 minutes.

"Good recipe to make ahead of time and serve from a crock pot. May be served as an appetizer or main dish with rice."

— SONDRA SIMMERS
  Narvon

Swiss Deer Steak

1 deer round steak

1 sliced onion

1 chopped green pepper

1 (8oz.) can tomato sauce

salt and pepper to taste

Place deer steak in a 9x13-inch greased roasting pan. Add the onions and pepper. Top with the tomato sauce. Add salt and pepper to taste. Bake covered at 350 degrees for 60 minutes.

"At our house I have hunters. We've tasted deer, turkey, rabbit, doves and pheasant which my husband and son have gotten over the years."

— SHIRLEY WEIDMAN
  Narvon

VEGETABLES & SIDES INDEX

Roasted Green Beans

Broccoli Casserole

French Carrots

Baked Corn

Kathy's Corn Fritters

Amanda's Corn Fritters

Corn Pudding

Baked Beans

Homemade Baked Beans

Buffet Potatoes

Chili-Seasoned Potato Wedges

Cheese Potato Puff

German Potato Salad

Linda's Potatoes

Lisa's Potatoes

Overnight Mashed Potatoes

Stand Up Baked Potatoes

Skillet Fried Sweet Potatoes

Sweet Potato Plus

Mom's Pan-Fried Filling (Bread Stuffing)

Bread Filling

Betty's Onion Pie

Mock Oysters

Fried Tomatoes

Stewed Tomatoes A-La-Greenbank

Spanakopeta (Spinach Pie)

Imitation Crab Cakes

Quick Zucchini Bake

Hot Fruit Casserole

Baked Pineapple

Pineapple Casserole

VEGETABLES & SIDES

Our Quilting Heritage

OFFERING A LARGE
SELECTION OF QUILTING
SUPPLIES, LOCAL-
MADE QUILTS AND
WALL HANGINGS.

Obies Country Store

Address   1585 Main St.
             PO Box 69
             Goodville PA 17528

Phone   (717) 445-4616

WOOD
LAMINATE
VINYL
CARPET

SERVING THE
COMMUNITY
SINCE 1985

Maitland's Flooring, LLC.

Address   2403 Main St.
             Narvon, PA 17555

Phone   (610) 286-1842

Fax   (610) 286-1843

Email   maitlandsflooring@dejazzd.com

VEGETABLES & SIDES

Our Quilting Heritage
A LANCASTER COUNTY TRADITION

The history of quilting in Lancaster County goes back to the early days of our country. When the English arrived in Chester and Lancaster Counties, they brought with them a tradition of quilt making, using fine, expensive, imported fabrics that came through the ports of Baltimore and Philadelphia. These quilts featured beautiful chintz and other printed cotton fabrics used in both pieced and appliqued designs.

Inked signatures became popular after the invention of permanent ink in the 1840s. About 1850, the sewing machine became available for home use and became "a standard part of sewing" in the decades following the Civil War. Machine stitching can appear in quilts as early as 1850, and is very commonly found after 1870.

During the nineteenth century, the many German residents of eastern Lancaster County, including the Amish and Mennonites, began adopting a tradition of quilt making that slowly replaced the use of woven coverlets for bedding. These women created exquisite quilted masterpieces that have been well preserved and are widely collected today.

In addition to being currently described as works of art, Amish and Mennonite quilts traditionally served a practical, functional purpose. Many were given as gifts, particularly to children and grandchildren, and as such, were seldom used.

Double Wedding Ring Quilt from the late 1950's.

The Pennsylvania German quilts are well known for their distinctive use of color – a deep saturation of primary colors of red, blue, green, yellow, purple, cheddar and pink. The early Amish quilts featured jeweltone wools, later supplemented with rayons and cotton twills, in a limited number of patterns. The quilts made by other Germanic religious denominations were made primarily of small cotton prints. These fabrics were inexpensive and easily available from the local dry goods stores, having been printed either in New England or the greater Philadelphia area.

The Amish began their quilting tradition using just 5 styles of designs. The other Pennsylvania German ladies used a variety of patterns, the same as their English neighbors were using, only in their distinctive color combinations. It is this use of color that sets quilts made in the southeastern counties of Pennsylvania apart from those made in other states.

The quilts of Caernarvon Township reflect this mix of styles and populations. While the Amish continued to make quilts in their own distinctive patterns during the first half of the twentieth century, most quilts made during this time do not have characteristics that can be identified with any one particular group or location. Beginning in the late 1800s, the mass marketing of quilting information, including patterns in newspapers and magazines, helped quilts to become more generic in style. With the advent of mail order catalogs, fabric and quilting supplies were available to women living anywhere in the US.

For generations, groups of women have gathered for quilting bees. The bee provides socialization and relaxation for these women as they sit around the quilt frame putting the important quilting stitches into the finished tops. It is a time when they can get together to visit and "catch up" with one another, exchange recipes and share fellowship.

Quilting day in the mansion.

Amish and Mennonite ladies of the area were among the groups that kept quiltmaking alive in the interim between WWII and the current quilt revival that began in the 1970s. More recently, many Plain women have developed cottage industries involving quilts. Many Amish and Mennonite women have opened small shops in their homes to supplement the family income. A handmade sign, stating simply "quilts sold here, no Sunday sales," announces the business. Many other ladies piece quilts in their homes to then be sold in other businesses. The current popularity of quilts and quiltmaking has made Lancaster County a destination for large numbers of quilters and collectors from around the country. Many older women growing up in the Depression recall making quilts out of necessity and learning to quilt from family and friends. Today, quilters are able to continue the quilting tradition using both "available" fabric and fabric purchased specifically for their quilting project. They also have available to them a wealth of information including books, magazines, television shows and Internet websites.

Quiltmaking is a fun and rewarding activity, enjoyed by people of all ages and skill levels. Quilting involves the creative expression of beauty and emotion that is conveyed through the thoughtful choice and preparation of fabric and the careful piecing, appliqué and quilting in the finished product.

Careful hand stitching.

When a quilter begins to think about making a quilt, there is a moment of inception when she actually decides the type of quilt she will create. For some, the moment may result from an outside event, such as the desire to make a wedding, birthday, or anniversary gift. For others, the inspiration might be the recognition of a need to recreate in fabric the emotional impact of the beauty of the natural world. Sometimes the impetus can be the desire to use a particular piece of fabric, or to explore a unique color combination or new technique. Frequently, quiltmakers are inspired by existing quilts found in their family closet, seen in a museum display, or pictured in a book or magazine.

Quilts can be a variety of sizes, including wall hanging, doll quilt, crib quilt, and twin through king size quilt. There are many different styles and themes to choose from, including Christmas, Cathedral Window, Yo Yo, Baltimore Album, Civil War, Amish style, Rag, Hawaiian style, Memory, Photo memory, 1930s reproduction and scrap quilts. Once the design decision has been made, there may be a period of incubation, during which the original idea is refined, materials are collected, and preparations are made.

When the time is right, the quiltmaker enters the implementation phase, beginning to work with the fabric. Historically, this often meant creating a template from paper or cardboard, tracing the shape onto fabric, and cutting the fabric with scissors.

Contemporary quiltmakers have a number of additional tools and techniques available to them, including freezer paper, rotary cutters, plastic templates and glue-sticks. During the process of cutting and

Applique covered bridge quilt by Mrs. David (Esther) Sauder.

sewing, the quiltmaker often realizes the need to modify or adapt the design. There is much give and take between the maker and the emerging quilt, and many quiltmakers report a high level of satisfaction during this process.

There is a point during construction when the quilt develops a life of its own, expressing its own "personality." As the abstract idea materializes into a quilt, the quilter may feel a sense of wonder that she has created a truly unique and new creation where nothing existed before. It is no surprise some quilters use metaphors of giving birth when speaking of their quiltmaking.

The quiltmaking process is not completed with the final binding stitches, for the quilt must fulfill its purpose. Whether it was intended to cover a bed, decorate a wall, serve as a gift, compete in a contest, or rest in a closet as evidence of personal achievement, the result is both satisfying and a true gift to the future. The best thing about making a quilt is that once finished, the quilter is able to share it with family and friends! Whether a quilt is used on a day to day basis or saved for special occasions, it serves as a reminder of the

Claudia Esh spinning.

love, care and attention to detail that went into its making. Many quilts are cherished and kept as family heirlooms to be passed down to future generations.

Historic Poole Forge hosted its first quilt show in the spring of 2008 and showcased more than fifty antique quilts from the eastern Lancaster County area. The historic mansion provided the perfect backdrop for the outstanding quilts, which dated from 1858 to 1952. Quilters, historians and visitors were thrilled with the variety of colors, patterns, and styles displayed. Many of the quilts were "best" quilts, made only for show or as gifts, and not designed to be slept under. Others showed wear, indicating that they were used for warmth and comfort.

The personal stories connected to many of the quilts added a special emotional personality to the exhibit. For instance, a crazy quilt, from 1876, that had won first prize at the Kentucky State Fair, is now living in Lancaster County after being lovingly handed down through the generations. The quilter was only sixteen when she made this fascinating quilt. A young Mennonite bride brought her friendship quilt with her when she moved here from Indiana. She continued to quilt on into her 90's, and her daughters and granddaughters continue that tradition here in Caernarvon.

We were able to show one room containing all Amish quilts, including a pink and white quilt made by a young girl and her mother, which seems to break the "rules" we have learned about typical Lancaster County Amish quilts. The young girl still treasures her quilt, more than fifty years after she made it. One moving quilt had been sent to Holland at the end of World War II as part of relief efforts, conducted primarily by the Red Cross

A variety of hand made local quilts on display at Obies General Store in Narvon, PA.

and Mennonite Central Committee. The young woman who received the quilt eventually came to the United States, keeping her treasured quilt until her death. It was then given to a special friend for continued care. The earliest quilt shown was a red and green applique with incredibly tiny quilting stitches, signed and dated 1858. It was made by a Lewistown area woman for her marriage, and now belongs to her great great granddaughter who lives locally. In the late 1890s, an 18 year old woman made her Chimney Sweep quilt using the unusual color combination of burgundy, purple and lavender. She never married and lived with various family members in the area. The quilt was handed down to a nephew, and then to his daughter. In the 1930's, two sisters each made a snowball quilt for their hope chests. One was red and green, the other red and blue. They were married on the same day in a double ceremony and later each made a Grandmother's Flower Garden quilt using dress scraps. The quilts are still treasured by family members. Also in the 1930s, a young woman in Iowa pieced a lovely pastel Trip Around The World top for her trousseau. It was never quilted and became a wedding gift for her granddaughter. Finally, the top was quilted by a Caernarvon quilter. One room in the mansion featured several examples of a local quilt pattern, currently known as The Bowmansville Star. It is a postage stamp quilt with the fabrics arranged in a distinctive large star pattern. One quilt was made in 1891, never used and in perfect condition. It is owned by the granddaughter of the maker. A 1930s version had larger blocks and had been lovingly used.

No doubt many quilts were made right at Poole Forge. We are aware of one resident of Poole Forge, Margaret McDowell, who made lovely appliquéd quilts in the 1960's and 70's. She often donated a quilt for fundraisers at Bangor Church. The owners of these quilts treasure their beauty and historic significance. The quilting traditions of Lancaster County bring visitors from around the world and we were honored to have many visit Poole Forge during the Spring Quilt show. We hope that the lovely setting of Poole Forge will host many more shows highlighting the exquisite quilts and the many talents of our local quilters. The quilts exhibited in the first "Quilts In The Mansion" Show at Poole Forge illustrated the diverse quilting styles of those living in the area. We are fortunate to be blessed with a long, deep and rich quilting tradition in this area.

Roasted Green Beans

2 lb. fresh green beans, trimmed, or

1 (16 oz.) pkg. frozen whole green beans, thawed

3 Tbsp. slivered almonds

1 1/2 Tbsp. lemon juice

1 Tbsp. olive oil

3/4 tsp. salt

1/2 tsp. garlic powder

1/2 tsp. basil

1/2 tsp. freshly ground pepper

Combine the green beans, almonds, lemon juice, olive oil, salt, garlic powder, basil and pepper in a bowl and mix well. Spread the bean mixture in a 10 X 15-inch baking pan. Roast at 450 degrees for 10 minutes or until tender and brown, stirring occasionally.

"Roasting green beans in the oven keeps them tender but still firm. This is a good dish for an outdoor party since it can be prepared in advance and held at room temperature."

— LIDA BENSINGER
Narvon

Broccoli Casserole

1 lb. broccoli, cut into pieces

1 can (10.75 oz.) cream of mushroom soup

2 large eggs, lightly beaten

1 cup mayonnaise

1 1/2 cups shredded cheddar cheese

1/2 cup butter, cut into pieces

pepper

1 sleeve Ritz® crackers, crushed

Preheat oven to 350 degrees. Mist a 9 X 13-inch baking dish with cooking spray. Steam broccoli until crisp/tender, about 7 minutes. Transfer to a bowl of ice water. Mix soup, eggs, mayonnaise, cheese, butter and pepper in a saucepan and cook over medium low heat, stirring until melted and well combined.

Drain broccoli, spread evenly in baking dish. Pour cheese mixture on top. Sprinkle with crackers. Bake for 30 minutes. *Serves 10*

"This is yummy and so light. It will make a broccoli lover out of everyone!"

— DARLENE MAY EMERY STAUFFER
Narvon

French Carrots

2 lb. carrots

2 chicken bouillon cubes dissolved in 1 cup boiling water

3 Tbsp. margarine

2 to 3 large onions

2 Tbsp. flour

1/2 tsp. salt

1 1/2 cups water

Grate carrots. Cook carrots and broth, covered, for 10 minutes. Melt butter and add onion. Cook covered for 15 minutes. Stir in salt, pepper, flour and add 1 1/2 cups water.

Bring to a boil and add cooked carrots. Simmer uncovered for 10 minutes; add pinch of brown sugar.

— CHERYL FOX

Baked Corn

4 cups creamed corn

2 cups milk

1 1/3 cups cracker crumbs

6 Tbsp. melted butter

1 tsp. salt

1/4 tsp. pepper

2 Tbsp. sugar

4 eggs

Beat eggs; add milk and crumbs, then add corn, seasoning and butter. Mix well. Pour into a greased casserole.

Bake, uncovered, at 350 degrees for 40 minutes.

— MARTHA NEWSWANGER
Narvon

Kathy's Corn Fritters

2 cups corn

1 well-beaten egg

1 1/2 tsp. sugar

1/3 tsp. salt

1/8 tsp. pepper

1 Tbsp. melted butter

1/4 cup flour

1/2 tsp. baking powder

Combine corn, egg, sugar, salt, pepper and butter. Mix flour and baking powder. Add to first mixture.

Drop into hot oil and brown on both sides. You can eat it plain or with table syrup.

— KATHY MARTIN
Narvon

Amanda's Corn Fritters

1 pt. grated sweet corn

1/2 cup flour

1/2 cup cracker crumbs

1/2 tsp. soda

1 tsp. salt

pepper

1 beaten egg

Mix all ingredients together. Drop by tablespoon on hot greased griddle. Fry to golden brown. Turn, fry other side. Serve with syrup.

— AMANDA SHIRK
  Narvon

Corn Pudding

1/2 cup butter or margarine

2 eggs, beaten

1 (16 oz.) can cream style corn (drain corn for less moist pudding)

1 (16 oz.) can yellow corn

8 oz. sour cream

1 (8 1/2 oz.) box Jiffy® cornbread mix

Combine melted butter, eggs, corn (I drain just a little), and sour cream. Add corn bread mix. Stir well. Pour into a 9 X 13-inch dish, sprayed with Pam. Bake, uncovered, at 350 degrees for 45 minutes.

"This recipe was given to me by my friend Cheryl Fox, whose husband does the chain saw carvings at Poole Forge."

— SHIRLEY WEIDMAN
  Narvon

Baked Beans

1 lb. dry beans

1/2 tsp. salt

3/4 cup King's® syrup

1 cup ketchup

bacon

1 small onion, diced

1/2 tsp. pepper

1 tsp. dry mustard

brown sugar

Cook beans and onions together. Add remaining ingredients and brown sugar to taste.

Bake, uncovered, at 350 degrees for 1 hour.

— MARYANN OESTREICH
  Narvon

Homemade Baked Beans

1 gallon can great northern beans, drained

1 cup ketchup

1 cup brown sugar

1 tsp. mustard

1/2 cup molasses

1/2 lb. bacon, fried and chopped

1 tsp. salt

1/4 cup chopped onions

1 tsp. Worcestershire sauce

Mix all ingredients together and bake at 350 degrees to desired consistency.

— Vera Jane Newswanger
Morgantown

Buffet Potatoes

4 medium potatoes

3 Tbsp. butter

dash salt and pepper

1 Tbsp. chopped parsley

1/2 cup grated American (or any cooking) cheese

1/2 cup cream or milk

Peel potatoes and cut like French fries. Place in 8 X 11 X ½-inch baking dish. Dot with butter. Sprinkle with salt, pepper, parsley and cheese. Pour cream all over top. Cover and bake at 325 degrees for 50 to 60 minutes.

"Very good and so easy!"

— Vera Jane Newswanger
Morgantown

Chili-Seasoned Potato Wedges

1 Tbsp. onion soup mix

1 Tbsp. chili powder

1/4 tsp. salt

1/4 tsp. garlic powder

1/4 tsp. pepper

4 large baking potatoes

2 Tbsp. vegetable oil

In a large re-sealable plastic bag, combine the soup mix, chili powder, salt, garlic powder and pepper. Cut each potato into eight wedges; place in the bag and shake to coat.

Arrange in a single layer in a greased 15 X 10 X 1-inch baking pan. Drizzle with oil. Bake, uncovered, at 425 degrees for 20 minutes. Turn; bake 15 to 20 minutes longer or until crisp. *Serves 8*

— Vera Jane Newswanger
Morgantown

Cheese Potato Puff

12 medium potatoes, peeled and cubed

2 cups shredded cheddar or Swiss cheese, divided

1 1/4 cups milk

1/3 cup butter

1 to 2 tsp. salt

2 eggs, beaten

Place the potatoes in a saucepan and cover with water; cover and bring to a boil. Cook until tender, about 15 to 20 minutes. Drain and mash. Add 1 3/4 cups cheese, milk, butter and salt; cook and stir over low heat until cheese and butter are melted. Fold in eggs. Spread into a greased 13 X 9 X 2-inch baking dish.

Bake, uncovered, at 350 degrees for 25 to 30 minutes. Sprinkle with the remaining cheese. Bake 5 minutes longer or until golden brown. *Serves 12*

— VERA JANE NEWSWANGER
Morgantown

German Potato Salad

6 to 8 red skin potatoes

1/2 lb. bacon

4 scallions

2 to 3 Tbsp. flour

2 Tbsp. red wine vinegar

2 Tbsp. sugar

1 tsp. salt

pepper

1 tsp. celery seed

1 tsp. dill weed

1 Tbsp. parsley

2 cups water

Cook halved potatoes with skin on one day before needed.

Peel and slice potatoes thinly. Cook bacon until crisp, drain but save the fat in frying pan. Crumble bacon. Cook sliced scallions in bacon grease, slowly add and stir in flour, vinegar, sugar, celery seed, salt and pepper. Add a little water at a time. Keep whisking until gravy is the thickness desired adding water gradually and cooking slowly. When thick and finished, add bacon, parsley and dill weed. Pour gravy mixture over potatoes. Bake uncovered at 350 degrees for 45 minutes. Serve hot. You can also make this a few hours ahead and cover to hold.

"Goes great with Sauerbraten!"

— SUSAN MARRIS
Goodville

Linda's Potatoes

2 to 3 lb. russet potatoes, cooked then shredded or 1 (30 oz.) pkg. frozen shredded potatoes

16 oz. sour cream

1/2 cup butter

2 Tbsp. dried onions

2 Tbsp. dried chives

2 Tbsp. dried parsley

1 1/2 tsp. salt

3 cups marble Jack shredded cheese (a blend of Colby and Montery Jack)

Combine all ingredients. Bake at 325 degrees in a greased 9 X 13-inch pan, uncovered, for 30 to 40 minutes.

— LINDA SAUDER
  East Earl

Lisa's Potatoes

8 to 10 potatoes of your choice

1 pint sour cream

1 can cream of chicken soup

2 cups grated mixture of cheddar cheese

1 Tbsp. chopped fresh parsley

1 tsp. dill weed

1 tsp. salt

1/2 tsp. black pepper

1/2 cup butter

1/3 cup Italian bread crumbs

Peel potatoes and cut into small chunks. Cook only until tender. Do not overcook. Do this the day before and refrigerate.

Combine all ingredients (except butter and bread crumbs) with potatoes. Put in deep casserole and top with butter and bread crumb mixture.

Bake at 350 degrees for 1 1/2 hours.

"Fantastic for a group or take anywhere – always finished to last bite. Easy to make ahead, refrigerate until ready to bake and serve."

— SUSAN MARRIS
  Goodville

Overnight Mashed Potatoes

2 1/2 lb. potatoes

1 (3 oz.) pkg. cream cheese with chives, cubed

2 tsp. butter

1/2 tsp. seasoned salt

1/4 tsp. pepper

1 cup light cream

1 1/2 Tbsp. butter

paprika

Cook potatoes with salt until tender, about 30 minutes. Mash potatoes and then add cream cheese, butter, seasoned salt and pepper. Mix until smooth. Turn mixture into greased baking dish. Refrigerate and cover with foil. When ready to bake, dot potatoes with 1 1/2 Tbsp. butter and paprika. Bake, uncovered, in 325 degree oven for 30 to 45 minutes.

"This recipe is great for holidays because it can be made the night before. It saves time when you're busy cooking your holiday meals."

— SHIRLEY WEIDMAN
Narvon

Stand Up Baked Potatoes

9 medium potatoes, washed well

salt and pepper to taste

garlic powder and chopped parsley to taste

9 slices Velveeta® cheese

1/2 lb. bacon, fried and crumbled

1/4 cup melted butter

Slice potatoes 1/4 inch thick, keeping the potatoes together, stand them in a greased 9 X 9-inch cake pan. Sprinkle salt, pepper, garlic powder and parsley over top. Pour 1 cup water over all. Cover and bake in 350 degree oven until soft, about 1 1/2 hours.

Drain off water. Pour melted butter over potatoes. Top with cheese and bacon. Return to oven until cheese is melted.

— ROSE NEWSWANGER
Narvon

Skillet Fried Sweet Potatoes

6 lb. sweet potatoes

1/2 cup butter

1 cup brown sugar

1/2 tsp. salt

1/4 cup water

Boil sweet potatoes until skin is soft. Cool and peel sweet potatoes. Combine butter, brown sugar, salt and water in electric skillet at 300 degrees. Add potatoes, sliced about 1 inch thick. Turn potatoes frequently until they have a nice brown coating and sauce thickens.

— CINDY DIEM
Narvon

Sweet Potato Plus

1/2 cup brown sugar

1 Tbsp. corn starch

1/4 tsp. grated rind and juice of 1 orange

3 Tbsp. sherry

1/2 cup butter

1/2 cup halved pecans

1 large can good yams or fresh cooked yams

Pour yams into deep casserole, having drained some of the juice off. Bring first 3 ingredients to a boil in small pan. Add butter, sherry and pecans. (I add 3 slices of orange halved into butter mixture also!)

Turn off heat to thicken. Pour mixture over potatoes. Sprinkle with cinnamon sugar and a pinch of dill weed on top. Bake at 350 degrees or lower for 1 1/2 to 2 hours, slowly basting. Do not let it get too brown, just golden.

"This is always a pleaser and try at least once! The recipe came from Buffalo NY in 1971 where I was a guest. Submitted it to a cookbook in Amherst, New Hampshire and now here we are in Pennsylvania sharing it around. It is great to take to a buffet or any dinner."

— SUSAN MARRIS
Goodville

Mom's Pan-Fried Filling (Bread Stuffing)

1/4 cup butter

1 small onion, finely chopped

1/2 cup finely chopped celery

1/2 cup finely chopped carrots

2 eggs, beaten

1 cup milk

pinch of saffron

1 loaf bread, cut into bite-sized chunks

4 Tbsp. chicken or turkey broth

Preheat large frying pan, or a 10 inch electric skillet to medium-low heat. Melt butter in frying pan; add vegetables, sauté about one minute. Add bread chunks. Stir to combine. Mix together eggs, milk and saffron; pour over bread, stir to combine.

Fry about 5 minutes, stirring frequently. Add broth, continue frying until liquid is absorbed and filling is beginning to show crispy edges. *Serves 6*

"My grandmother Betty served this traditional dish every Thanksgiving and Christmas. My mother Helen refined it a bit, and taught it to me."

— KAREN ZIMMERMAN
Narvon

Bread Filling

1/4 to 3/8 cups melted butter (not margarine)

1 onion, chopped

1 piece celery, chopped

salt

pepper

2 or 3 eggs

1/2 to 1 cup milk

1/2 loaf of bread, cubed

Simmer the butter, onion, celery, salt and pepper to brown. Add bread cubes. Mix eggs to milk, and then add to mixture. Put in a greased loaf dish, cover with foil and bake at 300 degrees for 30 minutes.

"This was my Grandma Brumbach's recipe. She gave it to me when I got married."

— Ginny Weber
Narvon

Betty's Onion Pie

1 pie crust, unfold and prick bottom

2 lb. sweet onions, cut up

1/2 cup butter

1/2 pint sour cream

4 eggs

Put sliced onions and butter in casserole. Cover and microwave for 15 minutes. Halfway, stir. Check to see if onions are tender. Cook longer if needed until tender. Beat 4 eggs.

To eggs, add 1/2 pint sour cream, salt and pepper to taste. Mix all together. Pour over onions into pie crust. Bake at 350 degrees for 45 minutes. Stick knife until clean, bake longer if necessary.

Our daughter Jody's mother-in-law Betty made this easy and yummy onion pie for every holiday and special occasion. And we are making it now as she has passed on. Enjoy!

— Barbara S. Nau/Schoolhouse Antiques
Goodville

My mother started teaching me to quilt when I was six. She gave me small squares which I would hand sew together into 4 patch blocks.

— Sara Newswanger

Mock Oysters

pancake or waffle batter

oil to deep fry

dandelion

confectioner's sugar

Pour 1 1/2 to 2 inches of oil in pan. Dip fresh, cleaned and washed, de-stemmed and drained dandelion flowers into batter. Fry in hot oil until golden brown. Dip in confectioner's sugar. Eat warm.

"Tastes like fried oysters. Great Grandma never wasted anything!"

— Ruth Lambert
East Earl

Fried Tomatoes

4 Tbsp. flour

2 Tbsp. sugar

1 1/2 tsp. salt

1/8 tsp. pepper

2 cups milk

Melt butter in pan. Mix flour, sugar, salt and pepper. Cut tomatoes into 1/2 inch slices. Dip in flour mixture and fry until brown.

Remove to a platter. Put milk in same pan and bring to boiling point, stirring until thickened. Use the remaining flour mixture to help thicken. Pour over tomatoes.

"In Memory of Ruth Trout"

— Deb Martin
Narvon

Stewed Tomatoes A-La-Greenbank

2 qt. tomatoes, peeled and chopped

2 cups onion, chopped

2 cups celery, chopped

2 Tbsp. Blackstrap molasses

6 Tbsp. vinegar

2/3 cup sugar

1 tsp. Worcestershire Sauce

2 tsp. crushed garlic

2 tsp. salt

1 tsp. pepper

1/8 lb. butter

thicken with clear gel

Heat tomatoes, onion and celery. Blend in balance of ingredients. Thicken slightly with cooking clear gel.

"This recipe was intended as a dish to be served with stuffed pig stomach but is good any time."

— Jack Hillard
New Holland

Spanakopeta (Spinach Pie)

1 lb. filo dough

2 lb. ricotta cheese

1/4 lb. butter

2 lb. chopped spinach

2 Tbsp. olive oil

4 eggs beaten

Place washed spinach, salt, pepper, butter, oil and eggs in bowl and mix. Into a buttered casserole pan use half of the filo dough brushing each sheet with butter. Pour spinach mixture on top of filo. Cover with remaining filo (buttering each sheet as before). Bake at 300 degrees for one hour.

"Delicious holiday treat. Lorraine always served this for Christmas Eve cocktail time."

— LORRAINE RAFFENSPERGER
Blue Ball

Imitation Crab Cakes

2 eggs, slightly beaten

2 cups grated zucchini

1 cup seasoned breadcrumbs

1 Tbsp. mayonnaise

2 tsp. Old Bay® seasoning

Make into cakes and fry in Canola oil. Drop by tablespoon full. It doesn't take much oil. Brown on both sides.

— ELNA NORDAHL
Lititz

Quick Zucchini Bake

1 Tbsp. butter

1 large zucchini, sliced thin

1 large onion, sliced

fresh tomatoes, sliced or 1 large can whole tomatoes

cheese

Melt butter in heavy fry pan on medium heat. Spread sliced zucchini out on bottom of pan. Spread onion slices on top of zucchini and tomatoes on top of onions.

Bring to a boil and then put heat on low and cook 15 minutes or until soft. Turn off burner and add 1 layer of either white American cheese or another cheese of your choice.

— ELEANOR HIBSHMAN
Narvon

Hot Fruit Casserole

1 (1 lb.) can sliced pineapple

1 (1 lb.) can peach halves

1 (1 lb.) can apricot halves

1 (1 lb.) can pear halves

1 (15 oz.) jar spiced apple rings

1/4 cup raisins

1/4 cup butter

1/3 cup light brown sugar

2 Tbsp. flour

1 tsp. curry powder

1 cup cream sherry

Drain fruits thoroughly. Arrange fruit in a buttered 2 qt. casserole. Stir butter, sugar, flour, and curry powder in top of double boiler until thickened and heavy. Add sherry and blend. Add to fruit, cover, and cool.

Can be refrigerated for a couple of days. Then bake before serving. Can be baked and served immediately. Bake, covered 350 degrees for one hour. *Serves 8*

— LORRAINE RAFFENSPERGER
Blue Ball

Local women spending a day quilting and sharing fellowship at the Caernarvon firehall.

Baked Pineapple

1/4 lb. butter

1 (16 oz.) can crushed
    pineapple

1 cup granulated sugar

6 slices bread, torn up

4 eggs

pinch of salt

Blend butter, sugar and salt until creamy; add eggs and then pineapple and mix all together. Fold in bread. Spoon into buttered baking dish.

Bake at 350 degrees for 45 minutes.

— MARY ANN GOOD
Terre Hill

Pineapple Casserole

1 (20 oz.) can crushed
    pineapple, drained

3/8 cup butter

1 cup sugar

4 eggs

5 slices of bread

Drain juice from pineapple. Cream butter and sugar together. Beat in eggs. Add drained pineapple. Beat slowly. Crumble in bread and stir well.

Bake at 375 degrees or lower for approximately 40 minutes until light brown and the middle is set. Eat warm.

— EVA BRUBAKER
East Earl

Snap Shots and Snippets

Along the Conestoga

Dr. Duttenhoffers Black Bag

Dr. Duttenhoffer lived across from the fire hall, which was known as the Conestoga Valley Fire Co. at the time. The fire alarm was actually set off from their house. Back in his time, he would make house calls and many of the women would give birth at home. Fran Trego remembers that many of the women did not have a doctor's care during pregnancy until they were ready to deliver the baby, and they never talked about it.

When Fran's mother was in labor with her, her father called the doctor and said that he better come over because his wife is having a baby. Her sister Jean went to school that day with the doctor's daughter, Betty. Betty went home for lunch that day and when she came back to school she announced to Jean that she has a new sister at home. Jean argued that she didn't have one there when she came to school in the morning. Betty responded by saying, "no, but, my daddy took one there today. You see, it came in the black bag!"

When Fran was older and visiting her sister for Thanksgiving, the doctor had forgotten his black bag when he left. She watched that black bag all day to see if a baby would appear! Anna Mary Ringler also remembers her siblings being delivered in that black bag too!

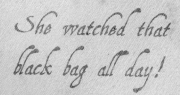

She watched that black bag all day!

"a good man who suffered many hardships during the great depression."

Wheatland

In the 1830's, Ironmaster Cyrus Jacob built a home across the road from Poole Forge for his daughter. He named it Wheatland. The Martin family purchased the farm in 1854 and has remained a working farm through six Martin generations. Today it is owned by the John David Martin family.

John remembers a story about his grandfather Eli, who was the tax collector for the township. He was a good man who suffered many hardships during the great depression. First he lost his wife, then all his cows got TB and died, then he ordered a trainload of cattle and when he went to pick them up at the East Earl train station, they opened the door and they all had died. He still said, "The lord is good to me", and he still prospered.

One day Dick Sandoe came to visit John David and wanted to share this story about Eli. "Your grandfather loaned my dad money for a house, and each week I would stop in and drop off whatever money we could afford and he always thanked me and never complained".

B&E Market

Buckwalter's store was located between what is now Gary Van Dyke's and Jeff Buckwalter's home. The post office was also located there for a period of time. Brenda Martin would always race to the store to beat Barb Shirk for the one blueberry pie that would be delivered from Tom's Pies in Bowmansville! The kids also enjoyed popsicles and the penny candy.

Most everyone's needs were met at the stores in Churchtown. They would barter for goods. If one person made butter, they would take it to the store and trade for other goods. If they traveled to a big town, they would go to Lancaster or Reading, especially for Christmas shopping. Floribel Styer recalled riding on the "Reading bus". Harvey Beiler was the driver and would travel from Morgantown to Churchtown, New Holland, and Terre Hill and then go back route 625 to Reading. Frank Weaver's family would sell produce at the livery stable in Lancaster. They would park the wagon, take out the shaft, and sell their goods from the wagon.

Rubinsons

Rubinson's not only had a store in New Holland, but also had one in Churchtown at one time, which was located at the current site of the fire hall. Jake Weaver's was the place to buy TV's, washing machines, and tractors. Brenda Martin recalls buying their first TV there when she got married. It was located where Churchtown Supply now resides. The undertaker was beside the current Deli in Churchtown. The post office was also located there for a period of time.

Harvey's Boots

Many local residents recall trips to Hauenstine's Store in Churchtown. It was owned by Maude and Hauney who provided groceries, shoes, and some clothing. If you wanted cheese, they would cut it off a huge block. Harvey Shirk purchased a pair of boots from there in 1962, had them patched once and is still wearing them to this day!

M
E
N
U

WASHINGTON INN

Route 23   Churchtown, Penna.

Conestoga Valley

You are now in the Conestoga Valley which extends eastward to Morgantown in Caernarvon Township. It is primarily a farming district unique in the fact that the majority of the farmers are Amish.

The Washington Inn was originally built in the 1700's. The exact date is not known. It is known however that the building was sold to Cyrus Jacobs in 1812 and started as an Inn after building a larger addition to the east side. The large east room was used at different times for balls, a store, a saddlers shop, a meeting room for the Methodists before building their Church, and for town meetings such as elections. After 1820 the Washington Inn became a stopping place for the mail stage because of the modern accommodations. The Inn was a favorite dining place for "coaching" parties until a few years after the turn of the century, and Tallyhos resting at the Inn was not an uncommon sight. Now, parties come to dine at Washington Inn in motor cars.

Other points of interest: Windsor Forge and mansion, 1733; Pool Forge, 1733; Bangor Episcopal Church, originally built about 1733 or 1734. Present church was erected in 1830.

There are of course other Histories and places of interest in this section too numerous to mention here.

MENU

APPETIZERS

Chilled Tomato Juice	$ .20
Chilled Fruit Juice	.20
Fruit Cup	.25
Home Made Soup (Served Week Days)	Cup .15 Bowl .25

PLATTERS
MADE TO ORDER

T-Bone Steak	$2.50
Rib Steak	1.75
Fried Oysters (Six) In Season	1.75
Fried Oysters (Three) In Season	1.25
Fried Ham	1.25
Roast Beef	1.50
Breaded Veal Cutlet	1.25
Chuck Wagon Steak	.90
Hamburg Steak	1.00
Vegetable Platter (Choice of Five)	1.00

Above Platters served with two vegetables, rolls and butter

SANDWICHES

Ham, Pork or Beef Barbecue	$ .30
Hamburger	.30
Cheeseburger	.30
Ham Salad	.30
Chicken Salad	.35
Egg & Olive	.30
Grilled Cheese	.30
Grilled Cheese & Bacon	.45
Grilled Ham & Cheese	.50
Ham & Egg	.50
Western	.50
Cliffertaburger	.45
Bacon, Tomato & Lettuce	.45
Cold Beef	.50
Baked Ham	.45
Egg Sandwich	.25
Hot Beef w. Potatoes	.75

"Good Morning"
BREAKFAST SUGGESTIONS

Tomato Juice	$ .20
Fruit Juice	.20
Coffee, Tea or Milk	.10
Buttered Toast	.10
Fresh, Crisp Cereal served with Top Milk	.25
Hot Cereal served with Top Milk	.20
Fruits in Season	.30
Hot Cakes w Butter & Syrup (5)	.40
2 Eggs, any style, Toast & Coffee	.40
2 Eggs, Hot Cakes & Coffee	.65
2 Eggs, Ham or Bacon, Toast & Coffee	.80
Home Fried Potatoes	.20
French Toast	.40

SALADS
Served on crisp lettuce with buttered toast

Potato Salad or Macaroni Salad	$ .40	
Pickled Egg Salad	.40	
Fruit Salad	.50	
Lettuce & Tomato	.40	
Egg & Olive	.40	
Ham Salad w Tomato Wedges	.50	
Chicken Salad w Tomato Wedges	.60	
Home Baked Pie	.20	With Ice Cream .30
Home Made Cake	.20	With Ice Cream .30
Ice Cream		.10 .20

The management thanks you for your patronage regardless of how large or small.

We also cater to private parties and banquets up to 60 persons. These served family style or platter style. Prices available.

If the food was not satisfactory, tell us; however if you enjoyed it tell others.

The Management

Best Dinner in Town

This is a menu from the Washington Inn (probably 1950-1960's) just prior to the time Hazel Lear closed and sold it. At that time a hamburger was just thirty cents. Ike Todd, who lived in Terre Hill, owned it next. At one time it was also owned by Harry Short. Mary Martin cleaned for them and they could never remember her name so they called her Honey or Dear! When Fran Trego was in her teens, they used to hold dances there once a week. They also had one of the first smorgasbords in the area serving lobster tail. People would be lined up outside to eat there.

Room for Forty

The Washington Inn served many folks over the years. At one time it was owned by Leah McClure who also owned the Wooden Bucket just east of Blue Ball. Then her sister Hazel took over. Sara Newswanger would stay there during the week and cook breakfast for the truckers who would park out back along the road and then come in the back door and wait for the restaurant to open at 8:00. Sometimes if the drivers got impatient they would call up the steps for Sara! Many of the drivers worked at the Terre Hill block plant and the Grace Mines. Brenda Martin washed dishes there while the owner, Hazel Lear waited on tables.

There was also room for forty borders and just one bathroom! They had a well and cistern that would run out of water during dry spells, so they had to buy water and have it hauled in. Most of the boarders were construction workers who would eat breakfast and supper at the inn and have their lunches packed for them to take along to work. One time the gas oven blew up. The door hit Hazel and threw her into the refrigerator on the other side of the room! Her nylon clothing melted to her body and she was burned quite badly. Dr. Duttenhoffer called around and had medicine flown into Lancaster Airport. The New Holland Ambulance picked it up and brought it to her. She doesn't know what it was, but, it worked wonders – she had no scarring at all!

The Big One

One big storm was in 1958. Tunnels were dug through town so people could move around. The snow and ice clung to wash lines and they were as big as stove pipes. The snow had a blue cast to it.

Opening Boot Jack Road

In 1962 another big storm came and they had to get Jesse Brubacher in with a big V-plow to open Boot Jack road.

Milk Delivery

Another big storm hit in 1978. When Wrights bakery delivered the bread they had to hand it over a huge snow bank so it could be dropped off in town. Milk was also handed over the snow bank.

Churchtown in Drifts

The west end of town facing east down Route 23 in 1958. The ESSO sign was at Jake Weaver's Churchtown Supply Store. The building past the fuel pumps is Maude Fink's house, where the Churchtown post office was located.

"If the Poole Forge Bridge could talk it would have many tales to share over the years..."

Stealing a Kiss

It became a tradition while driving through the covered bridge at Poole Forge, to stop in the middle of the bridge and steal a kiss from your date. John David Martin grew up just across from Poole Forge and recalls driving through the bridge many times to date his future wife, Mary. His farm was once part of Poole Forge.

Covered Bridge Romance

It was a crisp, clear Sunday afternoon in December of 1984 when Dr. Bob Owens invited his new neighbor, Vicki Nyul to join him for a walk around the Poole Forge property. She and her two daughters, Sarah and Colleen, had just moved into the East Tenant House the proceeding month, after Bob and Jeanette Beisel moved off the property. He suggested it was a nice day for doing some photography but she was puzzled when he stopped to take her picture before they reached the covered bridge. She had no idea what was awaiting for her at the bridge – a dozen red and white roses and a gold chain with two hearts connected by a diamond.

They had started dating just the preceding fall and were both surprised at how quickly and naturally their relationship had evolved. Bob had always vowed that he would have to date a person for at least 2 to 3 years before he would propose. Yet, after just three months of dating, he was prepared to pop the question.

Twenty four years and a son (Ryan) later is evidence that it was a good decision to take a walk through the covered bridge at Pool Forge. Dr. Owens, who is distantly related to James Buchanan, jokes that at least this engagement, unlike Buchanan's, has flourished!

— BOB & VICKI OWENS

POOL FORGE

Living at Poole Forge

Over the years many folks have been fortunate enough to actually live at Historic Poole Forge before it became a park. One such person was Gaynor Green. Having moved here while her husband Peter was still in England, she found comfort in finding the Wimer's living at Poole Forge also. Living in the East Tenant House with three small children and a fourth on the way, it was quite an adjustment. William and Dorothy Wimer lived in the mansion and raised beagles and hounds at the time.

"...with three small children and a fourth on the way, it was quite an adjustment."

Bill would take Gaynor to her doctor appointments, teach her how to write checks and other everyday tasks that we take for granted. There were always lots of ducks on the property which they loved to feed. On the other hand, they were not so thrilled about Barney Weaver's cows wandering onto the property to graze! Gaynor recalled trying to get them to "move along" on many occasions. Gaynor's fourth child Mel, who was less than 2 years old, remembers the swing set that was near the creek. One day the cows decided to charge it and needless to say, that was the end of the swing set. Speaking of animals, one year Gaynor decided to raise geese for Christmas gifts. Well, when it came time to give the "gifts" all the geese had names, so each recipient got a live goose as a pet, because they didn't have the heart to kill them.

Maggies Quilts

Margaret McDowell taught Gaynor how to quilt. She lived in the West Tennant House and walking into her house was like entering an antique store. The table was always set with gleaming silverware. She would take Gaynor upstairs where there were two bedrooms. She had a huge chest filled with quilts and when she opened it, you could smell the mothballs!

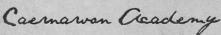

Caernarvon Academy

Many folks remember going to Caernarvon Academy which was later replaced by Caernarvon Elementary School. Stones from the academy were salvaged and used on the front of the new school which was torn down in 2008. The academy had four big rooms, 2 upstairs and 2 downstairs, where they would attend from first through eighth grade. At that time Amish, Mennonites and the "English" attended the academy. If one continued after eighth grade they would attend Terre Hill High School. At Caernarvon, Mrs. Buchanan taught first, second and third grade. Mrs. Shirk taught seventh and eighth. The kids could walk home for lunch or some went to the Washington Inn. Classes were taught in English and a lady would come to school once a week and teach from the Bible. Each morning, Mrs. Buchanan would read from the Bible, have prayer and they would salute the flag. If one of the boys got hurt, she would paint an animal on the cut with mercurochrome while the girls would get a flower.

Look, Jane.
Look, look.
See Dick.

See, see.
Oh, see.
See Dick.

School Books

Some of the books read in school included Bob, Nancy, Mac and Muff. Then in later years they read Dick, Jane and Spot books. One time Anna Mary Ringler had to stand up front in class and make up a story from pictures. When she came to the wheelbarrow she couldn't remember it in English, so she said it in Dutch and all the kids laughed at her!

Fun-n-Games

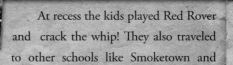

At recess the kids played Red Rover and crack the whip! They also traveled to other schools like Smoketown and Goodville to play baseball. Some of the neighborhood games included 'kick the can' and 'bag tag' (or in Dutch 'boom sock!'). Those who were just a bit ornery would get the bag wet to make it sting more. In Brenda Martin's backyard, they had a big light they could turn on to play cowboys and Indians at night. At public sales they played corner ball, which consisted of a rock wrapped in cloth. Needless to say this game was a bit rough!

The kids also enjoyed swimming. Ruthie Good went swimming on Boot Jack Road, while others would go swimming and fishing with Harry Zirt at the iron bridge on Churchtown Road. That spot was also used by locals to soak their iron wheels with wooden spokes for several days to tighten them.

"...Red Rover and crack the whip!"

Anna Mary Ringler also remembers the year school pictures were passed out and she didn't get her school picture. She was so disappointed. The photographer thought it was a double and threw it away — the other set of pictures belonged to her twin sister!

Turkey Supper

The biannual fire company turkey supper is an event that brings the Amish, Mennonites and "English" together to serve people from as far as Maryland, Delaware and New Jersey. Louis Trego remembers spending the evening tediously opening all the little cans of vegetables.

There were many colorful guests over the years. One gentleman from Georgia used to steal the silverware. Then there was the lady with two dogs in her coat. She would sit down to eat with her coat on, and inconspicuously feed the pups. The people across the table raised quite a commotion! When they offered her leftover turkey bones instead, she refused, saying she would never feed them bones! Another woman lined her purse with a bag and filled her plate with turkey. She then ate some turkey, so they couldn't take it back, and proceeded to fill up her purse with it!

Cakes

Delicious cakes are another staple at the turkey dinner. They are baked and donated by members of the community, and picked up by fireman. One time, Tom Stauffer. mentioned they aught to have a cake for themselves. Daryl Bensinger asked which one, and Tom said, "the one I just stepped in!" Another time Tom picked up a cake left on their porch, but the ants had first dibs! Tom yelled "go-go-go!" and threw it out the window before being attacked! During another cake pickup, Daryl thought Tom was taking too long of a time to get back in the jeep, but Daryl had rolled the tire on Tom's foot!

Heritage Day

Conestoga wagon.

Artisan Dean Fox carving a hawk with a chain saw.

Touring the mansion.

Shepherding the last turtle down the creek for the turtle race.

Beautifully situated along the Conestoga is the old iron plantation called Poole Forge. This property was purchased by Caernarvon Township with the vision to provide a passive park facility for the community and to preserve it's unique historical significance. The spectacular 1700's Iron Masters mansion, paymasters house, tenant houses, lime kilns and covered bridge, dating from 1859, create the perfect setting for special events, family reunions in the pavilion and playground and picnics throughout the park.

The Historic Poole Forge "Grand Opening" celebration on August 5, 2006 became the first Heritage Day event. Every year, near the end of summer, the volunteers at Poole Forge organize, plan and work to create an event to celebrate the rich heritage of the park and community. The day is filled with crafts and juried artisans, a car show, music entertainments, delicious food, the famous turtle race down the Conestoga and many other family oriented activities.

The park is open year round dawn to dusk. Historic Poole Forge is a nonprofit organization dedicated to the renewal of the property. Currently an all volunteer organization.

PUDDINGS & PIES INDEX

ALONG THE CONESTOGA

PUDDINGS & PIES

Windsor Forge

Windsor Forge

Just south of Churchtown along the Conestoga Creek lies Windsor Forge Mansion. The Windsor estate once occupied over three thousand acres of land, which was home to both the upper and lower forges. It all began in 1733 when John Jenkins, from Wales, contracted the purchase of 400 acres of land from William Penn, on behalf of the British Government. However, the patent was never carried out. Then, on December 28, 1742, William Branson, a hardware merchant from Philadelphia who owned the Reading Furnace, purchased the property. He declared that the name for the property would be Windsor, named after the Windsor Mansion in England, his homeland.

It was not long before Branson had both the upper and lower forges operating. It was then that he constructed the Eastern section of the mansion. Branson, along with his partners Samuel Flowers, Lynford Lardner and Richard Hockley, built various other dwellings in the area. The only partner to ever live at Windsor was Lynford Lardner, William Branson's son-in-law. The eastern end of the mansion may once have hosted two homes, each

Windsor Forge front around 1900.

sporting a walk-in-fireplace with a bake oven, front and back doors, a stair case, and attic. The floor of the attic above the kitchen is constructed of horse hair cement. Many declare the construction was to prevent chimney fires, while others claim it was to protect the home from flaming arrows launched to the roof tops by Indians. It was once thought that the eastern section of Windsor was constructed in two segments; however, recent renovations to the frontal exterior of the mansion indicate that the home was built as a twin house, for the stonework does not indicate any structural breaks. In 1765, the western end of the mansion was constructed by Lynford Lardner, as both forges had finally begun to prosper. This segment of Windsor hosts the original three-story mahogany railed staircase, which ascends from the foyer to the third floor. Within the western portion of Windsor, the ceilings are much higher, the latticed windows larger, and the rooms grander than those constructed in the earlier home.

Windsor Forge rear around 1900.

John Jenkin's son, David Jenkins, soon began working at the forges as a clerk. At that time, iron was being shipped to England from ports out of Philadelphia. On the property stood both forges, charcoal houses, wagon sheds, a smoke house, stables, a blacksmith shop, tenant houses, boarding houses, a large barn, a spring house, a carriage house and an office to the forges. The forges were finally operating at full capacity and it was then that David Jenkins began to purchase shares of land from Branson and his partners.

In 1776, prior to the Revolutionary War, David Jenkins had acquired the entire property. After acquiring the forges, David began to manage the iron business. He supplied artillary and ammunition to the troops, which aided the independence of our country. David prospered significantly and consequently was asked to represent the county at a meeting in Philadelphia to discuss the war at hand. David Jenkins was named to colonel, where he recruited and equipped a company of 100 soldiers in Caernarvon. These soldiers would soon become part of the 10th Battalion and would go on to fight in the war or guard the prison located in Lancaster. In August 1777, David Jenkins became justice of the peace. Soon after he married Martha Armour, daughter of General Armour of Pequea, with whom he had four sons: John, Robert, David, and William. John died at the early age of 25 in an accident, whereas Robert became the owner of the forges, and David a farmer. Their youngest son, William, became a lawyer in Lancaster, the president of the Farmers Bank, and also built Wheatland, which later became the home of President Buchanan.

It was in 1798 when David Jenkins' son Robert took ownership of the forges. Robert began purchasing property to add to the estate, which eventually totaled over 3000 acres. The business thrived for 50 years. Robert married Catherine Carmichael, the daughter of Reverend John Carmichael. Reverend Carmichael was pastor of the Forks of the Brandywine Presbyterian Church in Chester County. Robert Jenkins and Catherine Carmichael Jenkins had a son named David, after Robert's father, and a daughter, Elizabeth Jenkins Reigart. David inherited the estate after his father's death in 1848. It was then that he constructed the Twin Linden mansion, which is now a privately owned Inn. A couple of years after building Twin Linden, Robert died in a tragic accident. In 1850, the iron industry was beginning to fail significantly due to the increase in the production of steel. It was then that Catherine Carmichael Jenkins was forced to sell the land that was part of the iron forge estates. Prior to their deaths, Robert and Cathrine donated the land and a large sum of money to construct the Presbyterian Church, which is situated in Churchtown. They rest in the graveyard there, along with other family members.

Catherine Carmichael Jenkins died in 1856. Her daughter, Elizabeth Jenkins Reigart inherited the property. It would not be long until Elizabeth's daughter, named Catherine after Elizabeth's mother, acquired the land. In 1880, Catherine Reigart Cummins and her husband, a noted lawyer from New York, moved to the Windsor Mansion. They dwelled at Windsor until 1890, when they decided to move back to New York where he had practiced. The forges deteriorated at this time and the mansion sat empty for many years.

It was not until 1899 when Blanche Nevin, another granddaughter of Catherine and Robert Jenkins and daughter to Martha Jenkins and Dr. John Nevin, moved into Windsor. Dr. John Nevin was a profound Presbyterian minister and educator, who also served as a president to Franklin and Marshall College. Blanche Nevin had purchased the property from her cousin Catherine Reigart Cummins and would soon come to find Windsor an enchanting home. Blanche had become very familiar with Windsor as a young teen, as she lived there before moving to Lancaster. At the age of 21, Blanche studied sculpture and painting in Philadelphia and continued her education in Venice, Italy. Blanche entered her sculptures in world exhibitions, traveled freely throughout Europe, and spent much time in China and Japan. She loved to entertain and enjoyed an active social life, but never married. During the Wilson administration, Blanche entertained members of the First Family in Windsor mansion. Late in 1912, Woodrow Wilson's youngest daughter, Jessie, was a guest of "Auntie Blanche" at Windsor. It was here where Jessie met Francis Sayre, Blanche Nevin's nephew. Approximately one year later, on November 25, 1913, Jessie became Mrs. Sayre in a White House wedding.

Blanche Nevin is well know for her sculptures. She constructed the statue of General Muhlenberg, which can be found in Statuary Hall in Washington, D.C. She also created a bust of President Woodrow Wilson, as well as the bronze lion in Reservoir Park that was constructed in memory of her father.

Buddha sculpture in Windsor Forge garden.

Lion sculpture next to Buddha.

If you are ever traveling through the triangular intersection of West Orange Street and Columbia Avenue in Lancaster, Pennsylvania, be sure to note the beautiful marble horse drinking fountain that was constructed in memory of Blanche's mother. In addition to her more renowned work, there are two veracious lions sitting on their back haunches outside of Windsor that are guarding the mansion. There was once a Buddha that also sat elegantly on the front lawn of the Windsor Mansion that can now be found on display at the University of the Arts in Philadelphia. Blanche's nephew, Reverend John Nevin Sayre was deeded the mansion in 1913 where Blanche lived until her death in 1925. Heather Sayre Brown, John's daughter, was deeded the mansion in 1965; however, she and her husband never lived at Windsor. While the home was occupied by several individuals, it soon fell into despair.

Windsor Forge in 2009.

Lloyd and Sondra Simmers purchased the property in 1998 from Heather Sayre Brown. Brown was the last descendant of the Jenkins' family to own the property. The Simmers are restoring the property and mansion to its original state. It is very fortunate that no one has dramatically changed Windsor over the hundreds of years. The original office building, smokehouse, tenant house and spring house, as well as the mansion, are still situated on 34 acres of the original land. All eleven fireplaces are still intact, some of which have iron plates that were constructed at the forge surrounding their interior. The majority of the hardware and large doors are original to the home. The smokehouse has been left untouched with its iron hooks still snugly fitting into the beams. An iron arm for hanging large kettles still remains in one of the large walk-in fireplaces. If the walls of Windsor could talk, what a story they would tell!

Baked Barley Pudding

1 1/4 cups water

1/2 cup uncooked medium pearl barley

1/4 tsp. salt

2 cups milk

1 cup whipping cream

1/2 cup sugar

2 eggs

1 tsp. vanilla extract

1/2 cup golden raisins

1/4 cup cinnamon

In a saucepan, bring water to a boil. Stir in barley and salt. Reduce heat; simmer, uncovered, for 15 minutes, stirring occasionally. Add milk; cook over medium-low heat for 10 minutes or until barley is almost tender, stirring frequently. In a bowl, whisk the cream, sugar, eggs and vanilla; gradually stir into the barley mixture.

Spoon into eight greased 6 oz. custard cups. Sprinkle with raisins and cinnamon. Place custard cups in two 9-inch baking pans. Fill both pans with boiling water to a depth of 1 inch. Bake, uncovered at 350 degrees for 30 to 35 minutes or until a knife inserted near the center comes out clean. Pudding will appear layered when baked. *Serves 8*

"This is similar to rice pudding. For a special touch, top with cherry pie filling and whipped topping."

— VERA JANE NEWSWANGER
Morgantown

Blueberry Buckle

PIE

1/4 cup shortening

3/4 cup sugar

1 beaten egg

2 cups flour

2 tsp. baking powder

1/2 tsp. salt

1/2 cup milk

2 cups blueberries, drained

CRUMBS

1/2 cup sugar

1/3 cup flour

1/2 tsp. cinnamon

1/3 cup butter

Cream sugar and shortening together. Add egg. Sift flour, powder and salt and add to creamed mixture, alternately with milk.

Pour into a well greased 9-inch square baking pan and sprinkle blueberries over top. Combine sugar, flour, cinnamon and butter and make crumbs. Sprinkle over the blueberries.

Bake at 375 degrees for 40 to 50 minutes.

"Old family recipe that is great with a cup of coffee."

— DAISY LAMBERT
East Earl

Bread Pudding

2 eggs

2 cups milk

1/2 cup sugar

1 tsp. vanilla

4 slices of bread

cinnamon

Butter a medium 8 X 8-inch baking dish. Add eggs, milk, sugar, vanilla and stir. Cube bread and add to egg mixture. Stir lightly and sprinkle cinnamon on top.

Bake at 350 degrees for 45 minutes. Serve hot or cold with or without cream.

"Using day old bread is best, and also raisin bread, cinnamon bread or fruited bread works great too. The fruit gives a great taste."

— EDNA SWEITZER
East Earl

Cappuccino Mousse Trifle

2 1/2 cups cold milk

1/3 cup instant coffee granules

2 (3.5 oz.) pkgs. instant vanilla pudding

16 oz. whipped topping (thawed)

2 loaves of frozen pound cake thawed, cubed

1 oz. grated semi-sweet chocolate

1/4 tsp. cinnamon

In mixing bowl, stir the milk and coffee granules until dissolved; remove 1 cup and set aside. Add pudding to remaining milk mixture. Beat on low speed for 2 minutes, or until thickened.

Fold in half the whipped topping. Place a third of the cake cubes in a trifle bowl, layer with a third of the reserved milk mixture and pudding mixture and a fourth of the grated chocolate. Repeat layers twice.

Garnish with remaining whipped topping and chocolate. Sprinkle with cinnamon. Cover and refrigerate until serving.

— RUTH K. GOOD
East Earl

Caramel Custard

2 Tbsp. butter

1/2 cup sugar

1 egg yolk

1 cup milk

1 1/2 Tbsp. flour

1 tsp. vanilla

1 egg white

1 tsp. sugar

Brown butter in a saucepan. Combine butter, sugar, yolk, milk, flour, and vanilla. Thicken and then cool.

Pour into a baked pie shell.

Make egg white and sugar into a meringue.

Brown in oven at 350 degrees.

— RUTH LAMBERT
East Earl

Caramel Pudding

PART I

1 cup brown sugar

2 Tbsp. butter

1 Tbsp. heavy cream

PART II

Combine in a cup the first three ingredients below:

1/4 cup water

1/8 tsp. baking soda

1/2 tsp. salt

5 1/2 cups milk

PART III

Mix well in a small bowl and set aside:

1/4 cup cornstarch

1/4 cup flour

2 eggs

1/2 cup milk

OTHER

2 tsp. vanilla

2 Tbsp. whipped topping

In a heavy kettle, cook and stir Part I until nicely browned. Turn off and quickly add Part II.

Mix a little then add 5 1/2 cups milk. Stir on medium heat until all sugar is dissolved and milk is very hot.

Then whisk in Part III. Heat to a boil and turn off and add 2 tsp. vanilla.

When chilled, whisk well and then add 2 tablespoons whipped topping. This makes it extra creamy.

"This recipe was something Miriam's mom made almost every time they had company. She would add English walnuts to make it extra special. They were always glad for leftovers!"

— MIRIAM MARTIN
East Earl

Cherry Dessert

2 cups flour

1/2 cup brown sugar

1 cup nuts

1 cup margarine

8 oz. cream cheese

1 cup confectioner's sugar

1 large container of whipped topping

2 cans of cherry pie filling

Chop nuts fine. Mix first 4 ingredients as you would a pie crust. Pat into an ungreased 11 X 15-inch pan. Bake uncovered 15 minutes at 400 degrees (watch – it burns easily). Cool.

Mix cheese and sugar. Spread on crust. Cover with 2 cans cherry pie filling. Chill at least 12 hours. Add whipped topping.

"Barbara was asked to make this for a baby shower in Richmond, Michigan, during her third year of teaching."

— BARBARA POSSESSKY
Narvon

Coffee Carnival

1/4 cup tapioca

1/2 cup sugar

1/2 tsp. salt

1 1/2 cups water

1/3 cup raisins

1 cup strong coffee

1 tsp. vanilla

1 cup whipped cream or whipped topping

Combine in sauce pan the tapioca, sugar, salt water and raisins. Simmer about 5 minutes until tapioca is clear.

Remove from heat. Add coffee and vanilla. Cool, stirring occasionally. Chill. Add whipped cream before serving.

"This recipe has been in Sara's family at least 4 generations."

— SARA NEWSWANGER
Narvon

Cornstarch Pudding

3 Tbsp. cornstarch

1/3 cup sugar

1/2 tsp. salt

2 cups milk

1 tsp. vanilla

Combine cornstarch, sugar and salt. Gradually add milk and heat to boiling. Boil gently for 2 minutes, stirring constantly. Remove and add vanilla. Pour into molds rinsed with cold water or a bowl. Chill until firm.

Remove from mold and serve with cream and fruit.

— RUTH LAMBERT
East Earl

Grandma's Cracker Pudding

1 cup coconut

1 1/2 cup crushed crackers
(can use half saltines
and half Ritz crackers for
buttery flavor)

2 eggs, separated

1 cup granulated sugar

4 cups milk

2 slightly rounded Tbsp.
cornstarch

1 tsp. vanilla

Beat egg whites until stiff and set aside. Whisk together milk, egg yolks, sugar and cornstarch in sauce pan. Cook over low to medium heat until starting to thicken. Add crackers and coconut.

Stir constantly over heat until thick.

Pour into a 2 qt. greased baking dish. Top with egg whites.

Bake uncovered at 375 degrees for 3 to 5 minutes or just until egg whites are slightly browned.

"This recipe is submitted in memory of her Grandma, Elizabeth Good. During the depression era, people made their own recipes for special treats and desserts with the food they could afford. This is one of my Dad's favorites from that time and now."

— Linda Sauder
East Earl

Ice Cream Dessert

60 Ritz crackers

1/2 cup butter, softened

1/2 gallon vanilla ice cream,
softened

1 1/2 cup milk

2 pkgs. coconut cream
instant pudding

8 oz. whipped topping

Crush crackers and softened butter together. Save half cup of crumbs. Line a 9 X 13-inch pan with rest of crumbs.

Mix together in large mixing bowl the softened ice cream, milk and pudding. Pour on top of crumbs and chill until ready to serve.

Top with whipped topping and half cup of crumbs.

— Ruth K. Good
East Earl

Milk Tapioca

1 qt. milk

1 cup sugar

2 eggs

3 Tbsp. minute tapioca

1/4 tsp. salt

Scald milk in a double boiler or heavy 2 qt. sauce pan and add tapioca. Stir frequently. Cook for 15 minutes.

Then add 2 beaten eggs with sugar. Add to the tapioca and mix well. Cook for 3 minutes more.

Remove from heat and add vanilla. Cool a little, eat warm or serve cold with 1 cup of whipped topping to make more fluffy.

"This recipe was her grandmother Sauder's. It was a favorite for dessert when our 10 children were at home. Frequently it was served warm with chocolate cake. Anna Mae and her family own Shirk's Produce stand at the east end of Churchtown for the past 21 years."

— ANNA MAE SHIRK
Narvon

Mitch's Easy Ice Cream Pudding Dessert

1/2 gallon vanilla ice cream

1 1/2 cups milk

2 (3 1/2 oz.) pkgs. vanilla instant pudding mix

30 Oreo cookies

In a mixing bowl combine ice cream, milk and pudding mix until blended. In a large cake pan break 20 of the Oreos and place in the bottom for a crust. Pour mixture over broken cookies. Top with the remaining broken cookies. Can be stored in the freezer until ready to serve.

For a variation use Mint chocolate chip ice cream and Mint Oreos.

"This is a very easy dish to make for gatherings and we always come home empty-handed!"

— MITCHELL DIEM
Narvon

Old Fashioned Curtis Bay Rice Pudding

1 cup uncooked long grain
rice

1 qt. milk

1 (12 oz.) can of evaporated
milk

3/4 cup raisins

1 egg, well beaten

3/4 cup sugar

1/4 tsp. ground nutmeg

1 tsp. vanilla

1 Tbsp. lemon juice

1/2 tsp. ground cinnamon

Cook rice following label directions. In a large pan, combine cooked rice with milk and evaporated milk. Cook over low heat stirring occasionally until just a thin layer of liquid covers the rice (about 20 minutes). Rice expands even more during this step.

Plump raisins in 1 cup of boiling water for 2 minutes, drain. Remove rice mixture from heat, stir in egg, sugar, nutmeg, cinnamon, vanilla, lemon juice and raisins. Pour into large serving bowl. Lightly sprinkle top with extra cinnamon and nutmeg.

— BARBARA DIEM
Narvon

Pennsylvania Dutch Peach Pudding

BATTER

1/4 cup butter

1/2 cup sugar

1 egg

1 tsp. vanilla

1/2 cup milk

1 cup flour

1 tsp. baking powder

1/4 tsp. salt

PEACH MIXTURE

1 qt. sliced peaches, drained
canned or fresh.

1/4 cup sugar

whipped cream (optional)

Cream butter and sugar. Add egg and vanilla, beating well. Add milk and remaining dry ingredients. Mix well.

Combine peaches and 1/4 cup sugar in separate bowl. Spread peaches in buttered 8-inch pan. Cover with batter. Bake at 350 degrees for 45 minutes or until brown. Serve with whip cream.

"This recipe was found in the Ephrata paper back in the 1960's."

— SHARON COLON
Narvon

Rhubarb Crisp

4 cups (or more) of fresh or frozen cut up rhubarb

1 cup sugar

2 to 3 Tbsp. tapioca (small beads)

2 Tbsp. butter

1 cup sugar

1 egg

1 cup flour

1 tsp. baking powder

1 tsp. cinnamon sugar

Combine: rhubarb, sugar and tapioca. Stir often while making topping.

Mix together sugar and butter by hand until crumbly. Add 1 egg and mix well. Then add flour and baking powder until just crumbly. Pour rhubarb in an 8 X 8-inch baking casserole dish and spread topping over rhubarb. Sprinkle cinnamon sugar on top. Do not cover. Bake at 350 degrees for 45 to 60 minutes (until the center is cooked).

Rhubarb is wonderful cut up fresh or frozen to use year around. Do not thaw before adding it to something.

"This is a wonderful treat that was first made for us by a babysitter in the early 1970's. What a surprise to see my children sitting on the counter helping her when I came home from working a long day at a sports/skiing center. Always new and yummy in spring!"

— SUSAN MARRIS
Goodville

Windsor Forge summer kitchen. At one time this was the Windsor Forge office.

Strawberry Trifle

14 oz. can sweetened condensed milk

1/2 cup cold water

1 (3 oz.) pkg. instant vanilla pudding and pie filling

2 cups of whipping cream (or heavy cream) whipped till peaks

1 prepared loaf of pound cake (about 12 oz.) cut into 1 inch cubes

4 cups sliced fresh strawberries (2 quarts). Reserve some whole berries cake top

1/2 cup strawberry preserves

1/2 cup sliced almonds, toasted (enough to sprinkle on top of trifle)

In large mixing bowl combine milk and water. Add pudding mix; and beat until well blended. Chill for 5 minutes. Whip cream until it peaks; and fold into chilled mixture.

Spoon 1/3 of pudding mix into a clear glass trifle bowl. Top with 1/2 of the cake.

Then top with 1/2 of the strawberries and then 1/4 cup of the preserves. Repeat pudding, cake, strawberries, and preserves. Top with last 1/3 of the pudding mix.

Place whole strawberries (top down) around the edge of the bowl, and one in the center.

Sprinkle the almonds over the top of the pudding. Refrigerate a few hours. *Serves 16*

— THE INN AT TWIN LINDEN
  Churchtown

No Fail Pie Crust

4 cups flour

1 3/4 cups shortening

1 tsp. sugar

2 tsp. salt

1 tsp. vinegar

1 egg

1/2 cup water

Mix dry ingredients. Cut in shortening, and add the wet ingredients. Roll dough out to make two 8-inch pie shells.

— MARY ANN GOOD
  Terre Hill

Cream Puffs

PUFFS

1 cup hot water

1/2 cup butter

1 Tbsp. sugar

1/2 tsp. salt

1 cup sifted flour

4 eggs

FILLING

1 cup chilled whipping cream

3 Tbsp. sifted confectioner's sugar

1 1/2 tsp. vanilla extract, coffee beverage, fruit essence or fine liqueur

Bring first four puff ingredients to a rolling boil. Add flour. Beat vigorously with a wooden spoon until mixture leaves sides of pan and forms a smooth ball. Remove from heat. Quickly beat in eggs, one at a time, beating until smooth after each addition. Continue beating until mixture is thick and smooth. Dough may be shaped and baked at once, or wrapped in waxed paper and stored in refrigerator overnight.

Force dough through a pastry bag or drop by tablespoonfuls 2 inches apart onto a lightly greased baking sheet. Bake large puffs at 450 degrees for 15 minutes. Lower heat to 350 degrees and bake 20 to 25 minutes longer, or until golden in color.

Bake small puffs at 450 degrees 10 minutes. Lower heat to 350 degrees and bake 5 minutes longer, or until golden in color.

Remove to rack and cool.

Beat whipping cream in a chilled bowl with chilled rotary beater. Beat until cream stands in peaks when beater is slowly lifted upright. Fold or beat remaining ingredients into whipped cream with final few strokes until blended.

Cut off tops and fill shells with cream. Replace tops and sprinkle with sifted confectioner's sugar.

— FREDDY REY
Elverson

Apple Macaroon Pie

FILLING

5 medium apples, sliced thin

2 Tbsp. flour

1/2 cup sugar

cinnamon to taste

1 egg

TOPPING

1/2 cup sugar

1/2 cup flour

4 Tbsp. butter

Place apples in 9-inch pie pan. Mix together flour, sugar and cinnamon and sprinkle over sliced apples. Cream topping ingredients together. Add 1 well beaten egg to creamed mixture.

Spread on top of apples and dry ingredients (will make it's own crust on top of pie.) Sprinkle with chopped nuts and add whipped cream if desired.

Bake at 350 degrees for 45 minutes.

— MARY A. (BUNNY) PARMER
Narvon

Cheese Custard Pie

1 pt. cottage cheese

1 cup sugar

1 Tbsp. flour

1 pinch salt

3 egg yolks

3 egg whites

1 Tbsp. melted butter

Beat 3 egg whites till fluffy, set aside. Mix rest of ingredients together, then mix in egg whites. Do NOT grease or flour pans. Bake uncovered at 350 degrees for 40 minutes. *Makes 2 8-inch pies*

"This pie was served every Thanksgiving and Christmas at my Grandmother's house and it was handed down from her family."

— LUCY MERTZ
Narvon

Chocolate Funny Cake Pie

TOP

1 cup sugar

1/4 cup butter or lard

1/2 cup milk

1 egg beaten

1 cup flour

1 tsp. baking powder

1/2 tsp. vanilla

BOTTOM

1/2 cup sugar

4 Tbsp. cocoa

6 Tbsp. water

1/2 tsp. vanilla

unbaked pie shell

For top: Cream sugar and shortening. Combine milk and egg. Add to creamed mixture. Alternate with flour and baking powder. Add vanilla last. Set aside.

For bottom: Combine sugar, cocoa, water and vanilla. Pour into pie shell. Cover with topping. Bake at 350 degrees for 35 minutes. Chocolate will come up around the outside edge leaving a crusty edge on the finished pie.

— LINDA BOYER
Narvon

Chocolate Peanut Butter Pie

1 chocolate graham crust

1 1/2 pt. vanilla ice cream

2 cups creamy peanut butter

1 jar fudge topping

8 oz. Cool Whip®

Mix ice cream and peanut butter on low speed. Pour into pie crust. Freeze 3 hours. Top with 1 jar fudge topping. Return to freezer. Serve with cool whip on top of each slice.

— A.M. RINGLER
Narvon

Delicious Peanut Butter Pie

8 oz. softened cream cheese

1 cup powdered sugar

1 cup creamy peanut butter

1/2 cup milk

8 oz. cool whip

1 prepackaged chocolate cookie crust or graham cracker crust

Beat together the cream cheese and sugar in a large bowl. Add peanut butter, milk and cool whip. Spoon into the crust.

Cover and refrigerate for at least 4 hours. Garnish with chocolate or peanut butter chips if desired.

— BETTY STURLA
Life long resident of Churchtown now living in Lancaster

Creamy Pear Pie

PIE

4 cups sliced peeled pears

1/3 cup sugar

2 Tbsp. flour

1 (8 oz.) cup sour cream

1/2 tsp. vanilla extract

1/2 tsp. lemon extract

1/2 tsp. almond extract

1 unbaked pie pastry (9 inches)

TOPPING

1/4 cup flour

2 Tbsp. butter or margarine, melted

2 Tbsp. brown sugar

In a large bowl, toss pears with sugar and flour. Combine sour cream and extracts. Add to pear mixture and mix well. Pour into pie shell.

In a small bowl, mix topping ingredients until crumbly. Sprinkle over pears.

Bake at 400 degrees for 10 minutes. Reduce heat to 350 degrees. Bake 45 minutes more or until pears are tender. *Serves 6*

— VERA JANE NEWSWANGER
Morgantown

Impossible Pie

2 cups milk

4 eggs

2 tsp. vanilla

1/2 cup flour

3/4 cup sugar

3/4 cup butter

3/4 cup coconut

1 tsp. cinnamon sugar

Wisk together or in a blender combine all ingredients at once. Beat until foamy. Pour into a floured, buttered 10 inch pie plate. Sprinkle with the sugar. Place pie onto hot cookie pan. Bake at 350 degrees for 50 to 60 minutes. This will all puff up high and golden when it is finished baking. Carefully take out to cool on rack. Serve warm or cool. Eat same day.

"An old time favorite, often requested and always a good surprise. Easy as can be! The perfect magic pie."

— SUSAN MARRIS
Goodville

Lemon Sponge

1 large lemon and rind

1 3/4 cup sugar

4 Tbsp. butter

2 Tbsp. flour

2 cups milk

4 large or 5 small eggs
   separated

Mix all ingredients, except egg whites, until smooth. Whip egg whites last to hard peaks. Blend with first mix, can be white, still floating around. Pour into pie crust. Bake 15 minute at 400 degrees. Reduce to 350 degrees and bake until brown.

— REGINA CLARK
East Earl

Mahala's Minced Meat Pie

1 pt. minced meat

3 to 4 pt. chopped apples

1 1/2 cup raisins (or mix of
   raisins and currants)

3/4 cup sugar (granulated)

1/4 tsp. salt

4 Tbsp. softened butter

2 tsp. cinnamon

6 Tbsp. flour

red wine

2 pie shells

Mix everything together in large bowl except wine and pie shells.

Put into 2 pie shells. Drizzle with wine according to taste and put top crust on and score a few places. Put foil on crust edges for first 30 minutes of baking.

Bake at 425 degrees for 40 to 50 minutes.

"My grandmother made up a lot of her own recipes (which were kept only by memory). She made these pies nearly 60 years of her married life when her children brought wild game to her. Before she passed away at age 91, I spent a day with her making the meat and pies so I could write down the ingredients and preparations only she knew, so my family could continue to enjoy them."

"Grandma cooked venison meat in grapefruit juice (unsweetened). When cooled, she ground it and froze it in pint boxes or in earlier years canned it."

— LINDA SAUDER
East Earl

Molasses Coconut Custard Pie

2 Tbsp. flour

1/2 tsp. baking soda

1 cup sugar

1 cup molasses

2 eggs

1 cup milk or 1 1/2 cups half and half

1/2 cup cream

1 cup coconut

9 inch pie shell

Combine flour, soda, sugar. Add molasses and eggs. Mix. Add milk, cream and coconut. Bake 50 minutes or until set.

"Don't knock it until you've tried it" One of Pappy Mint's favorites

— LINDA BOYER
Narvon

Peach & Cream Pie

peach slices or halves

2/3 cup sugar

4 Tbsp. flour

salt

1/2 tsp. cinnamon

1 cup cream

pie shell

Place peaches in pastry shell. Combine sugar, flour, salt, cinnamon, and cream. Pour over peaches. Bake 40 minutes at 450 degrees or until set.

— EDNA SWEITZER
East Earl

Peaches & Cream Cheese Pie

CRUST & FILLING

3/4 cup flour

1 tsp. baking powder

1/2 tsp. salt

1 egg

1 small box regular vanilla pudding (not instant)

3 Tbsp. butter

1/2 cup milk

1 large can peaches

TOPPING

8 oz. cream cheese

3 Tbsp. peach juice

1/2 cup sugar

Combine first seven ingredients and beat 2 minutes. Pour into greased 9 inch pie plate. Drain one large can sliced peaches reserving 3 tablespoons juice. Place peaches over batter.

Combine topping ingredients and beat 2 minutes. Spoon to 1 inch of edge of pie plate. Combine 1 tablespoon sugar and 1/2 teaspoon cinnamon and sprinkle on top of filling.

Bake until brown, 35 to 45 minutes at 350 degrees.

"This has become a favorite dessert at all types of gatherings and has been requested many times by both family and friends."

— WANDA LONGER
East Earl

Pecan Pie

3 eggs

1/2 cup granulated sugar

1/4 cup melted butter

1 cup dark molasses (King syrup)

1 tsp. vanilla

dash of salt

1/2 cup pecans (or more), chopped

Beat eggs until light and beat in the sugar. Add next 5 ingredients in order given and mix together.

Pour into 8 inch pie crust and bake 1 hour at 350 degrees uncovered.

— EVELYN (GEHMAN) BUSH
Narvon

Rhubarb Pie

CRUST & FILLING

4 1/2 cups fresh rhubarb

2 cups brown sugar

3 eggs

2 heaping Tbsp. flour

CRUMBS

4 cups flour

1 cup brown sugar

1 cup lard (scant)

1 tsp. soda

pinch of cream of tarter

Put rhubarb into 3 pie shells. (You can omit the pie shells). Mix brown sugar, eggs and flour together. Pour on top of rhubarb. Mix crumb mixture together. Put on top of rhubarb mixture. Bake at 400 degrees for 10 minutes, then 370 degrees until done, about 30 minutes. (Can put into pyrex cake pan or 2 casseroles).

— EVA BRUBAKER
East Earl

Ruth Lambert's Lemon Meringue Pie

1 cup sugar

1/4 tsp. salt

4 Tbsp. cornstarch

2 cups water

1 egg yolk

juice and rind of 1 lemon

1 Tbsp. butter

3 egg whites

4 Tbsp. sugar

1 9-inch baked pie crust

In double boiler or saucepan combine sugar, salt and cornstarch. Add 1 cup water. Stir until dissolved. Add egg yolk to 1 cup water and beat until lemony. Add to sugar mix and cook until thick and clear.

Take off heat and add lemon and butter. Blend well. Cool. Pour into pie shell. Beat egg whites and add 4 tablespoons sugar. Spread into pie. Bake at 350 degrees until golden.

— RUTH LAMBERT
East Earl

COOKIES & CANDY INDEX

Baked Oatmeal Cookies

Blueberry Filled Cookies

Mary's Brown Sugar Cookies

Dottie's Brown Sugar Cookies

Buttermilk Cookies

Cherry Winks

Chip & Dip Cookies

Chocolate Cherry Chippers

Chocolate Chip Pudding Cookies

Chocolate Cookies

Coconut Crisps

Drop Sand Tarts

Eva's Filled Cookies

Floribel's Filled Cookies

Forgotten Cookies

Ginger Cream Cookies

Grammy Shirk's Cookies

Grandma Shirk's Sugar Cookies

Iced Sour Cream Cookies

Jewel Swirls

Kate Baxter Cookies (Cut Out Cookies)

Lepp Cookies

King Cookies

Meringues with Chocolate Chips

Pennsylvania Dutch Molasses Cookies

Peppernuts (Sugar Cookies)

Raisin Filled Cookies

Rich Chocolate Chip Cookies

Ginny's Sand Tarts

Bunny's Sand Tarts

Snicker Peanut Butter Cookies

Soft Sugar Cookies

Thumbprint Cookies

Very Good Soft Cookies

Welsh Picks

Cookie Dough Brownies

Auntie's Fudge

Granola Bars

Lemon Pie Bars

Revel Bars

Sour Cream Raisin Squares

Rhubarb Cheese Bars

Belly Guts (Black Walnut Candy)

Toffee Bars

Peanut Butter Fudge

Million Dollar Fudge

Potato Candy

Strawberries

ALONG THE CONESTOGA

COOKIES & CANDY
Churches of Churchtown

Churches of Churchtown

Many think that Churchtown got its name from the prevalence of its many churches. Churchtown is less than a mile long and is home to four active churches and one that now serves as the archive for the Caernarvon Historical Society. Churchtown was named after Bangor Protestant Episcopal Church who once owned the town. Bangor leased parcels of land to the early settlers which provided a source of income for the church.

Bangor Protestant Episcopal Church is located on the North side of Route 23 at Water Street. The oldest church in Churchtown, a log church was built in 1734 at its present location. The church was founded in 1722 with services held among Welsh settlers in the area, by missionaries from the Society for the Propagation of the Faith. A stone church was built in 1756 which replaced the log building. From 1776 to 1780 the church was closed because of the Revolutionary War. In 1830 the Gothic Revival style building was erected with local brownstone. A frame structure on the church grounds was originally used as a school. A stone wall still borders the property. Bangor retains her ties to the agrarian way of life every spring with the Rogation Sunday service. This service is performed to bless the fields, crops and farm animals,

Bangor Protestant Episcopal church built in 1756.

and has been a tradition for 200 years. At one time the service included a procession through fields and farms. Presently the service is performed on the church grounds with young farm animals, family pets and baskets filled with seeds and grains being blessed.

The Churchtown United Methodist Church located on the South side of Route 23 was built in 1879. Methodism began in Churchtown around 1800 with 625 members from the Springfield Circuit including Zion, Goodwill, Harmony, Waynesburg, Springton, Morgantown, Spring Forge, Cambridge, Forrest and Rockville. Initially services were held in various homes, and also the Bangor School and the Washington Inn. It was organized among workers at Windsor Forge and was supported by the Evans and Jenkins families. In 1838 the first stone church was built on the opposite side of the road where the cemetery is now located. The property was purchased from William Shirk for $100. The present church property was originally part of the Windsor Estate and the current

Churchtown United Methodist Church.

building was erected in 1879. It has been recorded that in 1883 a great revival was held by Reverend W.W. Cookman and lasted two months. During that time seventy one people were converted and became members of the church.

The Caernarvon Presbyterian Church is located on the South side of Route 23. It was originally built as the Jenkins' family chapel on the Windsor Forge estate in 1843. In 1846 it was chartered as a Presbyterian congregation, ministered by the Cedar Grove Presbyterian Church. In 1865 this congregation discontinued to meet. From 1867 to 1870 it became a congregation for a brief time. The building was placed in trust with presbytery. In 1957 it was used as the Grace and Truth Gospel Hall. Since 1983 it has been used by the Churchtown Historical Society.

Churchtown Mennonite Church.

The Churchtown Mennonite Church is located on the North side of Route 23, just east of Churchtown. It is part of the Lancaster Mennonite Conference. The first local Mennonite meetinghouse was built at Weaverland around 1766. During those days many people walked to services, some as far as 10 miles. Around 1830 the need was voiced for a meeting house in the Churchtown area. A group met about 1/2 mile south of the current church in an old log school known as Shirk's School in the village of Shirktown. Some time later a new stone school house was built on the east side of the Shirktown Road and Little Hill Road junction and it was later named Oak Glen School. Christian Shirk, a noted farmer, surveyor, and tannery operator who lived in Shirktown, was ordained in the Weaverland District in

Interior of the Churchtown Old Order Mennonite church, part of Wenger Mennonite Church..

1837 and served as the leader of this new congregation. He lived where Shirktown Day is presently held. The current frame church was built in 1879 when the church was founded and has been renovated and enlarged several times. In 1893 the church divided into two groups and worshiped on alternating Sundays. While one group became more progressive having Sunday school classes in English and evangelistic services, the other group remained more conservative. In 1910 the church was renovated with the pulpit being placed on the east with entrances on the east and west ends. The more conservative group was not in favor of these changes so they built their own meetinghouse about 1/2 mile west of the church which is now known as the Churchtown Old Order Mennonite Church.

The Churchtown Old Order Mennonite Church is part of the Groffdale Mennonite Conference which is also known as the Wenger Mennonite Church. It was founded in 1910 and the current frame meetinghouse was built at that time. The church is shared on alternating Sundays by the Wenger Mennonites, who use horse and buggies for their transportation, and the Horning Mennonites, who drive cars. A typical Sunday service for the Wenger Mennonites lasts from 9:00 until 11:00. The women and children are dropped off and enter the front of the church. Once entering the front of the church, there is an area for the women to hang their coats and there are several cribs for the women to use for their babies. The women congregate here before church, while the men tie

Outside of Churchtown Old Order Mennonite Church.

up their horses and enter in the back of the church. They too have a section to hang their coats and hats before entering the main part of the church. There are wooden benches in rows in a u-shape. In the center there is a long table with hymn books for the song leaders. The young married couples sit in the main section of benches, with the older children and then teens behind them. The married couples with young children sit near the front of the church so they have access to the crib area. The ministry sits in a row behind the u-shaped pews, with their wives sitting together in the same row. The service is in Pennsylvania Dutch while the hymns are in German. If guests are present, they also speak in English.

Baked Oatmeal Cookies

1 egg

1/4 cup oil

1/2 cup brown sugar

1/2 tsp. salt

1/2 Tbsp. baking powder

1/2 cup milk

1 cup oats

1/3 cup raisins

Beat eggs, sugar, salt, baking powder, milk and oil until blended. Add oats and raisins.

Bake at 350 degrees for 20 to 25 minutes. *Serves 4*

— JANESSA FISHER
  Narvon

Blueberry Filled Cookies

1 cup shortening

1 1/2 cups brown sugar

2 eggs

4 cups flour

1 cup rolled oats

2 tsp. baking powder

1/2 tsp. salt

1 tsp. baking soda

1/4 cup milk

2 tsp. vanilla

1 can blueberry pie filling

your favorite frosting

blueberry gelatin powder

Cream shortening and sugar together. Beat in eggs. Add dry ingredients with milk and vanilla. Roll out and cut with a round cookie cutter or cutter of choice. Put 1 teaspoon blueberry pie filling on a cookie, top with another cookie. Press edges together.

Bake at 350 degrees for 10 minutes. Cool, then ice with your favorite frosting. Sprinkle blueberry gelatin powder on top. *Makes 2 dozen*

— VERA JANE NEWSWANGER
  Morgantown

Mary's Brown Sugar Cookies

2 cups brown sugar

1 cup butter

3 eggs

4 cups flour

1/2 tsp. salt

1 tsp. baking soda

1/4 cup milk

1 tsp. vanilla

your favorite frosting

sprinkles

Cream butter and sugar together. Beat in eggs. Add flour with milk and vanilla. Drop by teaspoons on greased cookie sheet.

Bake at 350 degrees for 10 minutes. Cool.

Ice with your favorite frosting. Decorate with sprinkles for Christmas.

"This is an old recipe. A very good cookie."

— MARY JANE NEWSWANGER
  Morgantown

Dottie's Brown Sugar Cookies

2 cups brown sugar

1 cup butter

3 eggs

5 cups flour

1/2 tsp. salt

1 tsp. baking soda

1/4 cup milk

1 tsp. vanilla

chocolate chips, nuts,
   raisins, as desired
   (optional)

Cream together sugar and softened butter. Add eggs, milk, baking soda, salt and vanilla. Then add flour mixture one cup at a time.

Add any extras like chocolate chips, etc. Drop by rounded teaspoons. Bake at 375 degrees for 10 to 12 minutes on a greased cookie sheet.

"Dottie made up her own kind of chocolate chip cookie by using old fashioned sugar cookie style recipes and adding chocolate chips. Her children really enjoyed these."

— DOTTIE GOOD
  East Earl

Buttermilk Cookies

2 cups sugar

1 cup melted margarine

3 eggs

1 tsp. vanilla

4 cups flour

1 tsp. baking soda

1 tsp. baking powder

1 cup buttermilk

icing of your choice

sprinkles

Cream sugar and margarine. Add eggs and vanilla. Combine flour, soda and baking powder. Add buttermilk and flour mixture, alternating. Note – if batter seems too thin, add a bit more flour.

Drop by teaspoonful on lightly greased cookie sheet 2 inches apart. Bake at 350 degrees for 10 minutes.

Ice with icing of your choice. Decorate with sprinkles of your choice for special occasions. *Makes 6 dozen*

— BRENDA LEAMAN
East Earl

Cherry Winks

2 1/2 cups flour

1 tsp. baking powder

1/2 tsp. baking soda

1/2 tsp. salt

3/4 cup solid shortening

1 cup granulated sugar

2 eggs

2 Tbsp. milk

1 tsp. vanilla

1 cup chopped walnuts or
  pecans

1 cup chopped dates

1/2 cup chopped maraschino
  cherries

cherries halved for top of
  cookie

2 to 3 cups crushed corn
  flakes

Mix together the dry ingredients, set aside. In mixing bowl, blend shortening, sugar and eggs. Then add milk and vanilla, gradually add dry ingredients to the mixture, then remaining ingredients.

Shape into balls, according to size cookie you want and roll into corn flakes.

Place on greased baking sheet, put a half cherry on top and bake at 375 degrees for 10 to 12 minutes.

"From the time Linda was a very little girl, she remembers "helping" her Aunt Edna bake. Her favorite recipe was Cherry Wink cookies. Her favorite job was rolling the dough balls in the crushed corn flakes."

"In memory of Edna Ziemer."

— LINDA SAUDER
East Earl

Chip & Dip Cookies

1 cup butter, softened

1/2 cup sugar

1 egg yolk

1 teaspoon vanilla extract

1 3/4 cups all-purpose flour

3/4 cup coarsely crushed potato chips

3/4 cup coarsely crushed pretzels

1 cup semisweet chocolate chips

1 cup white chocolate chips

Preheat oven to 350 degrees. Combine butter and sugar; beat with a mixer at medium-high speed until light and fluffy. Add egg yolk and vanilla. Gradually add flour and mix well. Stir in potato chips and pretzels. Shape level tablespoons of dough into 3-inch logs. Place on an ungreased baking sheet, 1 1/2 inches apart. Bake 14 to 18 minutes, until edges are lightly browned. Cool completely on baking sheet.

Heat semisweet chocolate chips in microwave for 30 seconds; stir. Repeat until melted. Dip one end of each cookie into chocolate and place on wax paper. Refrigerate until firm, about 10 minutes.

Heat white chocolate chips in microwave for 30 seconds; stir. Repeat until melted. Dip other end of cookie into melted chips and place on wax paper. Refrigerate until firm, about 10 minutes. *Makes 2 dozen*

— ALEX DIEM
Narvon

Chocolate Cherry Chippers

1 1/2 cup flour

3/4 tsp. baking soda

1/2 tsp. salt

3/4 cup brown sugar

1/2 cup butter, softened

3 tsp. sugar

1 egg

1 tsp. vanilla extract

1/2 tsp. almond extract

1 cup chocolate cherry chips

1/2 cup maraschino cherries, chopped

1/2 cup slivered almonds

Beat brown sugar, butter and sugar. Beat in egg, vanilla and almond extracts. Add dry ingredients until well blended. Stir in cherries, almonds and chips.

Bake at 375 degrees for 10 to 12 minutes. *Makes 4 dozen*

"A unique variation of the chocolate chip cookie. Great for holiday brunches."

— JANESSA FISHER
Narvon

Chocolate Chip Pudding Cookies

2 1/4 cups unsifted all-purpose flour

1 tsp. baking soda

1 cup margarine, softened

1/4 cup granulated sugar

3/4 cup firmly packed light brown sugar

1 pack (4 serving size) vanilla instant pudding and pie filling

1 tsp. vanilla

2 eggs

12 oz. chocolate chips

Mix flour with baking soda. Combine butter, the sugars, dry pudding and vanilla in large mixing bowl. Beat until smooth and creamy. Beat in eggs.

Gradually add flour mixture. Stir in chocolate chips. Batter may be stiff.

Drop by rounded teaspoonfuls onto ungreased baking sheets about 2 inches apart.

Bake at 375 degrees for 8 to 10 minutes. *Makes 5 dozen*

"This recipe is from Louise's aunt when she started baking and she has been making it ever since.

— Louise Jennelle
Elverson

Chocolate Cookies

COOKIES

2 semi-sweet chocolate squares

1/2 cup shortening (Imperial margarine)

1 cup light brown sugar

1 egg

2 cups flour

1/2 cup milk

1/2 tsp. vanilla

1/2 tsp. baking soda

ICING

1/2 stick butter

1/2 box or 2 cups or more of confectioner's sugar

a little milk

Melt chocolate squares and shortening, mix together. Add brown sugar, milk, and egg. Add vanilla. Next add flour and baking soda, a little at a time. Drop by small scoopful onto ungreased cookie sheet. Bake 10 to 11 minutes in 350 degree oven.

For icing, mix butter and confectioner's sugar. Add a little milk, mix. Icing should be on firm side. If too thin add more confectioner's sugar.

"Handed down family recipe."

— Shirley J. Plank
New Holland

Coconut Crisps

1 cup butter

1 cup brown sugar

1 cup granulated sugar

1 1/2 cups flour

1 egg

1 1/4 cups rolled oats

3/4 cup coconut

1 tsp. baking powder

1/2 tsp. baking soda

1/2 tsp. salt

Mix all ingredients together and drop on a greased cookie sheet.

Bake at 350 degrees for about 10 minutes or until slightly golden brown. This recipe easily doubles.

— BETTY STURLA
Life long resident of Churchtown now living in Lancaster

Drop Sand Tarts

1 lb. butter

2 cups white sugar

2 eggs

4 cups flour

Cream butter and sugar. Add one egg at a time. Beat well. Stir in flour. Drop by teaspoon onto greased cookie sheet.

Bake at 375 degrees for 10 minutes. Can place nut on top of cookies or use a cookie stamp. *Makes 6 dozen*

— DAISY BOYER
East Earl

Eva's Filled Cookies

1/2 cup margarine

1/2 cup vegetable
shortening

1 1/2 cup brown sugar

2 eggs

4 cups flour

1 cup quick oatmeal

2 tsp. baking powder

1/2 tsp. salt

1 tsp. baking soda

1/4 cup milk

2 tsp. vanilla

blueberry or raisin pie filling

Mix shortenings and sugar. Add eggs and beat well. Sift together dry ingredients with milk and vanilla. Chill dough.

Roll out about 1/4 inch thick and cut with a round cutter.

Fill cookie sheet. Put 1 to 2 tsp. pie filling on each cookie, depending on size of cookie. Cover with another cookie.

Bake at 350 to 375 degrees until lightly brown.

Frost after cool.

— Eva Martin
Narvon

Floribel's Filled Cookies

5 cups sifted flour

2 tsp. baking powder

1 tsp. baking soda

1/2 tsp. salt

1 cup soft shortening

2 cups granulated sugar

2 eggs

1 tsp. vanilla

1 cup thick sour cream

Sift together first 4 ingredients. Mix until creamy the sugar, shortening, eggs and vanilla.

Mix in sour cream, then flour mixture a little at a time.

Chill. Roll with rolling pin about 1/4-inch thick, and then cut with round cutter. Put your favorite filling in center of cookie, and add another cookie on top. Press edges to seal. Bake at 350 degrees for 8 to 10 minutes or until golden brown. *Makes 4 dozen*

— Floribel Styer
Narvon

Forgotten Cookies

2/3 cup granulated sugar

2 egg whites

6 oz. chocolate chips (tiny ones, but any size will work)

Preheat oven to 375 degrees.

Beat egg whites, add sugar and beat until stiff. Fold in the chocolate chips. Drop by teaspoon on cookie sheet.

Place in oven and turn the oven off. Leave over night or about 8 hours.

Store in a tightly closed container.

"This is the cookie recipe that everyone should have. When you need something at the last minute or are low on ingredients, these are the best. Everyone loves them and they look elegant. They have been served many times at Bangor."

— MAURINE VANDYKE
  Narvon

The men's coat and hat room inside the Old Order Mennonite church in Churchtown.

A hand water pump and trough outside the church is reminiscent of simpler times.

Ginger Cream Cookies

1/4 cup soft shortening

1/2 cup brown sugar

1 small egg

1/2 cup dark molasses

1 tsp. baking soda

1/2 cup of hot water.

2 cups flour

1/2 tsp. salt

1 tsp. ginger

1/2 tsp. cinnamon

Mix first four ingredients together. In a separate bowl dissolve baking soda in hot water. Add to first four ingredients and mix. In a separate bowl sift flour with salt, ginger and cinnamon. Mix with wet ingredients. Chill the dough. Then drop by rounded teaspoonful about 2 inches apart on greased baking sheet. Bake at 350 degrees for 7 minutes. *Makes 2 dozen*

"This recipe was give to Floribel by Fannie Smucker of Narvon."

— FLORIBEL STYER
  Narvon

Grammy Shirk's Cookies

1 lb. brown sugar

1 1/4 cup butter

2 eggs

1/2 cup milk

1 tsp. cream of tartar

1 1/2 tsp. baking soda

4 cups flour

icing and sprinkles or nuts
  are optional

Mix sugar and butter well. Then add rest of ingredients. Drop by teaspoonful or larger depending on desired size, 2-inches apart. Bake on an ungreased cookie sheet at 350 degrees for 12 minutes. *Makes 5 dozen*

"Jessica's great grandmother's famous cookies have been in the family for years."

— JESSICA SHIRK
  Morgantown

Grandma Shirk's Sugar Cookies

2 cups granulated sugar

1 cup shortening

1 tsp. vanilla

3 eggs

1 tsp. baking soda

1/2 tsp. salt

1 tsp. baking powder

4 1/2 cups flour

cinnamon and sugar or
   vanilla frosting optional

Cream shortening and sugar; add eggs. Add dry ingredients, alternating dry ingredients with milk and vanilla. Bake at 375 degrees for 10 to 12 minutes. May sprinkle with cinnamon and sugar or with vanilla frosting. *Makes 5 dozen*

"This is Bob's mother, Bertha Shirk's recipe. A soft fluffy cookie that we always enjoyed especially at Christmas time."

— Paula Shirk
  Narvon

Iced Sour Cream Cookies

COOKIES

1 cup butter

2 cups light brown sugar

4 eggs

2 tsp. vanilla

1 pint sour cream

5 cups flour

2 tsp. baking soda

1 tsp. baking powder

1 tsp. salt

ICING

6 Tbsp. butter

1 tsp. vanilla

1 tsp. scalded milk

1 1/2 cup confectioner's
   sugar

Cream butter and sugar together. Add eggs and beat. Add vanilla. Set aside. Sift flour, soda, powder and salt. Add sifted ingredients and sour cream alternately to butter mix.

Refrigerate overnight. Drop by teaspoons onto ungreased cookie sheet. Bake at 350 degrees for 7 to 8 minutes. Cool.

Combine and beat icing ingredients until smooth. This will cover one half the batch of cookies. The icing tends to harden. *Makes 5 dozen*

"This recipe is Linda's husband, Leon's, favorite."

— Linda Boyer
  Narvon

Jewel Swirls

3/4 cup butter

1/2 cup sugar

1/2 cup sour cream

2 cup flour

1/2 tsp baking soda

1/4 tsp salt

1 pkg. of Jello®

Cream butter and sugar; add sour cream then the rest of ingredients. Cool dough in fridge for awhile, flour table and hands and make a ball and roll out dough, sprinkle dough with any flavor of jello then roll the dough, place on a dish in the fridge, continue making 2 to 3 logs. When the logs are chilled and easy to cut (1 to 2 hours) slice and bake cookies 6 to 8 minutes at 350.

"In memory of Galen's mom Minerva Jane Sauder."

— GALEN, AMANDA, HAYLEIGH AND ASHLEY SAUDER
  Lititz

Kate Baxter Cookies (Cut Out Cookies)

2 cups sugar – brown or white

1 cup butter or lard or margarine

6 Tbsp. milk or cream

2 eggs

1 tsp. vanilla

1 tsp. baking soda

5 cups flour

Cream together sugar, butter and milk. Add eggs, vanilla and baking soda. Add flour (may have to use hands to work in flour and may add more if it is too sticky to roll).

Roll on floured surface thickness of your cookie cutter. Bake at 350 degrees for 8 to 10 minutes or until done.

"This is a Pennsylvania Dutch recipe that has been in Sara's family for at least four generations and all enjoy eating them."

— SARA NEWSWANGER
  Narvon

Lepp Cookies

3 cups yellow sugar

1 1/2 cup shortening

1 egg

vanilla

8 to 9 cups flour

1 1/2 Tbsp. baking soda

1 1/2 tsp. cream of tartar

1 pint thick milk or buttermilk

Cream sugar and shortening. Add egg and vanilla. Sift all dry ingredients. Alternately add dry ingredients with milk to egg mixture. Chill overnight.

Roll on floured board and cut out. Bake at 400 degrees for 10 minutes.

"Great-Grandma Mint's dunking cookie. Keeps well in containers."

— LINDA BOYER
  Narvon

King Cookies

2 cups butter

2 cups brown sugar

1 1/2 cups white sugar

4 eggs (jumbo)

2 teaspoons vanilla

grated rind and juice of one orange

5 cups flour

2 tsp. baking powder

2 tsp. salt

2 tsp. baking soda

2 cups semi sweet chocolate chips

3 cups regular or golden raisins

3 cups chopped nuts

2 1/2 cups old fashioned rolled oats

3 cups granola

Blend the butter, brown sugar and white sugar together until creamy. Add the eggs vanilla orange rind and juice and beat until blended. Sift together the flour, baking powder, salt and baking soda. Stir into the wet mixture and mix just until blended. Add the remaining ingredients and mix until well blended.

Shape into rounded tsp. balls and bake on a greased cookie sheet 350 degrees for 12 minutes or just until just turning brown around the edges. Best when warm from the oven. Dough keeps refrigerated or frozen. Bake them fresh as needed.

"We keep a cookie jar at the back door, and we bake these Friday afternoon as the guests are arriving. We often hand them a fresh-baked cookie right off the cookie sheet. They love this!"

— CHRIS FARR
Churchtown Inn

Meringues with Chocolate Chips

2 egg whites

3/4 cup sugar

6 oz. chocolate bits

Set oven to 350 degrees. Separate egg whites. For best results let egg whites sit for 30 minutes before beating. Beat egg whites until very stiff. Add sugar very slowly and continue to beat. Fold chocolate bits into egg white mixture.

Drop by teaspoon on cookie sheet covered with waxed paper or aluminum foil. Place in oven then shut oven door and turn off the heat. Allow it to remain in oven for 6 hours or over night. *Makes 3 dozen*

"Dedicated to Vanessa"

— DEB MARTIN
Narvon

Pennsylvania Dutch Molasses Cookies

1 cup brown sugar

1 cup shortening

1 cup sour cream

1 bottle molasses

1 Tbsp. baking soda (put in sour cream)

6 cups flour

1 tsp. ginger

1 tsp. cinnamon

Mix ingredients. Top with granulated sugar or a beaten egg.

Bake at 325 degrees for 10 to 12 minutes on a greased baking sheet.

"This recipe was found in an old Ephrata newspaper from the 1960's. The cookies tasted like the molasses cookies her grandmother made."

— SHARON COLON
Narvon

Peppernuts (Sugar Cookies)

2 cups sugar

1 cup butter

3 eggs

1 cup sweet milk

4 1/2 to 5 cups flour

1 tsp. baking soda

1 tsp. Cream of Tartar

1/2 tsp. lemon extract

1/2 tsp. vanilla

nutmeg and sugar to sprinkle

raisins to top each cookie

Sift flour, baking soda and cream of tartar. In separate bowl cream butter, add sugar, and beat well. Add 1 egg at a time. Beat egg mixture in several portions, alternating with flour mixture and milk. Add lemon extract and vanilla and mix well.

Chill several hours or overnight. Sprinkle dough with nutmeg. Drop by teaspoons onto greased cookie sheets. Sprinkle with sugar. Place a raisin in the middle.

Bake at 375 for 7 to 8 minutes. *Makes 6 dozen*

— ALICE SMITH
East Earl

Raisin Filled Cookies

DOUGH

1 cup brown sugar

3/4 cup white sugar

1 cup lard or shortening

1 cup milk

2 eggs

1 tsp. baking soda

2 tsp. baking powder

2 tsp. vanilla

4 to 5 cups flour

FILLING

1 cup raisins, ground

1 cup sugar

1/2 cup water

Combine filling ingredients in blender and then cook until thick.

Mix dough ingredients together. Add flour until it is a soft texture to roll out 1/4 inch thick. Cut with round cutter. Make thumbprint and add 1 tsp. of filling. Put another dough on top. Press edges slightly.

Bake on lightly greased cookie sheets at 350 degrees for 10 to 12 minutes.

Cool. Frost with favorite icing. *Makes 2 dozen*

"This was a favorite cookie passed on from Lisa's great-grandmother going back to the 1900's or before."

— LISA W. SHIRK
Narvon

Rich Chocolate Chip Cookies

2 cups sugar

4 eggs

2 cups brown sugar, packed

4 tsp. vanilla

2 3/4 cups butter

8 cups flour

3 tsp. baking soda

12 oz. chocolate chips

1 cup chopped nuts
(optional)

Combine flour and baking soda in medium-sized bowl. In mixer bowl, cream sugars, eggs, vanilla and butter.

Beat 5 minutes. Add the flour mixture slowly while mixing. Stir in chocolate chips and nuts. Bake at 350 degrees on ungreased cookie sheet for 8 minutes. *Makes 8 dozen*

— SUSIE NEWSWANGER
Narvon

Ginny's Sand Tarts

3 cups granulated sugar

3 eggs

1 cup soft butter (1/2 lb.) –
not margarine

1/2 tsp. baking soda mixed
with a little warm water

1 tsp. cream of tartar

4 cups flour

Mix sugar and eggs together. Add the butter and mix. Mix in baking soda in warm water.

Separately mix flour and cream of tartar, then combine into the mixture.

Roll out portions of dough like you would pie dough. Cut with cookie cutters. Put on greased cookie sheets and bake at 350 degrees for 12 to 15 minutes depending on oven and thickness of cookie dough.

Brush with egg whites and sprinkle with nuts and colored sugars. *Makes 6 dozen*

"Ginny's mother gave this recipe to her when she got married."

— GINNY WEBER
Narvon

Bunny's Sand Tarts

1 egg

2 cups sugar

3 1/2 cups flour

1 lb. butter

cinnamon and sugar

Mix together and make into 2 or 3 rolls. Roll up and put into wax paper or plastic wrap and refrigerate overnight. Slice thinly and place on baking sheet. Sprinkle with cinnamon and sugar. Bake at 350 degrees for 12 minutes or until brown.

— MARY A. (BUNNY) PARMER
Narvon

Snicker Peanut Butter Cookies

1 cup butter, softened

1 cup peanut butter

1 cup brown sugar

1 cup sugar

2 eggs

1 tsp. vanilla

3 1/2 cups flour

1 tsp. baking soda

1/2 tsp. salt

2 (13 oz.) pkgs. mini-snickers

chocolate to drizzle

Combine all ingredients in order except snickers. Cover and chill for 2 to 3 hours. Shape dough around each snicker to form cookie. Bake at 325 degrees for 10 to 12 minutes. Drizzle melted chocolate over cookies. *Makes 4 dozen*

"Alex made this recipe for one of the events at Historic Poole Forge and had requests for them at future events!"

— Alex Diem
  Narvon

Soft Sugar Cookies

COOKIES

2 cups sugar

1 cup shortening

3 eggs, well beaten

1 cup sour milk (I sour mine with 1 tsp. lemon juice)

4 1/2 cups flour

2 tsp. baking powder

1 tsp. baking soda

1 tsp. salt

1 tsp. vanilla

CREME FROSTING

6 Tbsp. butter

dash of salt

4 Tbsp. milk

2 cups confectioner's sugar (approximate amount)

1 tsp. vanilla

Cream sugar and shortening. Add eggs. Blend in remaining ingredients, alternate the milk and the sifted dry ingredients. Use a tablespoon of dough for each cookie.

Bake on greased pan or use parchment paper to cover pans.

Sprinkle with plain or colored sugar before baking.

Bake at 375 degrees for 10 minutes. Blend frosting ingredients. *Makes 4 dozen*

— Shirley Hostler
  Mifflintown, Juniata County

Thumbprint Cookies

1/2 lb. butter or margarine

1/2 cup granulated sugar

3 hard cooked egg yolks put through a sieve

2 1/2 cups sifted all purpose flour

1 tsp. vanilla

your favorite jelly

Cream butter and sugar. Add flour, egg yolks and vanilla. Mix and roll into 1 inch balls and put on an ungreased cookie sheet. Press a dent with your thumb and put about 1/3 tsp. of jelly in it.

Bake at 375 degrees for 10 minutes. Cookies will get brown on the bottom but not on top. They scorch easy, so don't over bake. *Makes 2 dozen*

"Dedicated to Valerie."

— DEB MARTIN
Narvon

Very Good Soft Cookies

3 cups brown sugar

1 cup shortening

1 egg

2 cups buttermilk

1 1/2 Tbsp. baking soda

1 1/2 tsp. cream of tartar

1 1/2 tsp. baking powder

6 cups flour

Mix dry ingredients and add wet to mixture.

Bake at 375 degrees for about 10 minutes.

— ELEANOR HIBSHMAN
Narvon

Welsh Picks

1 1/3 sticks softened butter

3/4 cup granulated sugar

2 large eggs

1 tsp. best vanilla

3 cups of sifted all purpose flour

2 1/2 heaping tsp. baking powder

1/4 tsp. salt

1 1/4 tsp. nutmeg

1 1/2 tsp. cinnamon

3 Tbsp. pear juice (Grandma used pear juice from her own canning)

1 1/2 cups raisins

Beat the butter until smooth and slowly add sugar beating until mixed. Add eggs and vanilla and mix well. Set aside. Sift together flour, baking powder, salt, nutmeg and cinnamon. Incorporate flour mixture into batter alternately with pear juice. When combined, fold in raisins. Form dough into a ball and roll onto a lightly floured surface. Cut cookies with a 2 inch diameter juice glass or round cutter.

Use an electric frying pan (Grandma used her old cast iron pan) set to 275 degrees and grease the pan lightly with vegetable shortening and wipe out the pan until most of the oil is absorbed.

Place the cookies into the pan and cook until the top surface of the cookie has a slight sheen, careful not to let the bottoms burn. Turn and cook other side until lightly browned. Remove to a wire rack and allow to completely cool. Store in an airtight container.

— RAY & MEGAN SMECKER
Churchtown

This recipe, Welsh Picks, is from Eunice Watkins and her daughter, Megan Smecker, who are pure Welsh. Welsh immigrants came to the Churchtown area in the 1600's where they built most of the stone mansions (now occupied by the local Amish/Plain Folk) and forges and participated in the founding and building of the local Bangor Episcopal Church that was finally built in 1722 and is one of the first in America. Bangor is now on the National Historic Register.

Eunice and Megan moved to this old Welsh settled valley in 1991 and brought with them this recipe that has been shared with their local friends and is the one that the Welsh serve at a lot of church and social gatherings. The Picks were probably served at the Bangor Episcopal Church gatherings in the early 1700's too. This recipe is Great Grandma Edmunds' from Wales.

Cookie Dough Brownies

BROWNIES

2 cups sugar

1 1/2 cup flour

1/2 cup cocoa powder

1/2 tsp. salt

1 cup vegetable oil

4 eggs

2 tsp. vanilla extract

1/2 cup walnuts (optional)

FILLING

1/2 cup margarine

1/2 cup brown sugar

1/4 cup sugar

2 Tbsp. milk

1 tsp. vanilla

1 cup flour

GLAZE

1 cup chocolate chips

1 Tbsp. oil

3/4 cup walnuts (optional)

Brownies: Combine sugar, flour, cocoa and salt. Add oil, eggs and vanilla. Beat at medium speed for 3 minutes. Stir in walnuts. Bake in a greased 9 X 13-inch pan for 25 minutes at 350 degrees. Cool completely.

Filling: Cream margarine and sugars. Add milk and vanilla and mix well. Beat in flour. Spread over brownies. Chill until firm.

Glaze: Melt chocolate chips and oil in sauce pan. Stir until smooth. Spread over filling and sprinkle with nuts, if desired.

"Jeanette's son, Chris, hosted a "coffee-house" night for his youth group and she made these for him. These brownies were always the favorite."

— JEANETTE KLUMPP
Narvon

Auntie's Fudge

6 oz. pkg. of chocolate chips

1/4 lb. butter or margarine

1 cup chopped nuts of
    choice

1 tsp. vanilla

16 large marshmallows

6 oz. can of evaporated milk

2 cups sugar

Combine first four ingredients in a bowl. Combine next 3 ingredients in a heavy saucepan. Stir and heat slowly to boil. Stir occasionally and cook exactly 6 minutes to 238 degrees.

Pour over bowl of contents and mix until blended. Pour into 8 X 8-inch pan. Cool 1 hour. Keep in refrigerator.

In memory of Dorothy Morrissey and Avis Hamilton

— CHERYL FOX
New Holland

Granola Bars

1/4 cup butter

1/4 cup vegetable oil

1 1/2 lb. marshmallows

1/2 cup honey

1/4 cup peanut butter

4 1/2 cups rice crispy cereal

1 cup graham cracker crumbs

5 cups oatmeal

1 cup crushed peanuts

1 cup coconut

1 cup chocolate chips or M&M's®

1 1/2 cup raisins (optional)

Heat butter and oil on low heat until butter melts. Add marshmallows and stir until melted. Remove from heat and add honey and peanut butter. In a large bowl, add remaining ingredients.

Make a well in center and pour marshmallow mixture into the well. When using M&M's, cool the marshmallow mixture so the colors don't melt too much.

Stir and press into an 11 X 15-inch cookie sheet. Cool and cut.

— LORELLE NEWSWANGER
Narvon

Lemon Pie Bars

BARS

1 lemon cake mix

1 can (15.75 oz.) lemon pie filling

4 eggs

FROSTING

6 oz. cream cheese

3 cups confectioner's sugar

6 Tbsp. butter

1 tsp. vanilla

Mix bar ingredients together. Spread in 10 X 15-inch baking pan and bake at 350 degrees until done.

Combine frosting ingredients in a small bowl. Mix until well blended. Frost bars. Store in refrigerator.

— MARY JANE NEWSWANGER
Morgantown

Revel Bars

BARS

1 cup butter

2 cups granulated sugar

2 eggs

2 tsp. vanilla

2 1/2 cups flour

1 tsp. baking soda

1 tsp. salt

3 cups oatmeal

TOPPING

12 oz. chocolate chips

1 can condensed milk

2 Tbsp. butter

1/2 tsp. salt

Spread batter 2/3 inch deep in jelly roll pan. Save some crumbs for on top.

Melt the topping ingredients together and put on top. Then add the remaining crumbs.

Bake at 350 degrees for 25 to 30 minutes on a greased pan.

— SUSIE SMUCKER
Narvon

Sour Cream Raisin Squares

SQUARES

1 cup butter, softened

1 cup packed brown sugar

2 cups all purpose flour

2 cups quick cooking oats

1 tsp. baking powder

1 tsp. baking soda

1/8 tsp. salt

FILLING

4 egg yolks

2 cups (16 oz.) sour cream

1 1/2 cups raisins

1 cup sugar

1 Tbsp. cornstarch

In a mixing bowl, cream butter and brown sugar. Beat in flour, oats, baking powder, baking soda and salt. Mixture will be crumbly. Set aside 2 cups. Pat remaining crumbs into a greased 9 X 13 X 2-inch baking pan.

Bake at 350 degrees for 15 minutes. Cool.

Meanwhile, combine filling ingredients in a sauce pan. Bring to a boil. Cook and stir constantly for 5 to 8 minutes.

Pour over crust, sprinkle with reserved crumbs. Return to the oven for 15 minutes. *Serves 12*

— MARILYN HOOVER
East Earl

Rhubarb Cheese Bars

CRUST

1 cup flour

1/4 cup sugar

1/2 cup butter, softened

FILLING #1

3 cups fresh rhubarb, cut into pieces

1/2 cup sugar

2 Tbsp. flour

FILLING #2

1 1/2 pkgs. (12 oz. total) cream cheese, softened

1/2 cup sugar

2 eggs

TOPPING

1 cup sour cream

2 Tbsp. sugar

1 tsp. vanilla

Mix crust ingredients together. Press into bottom of 9 X 13-inch baking dish. Mix filling #1 ingredients together. Pour over crust.

Bake at 300 degrees for 30 minutes.

Mix filling #2 ingredients together. Pour over filling #1.

Bake at 350 degrees for 50 to 60 minutes.

Mix topping ingredients together. Spread over hot bars.

— JANESSA FISHER
  Narvon

Belly Guts (Black Walnut Candy)

1 cup molasses

2 cups sugar

1 Tbsp. apple cider vinegar

1 Tbsp. butter

1/2 cup water

1/2 lb. black walnuts, chopped (or your favorite nut)

Boil ingredients together until mix forms a ball in cold water test. Add nuts and cool.

Pour into buttered 10 X 12-inch pans and chill.

Break into pieces when cold. Keep cold.

— RUTH LAMBERT
  East Earl

Toffee Bars

1/2 cup butter

1/2 cup brown sugar

1 cup flour

1 cup brown sugar

1 tsp. vanilla

2 Tbsp. flour

1 tsp. baking powder

1/2 tsp. salt

2 eggs

1 cup coconut

1 cup chopped nuts (pecans or walnuts)

1/2 tsp. cinnamon sugar

Cream together first three ingredients. Spread on ungreased glass baking dish smaller than a 9 X 13-inch dish.

Bake at 350 degrees for 10 minutes.

Mix together remaining ingredients. Pour over crust. Sprinkle on cinnamon sugar and spread out and bake at 350 degrees for 25 minutes.

Mark while warm to cut later as desired shapes. Store in a tight container.

"A wonderful Christmas or holiday addition to everyone's busy cookie list. This was new to me in 1986. Sweet memories last!"

— SUSAN MARRIS
  Goodville

Peanut Butter Fudge

2 1/2 cups oatmeal

1/2 cup peanut butter

1/2 cup milk

2 cups sugar

3 Tbsp. cocoa

2 Tbsp. butter

1 tsp. vanilla

Mix first two ingredients in a bowl. In a saucepan combine next 5 ingredients and boil 1 minute. Pour over oats mixture. Mix lightly and drop by teaspoons on waxed paper. *Makes 4 dozen*

"This recipe was given to me by my friend, Fannie Smucker."

— FLORIBEL STYER
  Narvon

Million Dollar Fudge

5 oz. evaporated milk

1 3/4 cup granulated sugar

1/2 cup butter

2 1/2 cups milk chocolate chips

1 tsp. vanilla

1 3/4 cups miniature marshmallows

Mix milk and sugar in 2 qt. sauce pan and bring to a boil. Boil for 6 minutes on low heat. Remove from heat and cool for 2 minutes.

Add remaining ingredients to mixture. Stir until smooth. Pour into buttered 9 X 13-inch baking pan. Cool in refrigerator and cut into squares.

— JANESSA FISHER
Narvon

Potato Candy

1 tbsp. mashed potatoes

1 lb. or more of powdered sugar

1 tsp. vanilla

peanut butter

Put mashed potatoes in a bowl. Add vanilla and powdered sugar to mashed potatoes while hot, until roll out consistency. Roll out between waxed paper that is dusted with powdered sugar. Spread with peanut butter. Roll up like a jelly roll. Refrigerate for an hour or until stiff enough to slice. Keeps best if refrigerated.

"Betty Ann's mother made this recipe at Christmas time. It is good anytime."

— BETTY ANN JAMIESON
Trenton, NJ

Strawberries

1/2 cup butter

1 cup sugar

1 1/4 cup dates (8 oz.) cut fine

2 slightly beaten eggs

1/2 cup flour

1 tsp. vanilla

1 cup chopped nuts

2 1/2 cups rice krispies

1 1/2 bottle of red sugar

Heat butter and add sugar, eggs and dates. Cook for 5 minutes then turn to low heat and add flour. Cook stirring constantly for 7 to 10 minutes. Add vanilla, cereal and nuts and mix thoroughly. Cool to lukewarm and shape into strawberry shapes and coat with red sugar. Stem could be added with small tube of green icing. *Makes 3 dozen*

"This is Floribel's sister Mary's recipe"

— FLORIBEL STYER
Narvon

CAKES INDEX

ALONG THE CONESTOGA

CAKES
Historic Poole Forge

CHAPTER SPONSORED BY

Caernarvon Township

The Caernarvon Township Supervisors would like to express their appreciation to the many volunteers that give of themselves and their time to make Caernarvon Township a unique community in which to live.

- ▶ Caernarvon Fire Company
- ▶ Caernarvon Fire Company Ladies' Auxiliary
- ▶ Caernarvon Historical Society
- ▶ Caernarvon Memorial Society

- ▶ Caernarvon Township Agricultural Advisory Committee
- ▶ Caernarvon Township Planning Commission
- ▶ Caernarvon Township Zoning Hearing Board
- ▶ Historic Poole Forge

Historic Poole Forge

Perfectly situated along the southern side of Route 23, just outside of Churchtown, Poole Forge remains a vestige of another century. Just driving through the property with the stately fieldstone mansion nestled into the hillside, the spectacular sycamore trees towering over the property, the picturesque 150 year old covered bridge spanning the Conestoga Creek and the few remaining fieldstone outbuildings gives you the feeling of stepping back in time. The way the property is positioned with the fields, stream and mature landscaping, a sense of tranquility and isolation still exists. A visitor can almost envision the working iron plantation of 200 years ago and the generations of workers who lived their lives here. This peaceful place has managed to retain a visual sense of being buffered from the outside world.

"El" wing of the mansion.

Originally, the property was developed with a grist mill along the creek. It is thought the south section of the mansion was constructed first. It consisted of a fieldstone two-story structure with a walk-in fireplace for cooking on the north wall, with a staircase tucked beside in the northeast corner. The front door faced toward the west with a porch spanning the west side (remnants of this can be seen on the stone today). Documents show that in 1775, James Old, who formerly tended the Windsor forges, purchased this property. The Old family came from Wales. The family was reputed to be of great force, character and natural ability. They started as manual laborers at Windsor Forge but soon drifted toward owning and operating their own forges. Mr. Old built an iron forge on the property and named it Poole Forge after the large pool of water behind the dam breast. This dam was located on the southern part of the property. He also added the northern section of the mansion. The style of the rear wing was kept modest, because it was the new kitchen wing, and had many rooms on the second and third floors that appear to have been for boarders or workers. The most stylish items remaining of the rear wing or "El" wing are the dormers, with arched double hung windows which are Federal in style, indicating their date as after 1800. This renovation to the south section and the addition of the north end would have been considered a large undertaking.

Federal style dormer windows on roof of mansion.

James Old became a prominent ironmaster in the community. Records show he was elected to the State Legislature and became a Justice of the Peace. Mr. Old prospered and purchased the Speedwell forge and a forge near Lebanon. He lived at Poole Forge with his wife until his death in 1811. Old and his wife, Margaret, are buried at Bangor Church.

During the heyday of iron forge operations, the Poole Forge property housed families for the laborers. Of the nine tenant houses built only two remain; the small fieldstone tenant house to the east of the mansion and the newly restored west tenant house located in front of the covered bridge. The east tenant house is a fieldstone two-story structure with two rooms down and two rooms upstairs. A large, walk in stone fireplace on the first floor and originally, another on the second, complete the structure. The forge office, or Paymasters house, still stands today directly in front of the mansion. This structure is built of fine, smooth-surfaced sandstone. In the basement, an immense eight-foot fireplace with an impressive overhead lintel supporting the massive two-story stone structure above can still be seen. The actual forge building, where the men toiled, was just east of the Paymasters office and house. It was a long, one story, open space building with many windows and a large chimney at either end. Each chimney was an opening to two forges and anvils. A roof extended out over the large waterwheel and small over-shot wheel. The large wheel raised and powered the huge trip hammer. The forge building finally collapsed in 1910 but maps and forge records document the site.

The gatehouse to Poole Forge.

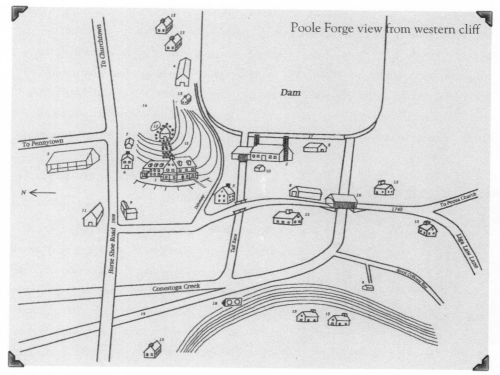

Poole Forge view from western cliff

(original drawing by Robert Simpson Sr.)

1. Mansion
2. Forge
3. Office
4. Carter's stable
5. Farm barn
6. Wash house
7. Ice house
8. Charcoal sheds
9. Spring houses
10. Scale house
11. Carriage shed
12. Aiwer
13. Terraces
14. Orchard
15. Tenant houses
16. Covered Bridge
17. Dam breast
18. Quarries and lime kilns
19. Tail race from early mill

South of the forge, charcoal was stored in a building and in front of the forge sat the scale house. Near the covered bridge and road stood another large charcoal building and shed to house the coal wagons. The coal wagons were of similar design as the Conestoga wagon with five-foot sides and a level loose bottom. The rear wheels stood almost six feet tall and front wheels almost five feet. These were heavy duty coal transports in the day and required strong horses to pull the loads. A stable was situated nearby east of the forge along the large dam. From records, it is estimated the stable was a two-story structure measuring eighty feet long. During the heyday of iron production, the heavy wagon teams hauled crude ore from the mine to the furnace, then the pig iron to the forges. The teamsters supplied the tons of charcoal to the furnace and forges. And lastly, they transported the finished iron product to Philadelphia, Reading and other destinations. Tons of iron was used in the war effort from the forges in this area. The forges made great profits for the Ironmasters during wartime, supplying raw metal and finished cast iron products.

By 1786, Poole Forge was one of seventeen furnaces, forges and mills within a thirty-nine mile radius of Lancaster. This area was considered a great iron center during this time according to the 1789 Pennsylvania Gazeteer which published an article stating the two forges around Churchtown (Poole and Windsor) were producing four hundred and fifty tons of bar iron annually. This was considered high productivity. Mr. Old sold his forge and over 700 acres of land to his son David in 1795. Ironmaster Old was more interested in the Birdsboro iron works. Four years later, David Old sold Poole Forge again to Cyrus Jacobs, his brother-in-law who owned Spring Grove Forge. Mr. Jacobs continued to run a very prosperous charcoal-iron business.

Original marble fireplace in the mansion parlor.

Life on an eighteenth century iron plantation is hard for people to imagine today. These were actual vestiges of old world landed estates, where a society of ironmasters controlled the lives of their workers. In the beginning, these estates were self-sufficient, taking care of all the needs of the workers and his family. The estate managed a general store, food production, and health needs. Gradually, as more towns sprang up nearby, the responsibilities of the estate moved to the town. No record has yet been found showing a general store on the Poole Forge property, although from 1806 ledgers, documents list small necessities purchased by the workers on site. With the town of Churchtown so close, most likely the forge community walked to town for their general needs. By 1779, Churchtown had tailors, shoemakers, blacksmiths, tinsmiths, hat makers, cabinet makers, saddlers, carpenters, doctors and undertakers to take care of all their needs and wants. A gradual dependency in town life evolved and dismantled the large self-sufficient estates. Although the average worker relied heavily on the ironmaster and his family, they were paid wages and bought their own supplies. The workers were free to leave the forge at anytime. Records show that life must have been pretty good on the estates because second and third generations stayed on at the same forge community.

The mansion house is an imposing structure nestled in to the hillside with the south end built over 200 years ago. It was the social and culture center for the estate. After the Old's purchased the property in 1775, they decorated the place in high style appropriate for the day. They remodeled the front section adding Federal-styled dormers. The west door was filled in, the cook fireplace taken out, other fireplaces added, the staircase changed and enlarged, and the orientation of the entry door moved to the south, where it is now. This renovation gave the entry a wide hall and stairs. All the bedrooms now had fireplaces. They installed a marble fireplace in the front parlor. This is still in place today. Most likely, in the eighteenth century, the furnishings were imported from Europe and many luxuries graced the interior making life quite comfortable for the ironmaster and his family.

West Tenant house.

Behind the mansion, where the garage exists today, a washhouse stood and behind that was the icehouse. The remnants of the icehouse still are visible on the hillside to the east of the mansion. Icehouses were a necessity to keep food from spoiling and having it situated close to the kitchen was important. Across the road was a large stone stable for housing the saddle and coach horses. Beside the stable was the shed for storing the coaches and equipment. The springhouse (gatehouse) still sits at the entrance corner of the property. It is a charming fieldstone cottage with a natural spring keeping it cool and damp. At one time, the spring fed a fountain on the front lawn of the mansion. It was a wooden sculpture of a boy and his dog. Fresh water spilled from the dog's mouth.

Behind the mansion the hillside was terraced with beautiful flower beds, scented shrubs and lots of greenery. A central walk bordered by boxwood and flowers lead the way from the house to the upper meadow. At one time, there existed a latticed summer house where family and friends spent the hottest days of the summer enjoying the shaded trees, cool breezes and relaxing. The very popular yard game of croquet was played on the upper meadow too. An orchard spanned the back of the meadow. Many community events were held in the orchard such as Sunday school celebrations and holiday gatherings enjoyed by everyone.

Today, Poole Forge still looks much like it did 150 years ago. Of course, the once 3000-acre estate has been chiseled down to a mere 24 acres and has survived many owners and renovations. Some of the renovations have been positive for the estate and others have left a negative footprint on the land. Since Caernarvon Township purchased the property in 2005, for the purpose of a community park and historical preservation, many positive changes have occurred. The many volunteers who share a common interest in preserving

Historic Poole Forge pavilion erected in 2007 and playground erected in 2006.

and restoring this special place have spent countless hours working and sharing their talents in the hope of creating a park for generations to share.

OWNERS OF POOLE FORGE:

▸ James Old purchased from Edward Hughes in 1775. He turned it into a working forge

▸ Robert Coleman purchased Poole Forge in 1785 from James Old (Coleman married Old's daughter)

▸ Cyrus Jacobs purchased Poole Forge from his brother-in-law, Davis Old (Jacobs married Old's other daughter)

▸ Willed to grandsons Hanson & Cyrus Jacobs in 1830

▸ Hanson Jacobs took Poole Forge as his share in 1836 after his marriage to Catherine Jenkins

▸ In 1852, Ironmaster, Jacob Jamison purchased Poole Forge.

▸ In 1854, Isaac Blight purchased Poole Forge (he farmed & continued the iron business)

▸ In 1862, sold at sheriff's sale to James DeHaven

▸ The DeHaven family owned the property until 1925.

▸ Sold to Walter Hager (summer home) in 1925

▸ In 1931, sold to William Troop (local farmer). He split the mansion in half.

▸ Walter Troop sold the property to Charles Hess in 1936

▸ Charles Hess & Harold Brecht purchased Poole Forge in 1936

▸ In 1948, sold to Katherine McDowell and family

▸ Dorothy Wimer purchased the property in 1981, became a dog kennel

▸ In 1981 Harry & Sara Kruppenbach purchased the property

▸ In 2005 Caernarvon Township purchased the 24 acre site and created Historic Poole Forge Inc. to operate and maintain it.

Black Walnut Cake

CAKE

2 cups sifted + 2 Tbsp. sifted flour

1 1/3 cups sugar

3 1/2 tsp. baking powder

1/2 tsp. salt

1/2 cup margarine

1 cup milk

2 tsp. vanilla

1/2 cup egg whites (unbeaten)

1/2 cup black walnuts

FROSTING

1 cup sugar

1 cup black walnuts

1 cup coffee cream

Place in a large mixing bowl the flour, sugar, baking powder and salt. In a separate bowl mix margarine, milk and vanilla. Add to dry ingredients and mix for 2 minutes. Add the egg whites and beat 2 minutes more. Fold in black walnuts. Grease and flour a 13 X 9-inch or two 8-inch pans. Bake at 350 degrees for 30 to 35 minutes.

Combine frosting ingredients. Place in heavy aluminum pan and heat slowly. Cook about 15 to 20 minutes. Do not stir. Cool and spread on cooled cake.

"A favorite Raffensperger cake!"

— LORRAINE RAFFENSPERGER
  Blue Ball

Milkless, Eggless, Butterless Cake

1 cup very dark brown sugar

1 cup water

1 1/2 cup seeded raisins

1/3 cup lard

1 tsp. ground cinnamon

1/3 tsp. ground cloves

1/4 tsp. salt

1/4 tsp. ground sugar

1 tsp. baking soda

1 Tbsp. warm water

2 cups sifted flour

1/2 tsp. baking powder

Boil the first 8 ingredients for 3 minutes, cool, stir in baking soda dissolved in 1 tbsp. warm water. In a separate bowl sift 2 cups flour. Resift with baking powder. Add to boiled ingredients and mix. Add sifted flour, resifted with baking powder. Bake in an 8-inch square pan or a 10-inch cast iron skillet at 350 degrees for 35 minutes.

"It resembles an applesauce cake. When times were lean this was a treat."

— RUTH LAMBERT
  East Earl

Pop's Coffee Cake

1 lb. brown sugar

3 cups flour

1 stick butter

3 eggs

1 cup butter milk

1 tsp. baking soda

Mix brown sugar, flour and butter to make crumbs. Keep 1/2 to 1 cup out for topping. Add eggs, butter milk and baking soda. Pour into 3 ungreased 8 or 9-inch pie pans. Sprinkle tops with crumbs. Bake at 350 degrees for 30 to 40 minutes, checking with a toothpick until done.

"My dad's favorite dunker."

— LINDA BOYER
Narvon

Rum Cake

CAKE

1 yellow cake mix

4 eggs

1/2 cup vegetable oil

1 (3 3/4 oz.) pkg. instant vanilla pudding

1/2 cup cold water

1/2 cup dark Bacardi rum (makes a difference in the taste)

RUM GLAZE

1 stick butter

1/4 cup cold water

1 cup sugar

1/2 cup rum

Mix all cake ingredients together. Grease and flour a 10-inch tube pan. Pour cake batter in pan.

Bake at 350 degrees for 1 hour. Cool in pan for 25 minutes before removing.

Meanwhile, melt butter in saucepan and stir in water and sugar. Boil for 5 minutes. Remove from heat. Stir in rum.

Prick top of cake and drizzle glaze over cake.

— DARLENE MAY EMERY STAUFFER
Narvon

Southern Cinnamon Cake

1 cup sugar

2 Tbsp. butter

2 cups flour

1 1/2 tsp. baking powder

1/2 tsp. salt

1 cup milk

1 egg

pinch of nutmeg

Cream the butter and sugar, then add the egg. Mix dry ingredients together. Alternate dry ingredients and milk when mixing into creamed mixture. Sprinkle cinnamon and sugar on top before putting in oven. Bake in greased 8-inch pan at 350 degrees.

"A recipe handed down from my mother. She made many cakes at one time and put a supply in the freezer."

— SHARON COLON
Narvon

Wedding Cake

2 cups sugar

3/4 cup butter

2 cups flour sifted

1 cup cornstarch

1 tsp. baking powder

1 cup milk

1 tsp. vanilla

Cream the sugar and butter together. Sift flour, baking powder and cornstarch together. Add these alternately with milk and vanilla to creamed mixture. Bake at 350 degrees in 2 8 inch layer pans for 25 to 30 minutes.

"Traditionally the wedding cake."

— EDNA SWEITZER
East Earl

1700 Pound Cake

3 cups sugar

2 sticks butter

5 eggs

1 tsp. lemon flavoring or juice

2 tsp. vanilla

1 Tbsp. buttermilk

1/2 tsp. almond extract

3 cups sifted cake flour

1 cup sweet milk

Cream the sugar and butter. Add eggs one at a time and beat well. Add lemon, vanilla, buttermilk, almond and mix well. Add flour and milk alternately. Bake in greased and floured 12-cup tube pan for 1 hour and 15 min. at 300 degrees. Do not open door for first hour.

Optionally, add 1/2 cup cocoa to flour mix to make chocolate cake. Bake at 350 degrees and use loaf pans for smaller cakes.

"Old German Hand-written recipe I had translated. Great with ice cream and fruit."

— LINDA BOYER
Narvon

Butter Dips

2 1/4 cup flour

1 tbsp. sugar

3 1/2 tsp. baking powder

1 1/2 tsp. salt

1 cup milk

1 stick margarine or butter

1/2 tsp. seasoned salt

1/2 tsp. garlic powder

Sift dry ingredients, then add milk and turn with fork, just until dough clings together. Put on well floured board and knead lightly, then roll to 1/2 inch thick rectangle; cut into strips about 3/4 inch x 4 inches. In a 9 x 13 pan melt butter and add seasonings. Roll strips in butter, and then lay side by side in pan. Bake at 450 degrees for 15 to 20 minutes.

Can use different spices or add grated cheese, herbs, spices to dough.

— SALLY KELLERMAN
South Coventry

Applesauce Cake

1 2/3 cups sifted flour

1 1/3 cups sugar

1/4 tsp. baking powder

1 tsp. baking soda

3/4 tsp. salt

1/2 tsp. cinnamon

1/4 tsp. cloves

1 1/4 tsp. allspice

1/3 cup shortening

1 large egg

1/3 cup water

2/3 cup raisins

1 cup applesauce

Sift together all the dry ingredients in a bowl. Then add the shortening, egg, water, raisins and applesauce. Grease and flour 2 8-inch pans. Bake at 350 degrees for 50 to 55 minutes.

"This was my grandmother's recipe. She used to live on Boot Jack Road. There was a house on the side of the hill where the landfill is now. You could see the house from Route 23. I talked to my family and we figured it to be around 1920 when her family moved there. My grandmother used to make this cake for her kids and we are sure she got it from her mother. We are not sure how long she lived there."

— CATHERINE HAWK STROCK
Narvon

Banana Chiffon Cake

2 1/4 cups cake flour

1 1/2 cups sugar

3 tsp. baking powder

1 tsp. salt

1 tsp. vanilla

1/2 cup vegetable oil

5 egg yolks

1/3 cup water

1 cup mashed banana

Mix dry ingredients together. Make a well and add wet ingredients. Beat until smooth. Beat 1 cup egg whites and 1 tsp. cream of tartar until very stiff. Fold into batter.

Bake in tube cake pan at 325 degrees for 1 hour or until golden brown. Ice with your favorite frosting. Sprinkle chopped walnuts on top.

— MARY JANE NEWSWANGER
  Morgantown

Butternut Squash Layer Cake

LAYERS

1/2 cup butter or margarine,
  softened

1 cup sugar

1 cup packed brown sugar

2 eggs

1 cup mashed cooked
  butternut squash

1 tsp. maple flavoring

3 cups cake flour

4 tsp. baking powder

1/4 tsp. baking soda

1/2 cup milk

1 cup chopped walnuts

FROSTING

1 1/2 cups packed brown
  sugar

3 egg whites

6 Tbsp. water

1/4 tsp. cream of tartar

1/8 tsp. salt

1 tsp. vanilla extract

In a mixing bowl, cream the butter and sugars. Add eggs, one at a time, beating well after each addition. Add squash and maple flavoring; mix well. Combine flour, baking powder and baking soda; add to creamed mixture alternately with milk. Stir in walnuts. Pour into two greased and floured 9-inch round baking pans. Bake at 350 degrees for 25 to 30 minutes or until a toothpick inserted near the center comes out clean. Cool 10 minutes before removing from pans to wire racks.

For frosting, combine the brown sugar, egg whites, water, cream of tartar and salt in a heavy saucepan. With a portable mixer, beat on low speed for 1 minute. Continue beating over low heat until a thermometer reads 160 degrees, about 8 to 10 minutes. A stand mixer is recommended for beating the frosting after it reaches 160 degrees.

Pour frosting into a large mixing bowl; add vanilla. Beat on high speed until stiff peaks form, about 3 minutes. Spread between layers, and over top and sides of cake. Refrigerate.

— VERA JANE NEWSWANGER
  Morgantown

German Raw Apple Cake

CAKE

1/2 cup vegetable oil

1/2 cup brown sugar

1 cup granulated sugar

2 eggs

2 1/4 cups flour

1/2 tsp. salt

2 tsp. pumpkin pie spices

2 cups raw peeled and sliced apples

1 cup sour milk

2 tsp. baking soda

TOPPING

1/2 cup brown sugar

1/2 cup granulated sugar

1/2 tsp. pumpkin pie spice

Cream all cake ingredients together, with apples last. Pour into 9 X 13-inch pan.

Then take 1/2 cup brown sugar and 1/2 cup granulated sugar, mix. Then add 1/2 tsp. pumpkin pie spice mix together.

Spread topping mixture on cake.

Bake at 350 degrees for 45 minutes.

"I love this cake and I always double the topping and add some pecan pieces before cake goes in oven."

— MARY ANN GOOD
Terre Hill

Grandma's Fruit Cake

1 1/2 cup fresh fruit (any kind)

3 cups flour

1 1/2 cups sugar

1/2 tsp. salt

3/4 cup butter, melted

1 cup sour cream

3 large eggs

1/2 cup chopped nuts (your choice)

2 tsp. baking powder

1 tsp. baking soda

Combine flour, sugar, and salt. Add melted butter, sour cream and eggs. Mix to moisten. Add nuts, baking powder and baking soda. Beat until blended. Fold in fruit; quickly turn into greased and floured pans. Bake at 350 degrees for 55 to 60 minutes. Cool 20 minutes and invert.

You can use a 9 X 13-inch pan or 9 to 10-inch pans. Just remember to cool well before turning out. This cake needs only powdered sugar to top.

— EDNA SWEITZER
East Earl

Heavenly Lemony Cheesecake

CRUST

1 cup sifted flour

1/4 cup sugar

1 egg yolk

1/2 cup soft butter

FILLING

5 pkgs. (8 oz.) cream cheese

1 3/4 cup sugar

3 Tbsp. all purpose flour

1/4 tsp. salt

grated rind from 1 lemon

grated rind from 1/2 orange

5 eggs

2 egg yolks

1/2 cup heavy cream

For crust, mix everything together, slightly chill in refrigerator for about 20 minutes.

Butter pan bottom and cover it with chilled crust, press out. Bake for 8 minutes at 400 degrees. Butter sides of pan. Let cool. Press crust around sides.

For filling, beat cheese until soft. Mix sugar, flour, and salt, gradually blend into cheese, keeping mixture smooth. Add grated rinds. Add eggs and egg yolks, one at a time, beat thoroughly after each. Blend in cream. Pour into pan with crust.

Bake in preheated oven at 475 degrees for 15 minutes. Reduce heat to 225 degrees and bake for 1 hour longer.

Turn off heat and leave cake in oven for 15 minutes. Remove from oven and let stand until cool. Chill. When ready to serve, remove from sides of pan.

— CHRISTI DOWNES
  Garnet Valley

My Hubby's Favorite Strawberry Shortcake

1 cup granulated sugar

1 Tbsp. butter

1 egg

3 tsp. baking powder

1 tsp. salt

1 cup milk

3 cups flour

1 pint sliced strawberries

Mix all ingredients together. Then add strawberries.

Bake at 350 degrees for almost an hour, check for doneness.

— MARY ANN GOOD
  Terre Hill

Pineapple Angel Food Cake

1 (16 oz.) pkg. angel food cake mix (must be the one-envelope type of mix)

1 (20 oz.) can crushed pineapple with juice

1 (12 oz.) container of Cool Whip

Preheat oven to 350 degrees. Spray 9 X 13-inch pan with vegetable oil. In large bowl, combine cake mix and pineapple with juice. Mix until well blended. Pour batter into prepared pan.

Bake for 25 minutes or until golden brown. Let cool upside down or the cake will sink. Serve with Cool Whip.

— LIDA BENSINGER
Narvon

Martha's Pumpkin Cake

4 eggs

1/2 cup olive oil

1/2 cup maple syrup

2 cups pumpkin

1 tsp. salt

2 tsp. cinnamon

1 tsp. baking powder

1 tsp. baking soda

2 1/2 cups flour

1 cup or more chocolate chips

Sift together dry ingredients, add remaining ingredients and beat for 2 minutes. Pour into 9 x 13-inch greased cake pan. Top with chocolate chips.

Bake at 350 degrees for 30 to 35 minutes.

— MARTHA NEWSWANGER
Narvon

Betty's Pumpkin Cake

CAKE

1 pkg. yellow cake mix

1 egg

1/2 cup melted margarine

FILLING

1 large can of pumpkin

2 eggs

2 tsp. nutmeg

1/2 tsp. ginger

1/2 cup sugar

2 tsp. cinnamon

2/3 cup milk

TOPPING

1 cup cake mix

1/4 cup sugar

1/4 cup cold oleo

Take out 1 cup yellow cake mix, set aside. Fork beat one egg, and add to rest of cake mix. Add melted margarine. Mix together and pat into oblong pan that is greased on the bottom only.

For filling, mix ingredients and pour over crust.

For topping, mix together to make crumb topping.

Bake in greased and floured 9 X 13-inch pan at 350 degrees for 45 minutes.

"It's like pumpkin pie but has a cake bottom. Feeds a lot of people. Good for a church supper."

— BETTY ANN JAMIESON
Hamilton, NJ

Surprise Fruit Squares

1 cup butter or margarine

1 1/2 cups sugar

2 cups flour

4 eggs

1 tsp. vanilla

1 can cherry or any flavor fruit pie filling

milk and confectioner's sugar for icing

Cream butter, and gradually add sugar, beating until light and fluffy. Add eggs, beat well. Stir in flour and vanilla. Pour into a lightly greased jelly roll pan 15 1/2 X 10-1/2-inches, spreading evenly into the pan. Drop pie filling by the tablespoonful on top of the batter until the pie filling is all used. Bake at 350 degrees for about 40 to 45 minutes or until slightly brown on the top. The batter will puff up around the pie filling while baking. Cool. Drizzle icing across the pan (mix a little milk and confectioner's sugar to make the icing). Cut into squares and serve.

— COLLEEN COLDREN
East Earl

Amish Chocolate Chiffon Cake with Seven Minute Frosting

CAKE

1/4 cup cocoa

3/4 cup boiling water

1 3/4 cups sugar

1 3/4 cups flour

1 1/2 tsp. baking soda

8 eggs separated

2 tsp. vanilla

1 tsp. salt

1/2 cup vegetable oil

1/2 tsp. cream of tartar

FROSTING

2 egg whites

1 cup white sugar

2 tsp. white Karo

5 tbsp. water or less

1 tsp. vanilla

First mix cocoa with boiling water (let cool). Take sugar and flour and make a well, put in egg yolks, vanilla, salt, baking soda, and vegetable oil. Mix well. Add cocoa water, mix well again. Put cream of tartar in egg whites. Beat till very stiff. Fold into mixture, bake in tube pan at 325 degrees for 60 to 65 minutes.

For frosting, combine egg whites, sugar, Karo in top of double boiler. Beat until well mixed. Place over boiling water. Beat constantly for 7 minutes. Remove from heat, add vanilla. Beat until thick enough to spread.

— RAY & MEGAN SMECKER
   Churchtown

Black Joe Cake

1/2 cup margarine

2 cups brown sugar

2 eggs

1/2 cup cocoa

1 1/2 tsp. baking soda

1 3/4 cup flour

1 cup thick milk

Cream sugar and margarine. Beat until fluffy. Add eggs, one at a time. Add baking soda, cocoa, and flour alternately with milk. Stir to bind (do not beat) by hand. Bake in a 9-inch square pan at 350 degrees until done. Delicious with Pillsbury Whipped Supreme white icing.

"From Leah McClure's sister Jo."

— LINDA BOYER
   Narvon

Caramel Cake

2 cups brown sugar

1/2 cup shortening

2 eggs

1 tsp. vanilla

2 cups flour

1/2 tsp. salt

1 tsp. cocoa

2 tsp. hot water

1 cup sour milk

1 tsp. baking soda

Cream sugar and shortening. Add eggs, vanilla, flour, and salt. Pour water in 2 cup measuring cup; add cocoa, milk and baking soda. Stir until cocoa is dissolved. Pour into batter.

Bake in 9 X 13-inch pan at 350 degrees for 35 to 40 minutes.

— DAISY LAMBERT
East Earl

The Amish are always open to learning, and only go to school in a one room school house up to the eighth grade. Then they finish off with several years of learning a trade. Amish children are taught Pennsylvania Dutch first and then English as their second language.

One day Amish Raymond E. Smecker, spent a summer reading some English classics. He especially was fascinated by the story of Rip Van Winkle by Washington Irving. Soon after finishing the story Raymond was relaxing and listening to a group of grownups.

He remembers his father saying "I'm really having a rough time sleeping, all the problems, bad cows, splitting the farm..... bad milk prices... I just need to get some sleep."

This statement sparked Raymond's imagination. He jumped up and said " Dad, I just read about this man who slept for 20 years. He drank something? Why don't you call the doctor and ask him to give you some medicine like that Mr Winkle?"

"Oh Raymond," said his father, " I know that story but I don't want to sleep that long."

— BY RAY & MEGAN SMECKER

Chocolate Kahlua Cake
with Bailey's Cream Cheese Icing

CAKE

2 cups flour

2 cups sugar

3/4 cups cocoa

2 tsp. baking soda

1 tsp. baking powder

1/2 cup oil

1 cup milk

1 cup hot coffee

2 eggs

1 tsp. vanilla

1/2 cup Kahlua

IRISH CREME
ICING

1 (2 lb.) bag of
confectioner's sugar

1/2 cup shortening

4 oz. cream cheese

1/4 cup milk

Bailey's Irish Cream

Sift together first five ingredients, make a well and add next five ingredients. Mix 2 minutes on low speed.

Bake in greased and floured 13 X 9-inch baking pan at 350 degrees for 30 minutes or until toothpick comes out clean.

Mix Irish creme icing ingredients, adding Bailey's Irish Cream until spreading consistency.

When cake is warm, poke holes about every 3 or 4 inches into cake and pour 1/2 cup Kahlua into the holes. Finish with Irish cream cheese icing.

For icing, mix all ingredients together until fluffy. Spread on Chocolate Kahlua cake.

— SONDRA SIMMERS
Narvon

Chocolate Sundae Cake

1 box chocolate cake mix

1 bottle of caramel ice cream topping

1 (12 oz.) bag 5th Avenues, crushed

1 (8 oz.) container of cool whip

Bake cake as directed in a 9 X 13-inch pan. When it comes out of oven, poke hole in the top of hot cake, with wooden spoon handle, about 10 to 12 holes. Squeeze caramel topping over top of cake and sprinkle about 1/2 candy over that then put in fridge to get cold. Then when cool cover with cool whip and top with the rest of the candy.

— MARY ANN GOOD
Terre Hill

Chocolate Mayonnaise Cake with Chocolate Icing

CAKE

1 3/4 cup flour

2 tsp. baking soda

1 cup sugar

1/2 cup cocoa

1 tsp. vanilla

1 cup cold water

1 cup mayonnaise

ICING

1/2 cup butter

5 cup confectioner's sugar

1/2 cup cocoa

1 tsp. vanilla

1/2 cup + 2 Tbsp. milk

Sift dry ingredients. Add vanilla and water. Mix until smooth. Fold in mayonnaise. Bake in a greased and floured 8 X 8 inch pan at 350 degrees for 45 minutes.

For icing sift sugar and cocoa into bowl containing butter. Cream together and add vanilla. Gradually add milk and beat until smooth.

"So simple my daughter made it when she was 5 years old!"

— SALLY KELLERMAN
  South Coventry

Ice Cream Cake

1 box yellow cake mix

1 small box instant chocolate pudding

4 eggs

1/2 cup oil

2 tsp. vanilla

1 cup water

1 qt. ice cream or less

strawberries and Cool Whip® (optional)

Mix all ingredients together. Line a 9 X 13-inch baking pan with foil. Pour batter into pan and bake according to cake mix box instructions.

When cool, cut cake in half horizontally and put ice cream in middle. Optional: Serve with strawberries and Cool Whip®.

— JANESSA FISHER
  Narvon

Our Favorite Chocolate Cake with Peanut Butter Frosting

CAKE

2 cups flour

1 tsp. salt

1 Tbsp. baking powder

2 tsp. baking soda

3/4 cup cocoa

2 cups sugar

1 cup hot coffee

1 cup vegetable oil

1 cup milk

2 eggs

1 tsp. vanilla

ICING

2 Tbsp. peanut butter

1 stick of butter, creamed

1 box confectioner's sugar

1 Tbsp. light colored Karo

2 Tbsp. milk

1 tsp. vanilla

Put all dry ingredients in a mixing bowl. Add eggs, milk, oil and vanilla. Beat 2 minutes. Add hot coffee and beat another minute.

Bake at 350 degrees for 35 to 40 minutes.

For icing, mix peanut butter and creamed butter well. Add confectioner's sugar. Mix milk in until nice and creamy. Then add Karo and vanilla. If thinner frosting is desired, just add a little more milk 1 tablespoon at a time.

— ELEANOR HIBSHMAN
Narvon

Pete's Chocolate Cake

2 eggs

1 cup white sugar

3/4 cup brown sugar

1/2 cup shortening

1 cup milk

2 cups flour

1/2 cup cocoa

1 tsp. baking soda

1 tsp. salt

1/4 cup boiling water

Mix together eggs, sugars and shortening. Then add milk and mix. Add flour, cocoa, baking soda and salt and mix well. Add boiling water last.

Put in a greased 9 X 9-inch pan and bake at 350 degrees for approximately 30 minutes or until toothpick comes out clean.

"A family favorite to eat with warm chocolate pudding."

— EVA BRUBAKER
East Earl

Tickle Cake

CAKE

3 cups flour

2 cups sugar

2/3 cup cocoa

1 1/2 tsp. salt

2 tsp. baking soda

1 cup boiling water

1 cup sour milk

2 eggs

1 cup oil

2 tsp. vanilla

FILLING

1/2 cup shortening

1/2 cup margarine

1 cup sugar

1 tbsp. vanilla

1/2 cup hot milk (scant)

FROSTING

1/2 cup margarine

1 cup brown sugar

1/2 cup milk

3 tbsp. cocoa

confectioner's sugar

Mix first four cake ingredients. Dissolve baking soda in hot water. Add to flour mixture with rest of cake ingredients. Mix well. Pour in greased pan and bake at 350 degrees for 25 minutes. Do not over bake. Cool.

For filling, cream together shortening and margarine. Add vanilla and sugar and beat. Add hot milk 1 tablespoon at a time beating until creamy, spread on cake and freeze.

For frosting boil together and cool until warm. Thicken with confectioner's sugar until it reaches a spreadable consistency. Remove cake from freezer and top with frosting. Cake keeps best in refrigerator.

— ADA MAE BRUBAKER
Narvon

Tips for Cake Mix (For a Bigger & Better Cake)

1 egg

3/4 cup flour

1 tsp. baking soda

1 Tbsp. cooking oil

1/3 cup water

1/2 cup sugar

Flavoring to your taste.

Mix cake as directed on box and add all ingredients. Mix well. Bake as directions call for on cake mix box.

— EVA BRUBAKER
East Earl

CANNING, FREEZING, & THIS 'N THAT INDEX

ALONG THE CONESTOGA

Canning, Freezing, & This 'n That

Shirktown Day & Churchtown Day

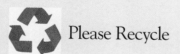

Shirktown Day & Churchtown Day

The first Saturday in August has found a faithful group of neighbors working together with Bob and Paula Shirk to host the Shirktown Threshers Show. It is a day devoted to keeping history alive by the demonstration of threshing methods used in bygone days, as well as farm-related exhibits and home-craft demonstrations.

How did Shirktown Threshers get their start? It all began in 1985 when a friend gave Bob a wooden hand-fed Pottstown Ellis Keystone threshing machine. Thus began a more serious search for other threshing machines, horse-drawn equipment, corn shellers, planters, cultivators, John Deere tractors, engines, plows and other farm-related items. There was an interest in the neighborhood to try to cut wheat using a grain cradle. Later, a binder was used to cut the wheat. We still use this binder to cut the wheat for our show each year. If we cut the wheat, why not try the Ellis Keystone threshing machine to thresh the grain from the stalks of wheat? So one Saturday afternoon, a few neighbors and friends gathered to try threshing. We used a New Holland 4 horse power gas engine to run the thresher. This event happened on a small scale for several years, moving from a small hill across the road to a larger area in front of the tobacco shed. We experimented with gas engines, tractors, and a small steam engine to run the thresher. Each year brought a few more neighbors and friends who "played" with threshing. We had fun and still do!

Children watching the threshing.

In 1992 we wanted to celebrate the bicentennial anniversary of our farm which was purchased in 1792 by Joseph Shirk. He bought 201.5 acres. Our farm is just one of the five farms that Joseph divided and willed to his five sons in 1825. All of the farms are still in operation but there are only two that have been farmed by the Shirk's continuously since 1792. We decided to have a larger threshing demonstration in 1992, displaying Bob's growing farm collection, inviting family, friends, and neighbors, and providing food to help celebrate this rare occasion. We had a wonderful time and people urged us to have a threshing again the following year. We discussed this with our neighbors and everyone was excited about making this an annual event. As you can tell, this is not about Bob and

Bob & Paula Shirk.

Paula. We could not put on a show ourselves. It is the combined effort of our neighbors. We took the neighborhood name of Shirktown and came up with Shirktown Threshers. Since then we are still having a good time. Bob says that when it ceases to be fun, we will no longer do the show.

Bob and the threshers demonstrate the progression of threshing several times throughout the day. They begin by flailing the wheat on the ground. Then they use a groundhog threshing machine which literally shakes the grain from the stalks. The grain falls through the screen of the thresher to a covering on the ground below. This thresher is run by a small gas engine. Next, one of our neighbor's mules walks up the tread power machine which is belted to a threshing machine. The mule proceeds to tread enough power to run the threshing

Bob Shirk driving his father's tractor in the parade.

machine. Another demonstration uses two of the mules walking in a circle hooked to a sweep which runs another threshing machine. The next step is to use the larger metal Frick threshers using gas engines, tractors, and a steam engine, which is owned by one of our neighbors, to run them.

Demonstrating a machine.

Each year we try to include some of the bigger and newer farm equipment to contrast with the old. One year we used a 9500 John Deere combine to harvest some rye that was still standing. We then used a John Deere 7810 and a round baler to bale the straw. Not many people get to see these large machines at work. It was a successful demonstration.

Besides Bob's collection we have friends who bring their tractors and engines for display. Many engines are running with exhibitors anxious to explain how they work and what they were used for. One year we had a miniature steam engine and bailer producing small bales of straw. We also had a homemade tractor running a miniature threshing machine. A small saw mill was run by a gas engine. A large New Holland stone crusher was in operation.

Some folks exhibited their special collections. There were wrenches on a display board of all shapes and sizes. We also had a display of colorful metal tractor seats. Old chain saws were on display. Another person had their tool collection to show. Beautifully hand crafted quarter scale wagons were exhibited. One of the collectors entertained us with his banjo.

Linda Beiler demonstrating wheat weaving.

A group of ladies gather around the "old house" to demonstrate open fire cooking, wool and yarn dying, rug braiding, spinning, weaving, making felt, basket making and wheat weaving. Children are often involved in the sewing crafts during the day. People of all ages can be seen trying to weave a wheat design to take home. We had a quilt prepared for quilting one year. Several ladies took time to add their stitches to the quilt.

An older resident of our community helped to burn lime as a boy. We have no lime kiln but we worked with him until a heavy brick lined smokestack, which he purchased from Birdsboro Steel, was positioned on a wooded hill above the farm lane. The smokestack acts as a lime kiln and we have produced some very good lime in the past years. The actual task of burning the lime was easy in comparison to getting the stack in place! Several days prior to the show we fill the stack with limestone, coal, and wood. We light it and it burns day and night. By Saturday, we usually have the final product. It attracts a lot of attention as it was a necessary part of farming long ago. They needed the lime to fertilize their crops.

Our food is provided by the parents of three local Amish and Mennonite schools in the community. All proceeds go to the schools to help them cover student and school expenses. They do make a donation to the local volunteer fire company. Much of the food is homemade, especially the soup, pies, root beer, and tea. We do have homemade

Crowds watching Shirktown Day events.

ice cream which is churned with a small gas engine. Another homemade treat is our bread which is baked in our outside bake oven. Our baker makes the best French bread! People stand in line to sample these delicious treats.

We also have a display of the Shurch – Shirk family history from those who came from Switzerland to those in Shirktown, Caernarvon Township, Lancaster County, Pennsylvania. Paula has recorded this history on charts for public reading. Bob and his brothers and sisters represent the eighth generation of Shirks in America. Bob is the sixth Shirk descendent to live on this farm. The restored home that Christian Shirk built in the early 1800's is still standing the test of time. A four square garden is near the house with its herbs, vegetables, and flowers in abundance.

This event is free to the public and is not commercialized. You will find a mixture of friendly people enjoying the day. All are here for the purpose of seeing how farming was done a hundred or more years ago. Preserving a piece of history is our goal. Let the young people get a glimpse of the past and enjoy taking part in the day's events!

If this event doesn't peak your interest you may want to venture into Churchtown for the annual Churchtown Sale Days. When sixteen-year-old Travis Martin thought of the idea for a community garage sale, he didn't plan on it becoming a yearly event, but, the 25th annual Churchtown Sale Day was held in August 2008. The day's events now begin with a pancake breakfast, served at the Churchtown Fire Hall and prepared by the Ladies'

Auxiliary. Then visitors stroll through town to inspect a variety of goods available on the lawns of the various residences. Those who live outside town usually bring their sale items to a friend or family members' house for display.

It was in 1983 when his mom, Betty, decided to have a garage sale, that Travis conceived the idea of involving the whole community. "I thought it would be much better if we had a lot of people do it", he explained. At the time, Travis and his family, lifelong residents of the area, lived at Twin Linden in Churchtown, and owned and operated Pebble Rock Campground located two miles north of town.

Travis was delivering the Penny Saver each week and when he made his rounds, he talked to residents explaining his idea. The following spring, as he covered his newspaper route, there were inquiries as to when he was planning the next sale day. Travis did some coordinating and the event expanded in 1984 to include the pancake breakfast.

Travis, who enjoys running and was on the track and field team at Garden Spot High School, began thinking that winter of adding a race to the day's event. He began mapping out a route and planning the many details of such an endeavor. With the aid of experienced race planners, timing was arranged, a zoning waiver obtained from the township supervisors (Travis's dad is Jerald Martin, then chairman of the supervisors), and the help of thirty people enlisted as timers, split timers, and registrars for the day of the race.

Finding that many volunteers wasn't easy, but Travis found willing workers at the fire company, Red Rose Alliance, and among school friends and campers at Pebble Rock where he worked summers as athletic director and lifeguard.

Thus in 1985 the First Annual Churchtown Alliance Run was introduced. Proceeds from the 10,000 meter race and two-mile fun/run benefited the Red Rose Alliance, a local citizen's action group organized in 1981 in opposition to the hazardous waste landfill proposed for the former Narvon clay mine property. Travis overlooked no detail in planning the 6.2 mile race which began at Pebble Rock Campground, the sponsor of the race.

"It was a scenic route and challenging," he recalls. "There were some hills and there were water stations and spray-down stations for the runners along the way." The race took place on secondary roads with split times at the one-, three- and four-mile marks. Course safety was provided by police and ambulance service. Awards were presented to the winners in several categories following the race.

— CHURCHTOWN DAY STORY FROM RECOLLECTIONS OF CAERNARVON TOWNSHIP
  BY MARY PETROFSKE, FRIENDS OF BANGOR

Canning 101

The canned recipes in this section are processed with the boiling-water canning method. They are either A) cold packed, which means the ingredients in the jar starts out cold before entering the canner, or B) hot packed, the ingredients are heated before entering the canner. It will be stated in each recipe which one to follow. [1]

A) Using Boiling Water Canners

Most boiling water canners are made of aluminum or porcelain-covered steel. They have fitted lids and removable racks that are either perforated or shaped wire racks. The canner must be deep enough so that at least one inch of briskly boiling water will be over the tops of jars during processing. Some boiling water canners do not have completely flat bottoms. A flat bottom must be used on an electric range. Either a flat or ridged bottom may be used on a gas burner. To ensure uniform processing of all jars with an electric range, the canner should be no more than 4 inches wider in diameter than the element on which it is heated. (When centered on the burner or element, the canner should not extend over the edge of the burner or element by more than 2 inches on any side.) Follow these steps for successful boiling water canning:

1. Before you start preparing your food, fill the canner half full with clean warm water for a canner load of pint jars. For other sizes and numbers of jars, you will need to adjust the amount of water so it will be 1 to 2 inches over the top of the filled jars.
2. Center the canner over the burner and preheat the water to 140 degrees F. for raw packed foods and to 180 degrees F. for hot-packed foods. You can begin preparing food for your jars while this water is preheating.
3. Load filled jars, fitted with lids, into the canner one at a time, using a jar lifter. When moving jars with a jar lifter, make sure the jar lifter is securely positioned below the neck of the jar (below the screw band of the lid). Keep the jar upright at all times. Tilting the jar could cause food to spill into the sealing area of the lid. If you have a shaped wire rack that has handles to hold it on the canner sides, above the water in the canner, you can load jars onto the rack in the raised position and then use the handles to lower the rack with jars into the water.
4. Add more boiling water, if needed, so the water level is at least one inch above the jar tops. For process times over 30 minutes, the water level should be 2 inches above the jars.
5. Turn the heat setting to its highest position, cover the canner with its lid and heat until the water boils vigorously.

---

1) Instructions for water batch canning are taken with permission from the USDA canning guide, for more detailed instructions please visit their website http://www.uga.edu/nchfp/.

2) Elizabeth L. Andress, Ph.D., Professor and Extension Food Safety Specialist. The University of Georgia and Ft. Valley State University. http://www.uga.edu/nchfp/publications/uga/uga_using_bw_can.pdf

6. Set a timer (after the water is boiling) for the total minutes required for processing the food.

7. Keep the canner covered for the process time. The heat setting may be lowered as long as a gentle but complete boil is maintained for the entire process time.

8. Add more boiling water during the process, if needed, to keep the water level above the jar tops.

9. If the water stops boiling at any time during the process, turn the heat on its highest setting, bring the water back to a vigorous boil, and begin the timing of the process over, from the beginning (using the total original process time).

10. When the jars have been processed in boiling water for the recommended time, turn off the heat and remove the canner lid. Wait 5 minutes before removing jars.

11. Using a jar lifter, remove the jars one at a time, being careful not to tilt the jars. Carefully place them directly onto a towel or cake cooling rack, leaving at least one inch of space between the jars during cooling. Avoid placing the jars on a cold surface or in a cold draft.

12. Let the jars sit undisturbed while they cool, from 12 to 24 hours. Do not tighten ring bands on the lids or push down on the center of the flat metal lid until the jar is completely cooled.

13. Remove ring bands from sealed jars. Put any unsealed jars in the refrigerator and use first.

14. Wash jars and lids to remove all residues.

15. Label jars and store in a cool, dry place out of direct light. [2]

B) Cooling Jars & Testing / Reproducing Jar Seals

When you remove hot jars from a canner, do not retighten their jar lids. Retightening of hot lids may cut through the gasket and cause seal failures. Cool the jars at room temperature for 12 to 24 hours. Jars may be cooled on racks or towels to minimize heat damage to counters. The food level and liquid volume of raw-packed jars will be noticeably lower after cooling. Air is exhausted during processing and food shrinks. If a jar loses excessive liquid during processing, do not open it to add more liquid. Check for sealed lids as described below. After cooling jars for 12 to 24 hours, remove the screw bands and test seals with one of the following options:

▸ Option 1: Press the middle of the lid with a finger or thumb. If the lid springs up when you release your finger, the lid is unsealed.

▸ Option 2: Tap the lid with the bottom of a teaspoon. If it makes a dull sound, the lid is not sealed. If food is in contact with the underside of the lid, it will also cause a dull sound. If the jar is sealed correctly, it will make a ringing, high-pitched sound.

▸ Option 3: Hold the jar at eye level and look across the lid. The lid should be concave (curved down slightly in the center). If center of the lid is either flat or bulging, it may not be sealed.

If a lid fails to seal on a jar, remove the lid and check the jar-sealing surface for tiny nicks. If necessary, change the jar, add a new, properly prepared lid, and reprocess within 24 hours using the same processing time. Headspace in unsealed jars may be adjusted to 1 1/2 inches and jars could be frozen instead of reprocessed. Foods in single unsealed jars could be stored in the refrigerator and consumed within several days.

Dilley Beans

1/4 cup canning salt

2 cups vinegar

2 cups water

garlic

dill head or 1 Tbsp. dill seed

1 clove garlic or 1 Tbsp.
  minced dry garlic

2 lb. fresh beans

Wash and trim beans.

Place in each jar: dill head or dill seed, garlic clove or minced garlic. Pack with whole beans. Combine salt, vinegar and water. Bring to a boil.

Add beans. Process 5 minutes in boiling water bath. *Makes 4 pints*

— DAISY LAMBERT
  East Earl

Dried Corn

corn on the cob

water

1 tsp. salt

sugar

2 cups milk

2 Tbsp. butter

Husk and clean corn. Cook corn on the cob just until it comes to a boil. Let cool. Cut off cob, but do not scrape. (Avoid creamed corn as it would brown too much in the vegetable dryer)

Stir and scrape every 30 minutes and spread out again. It's best to dry on low heat so it doesn't brown too much – a light golden brown – until kernels feel dry. Approximately 3 to 4 hours.

To prepare dried corn cover with about 1 1/2 cups water and 1 teaspoon salt and a bit of sugar if desired. Heat on low heat and simmer until the water is absorbed. Add 2 cups milk or part cream – 2 tablespoons butter. Boil on low for 1 hour adding milk if it becomes dry. *Serves 6*

— EVA MARTIN
  Narvon

Dried String Beans

string beans

water

salt

ham or pork (optional)

To dry string beans, nip and wash beans. Boil about 30 minutes. Drain and dry on a vegetable dryer. It will take 4 to 5 hours until the beans are completely dry.

To cook beans, soak covered with plenty of water for a few hours or overnight. Drain and boil again for 30 minutes adding fresh water and salt.

"They are good cooked with ham or fresh pork roast. Can be baked with meat by placing on top of roast. This is a bit old-fashioned but we enjoy them for a change."

— Eva Martin
Narvon

Pickled Red Beets

beets

2 cups red beet juice

2 cups sugar

1 cup vinegar

1 Tbsp. salt

pepper

Cook beets until tender. Leave 2 inches of stems and top root. Peel, slice and place in jars. Pour remaining ingredients over beets.

Put in canner and cold pack 15 to 20 minutes.

— Rachael Lapp
Narvon

Dill Pickles to Can

Fresh medium-sized pickles to fill 4 one-quart jars

4 tsp. dill seed

2 tsp. minced garlic

1 qt. water

1 cup vinegar

1/4 cup uniodized salt

3 tsp. sugar

pinch turmeric

Enough fresh medium-sized pickles to fill four one-quart jars. To each jar add 1 tsp. dill seed and 1/2 tsp. minced garlic.

Bring the following ingredients to a boil: water, vinegar, uniodized salt, sugar and a pinch of turmeric. Fill jars with syrup and close. Place in boiling water batch for 15 minutes.

— Janessa Fisher
Narvon

Sauerkraut A-La-Greenbank

4 large heads of cabbage

water as needed

1/2 cup sea salt

1/2 cup vinegar

1/4 cup white wine

Save some of the outer leaves and remove heart before shredding. Using a medium cut slaw board shred cabbage into a large container for mixing purposes. Mix in sea salt. If mixture does not taste salty after mixing, add more salt. It must taste salty! Sprinkle with vinegar and white wine, mix thoroughly. Layer mixed cabbage into a large crock and compact as filling. Add water to cover cabbage as you fill the crock. Cover contents with outer cabbage leaves and place a weight on top for compacting. Let stand for about 10 days at room temperature.

A mold will form on top of the water that covers the leaves. Remove the mold and all top leaves and discard. Take sauerkraut from crock and place in kettles for heating. Bring to a boil. While hot place sauerkraut and juice in jars and turn lids down tight. Leave air space in neck of jar. They will seal by themselves. Your sauerkraut is now canned and ready to be used as desired.

"I have family and friends requesting the sauerkraut, not the recipe!"

— JACK HILLARD
New Holland

Pauline's Pickles

2 qts pickle chunks into 1/2 to 3/4 inch chunks

1 cup vinegar

1 cup water

2 cups sugar

1 tsp. salt

1 tsp. pickling spices

Heat above ingredients to boiling and then add the pickle chunks. Bring to a boil again. Put in jars and seal. Process 10 minutes in boiling water bath.

"I received this recipe from two older Churchtown friends, Mary Pyfrom and Pauline Martin. I've made this recipe for years and have passed it on to my daughters, neighbors and friends. They are still called 'Pauline's Pickles'!"

— PAULA SHIRK
Narvon

Banana Pickles

1 1/2 cup vinegar

2 cups water

3 cups sugar

1 tsp. mustard seed

1 tsp. salt

1 tsp. celery seed

1 tsp. turmeric

"Pare large cucumbers. Cut in length and pack in jars.

Mix ingredients together. Bring liquid to a boil. Fill jars with syrup, put lids and rings on and cold pack for 10 minutes. *Makes 3 quarts*

"I received this pickle recipe from my neighbor Ella Newswanger. My girls liked these pickles because they have a yellow banana color!"

— Paula Shirk
Narvon

Kosher Dill Pickles

1 (9 oz.) pkg. Mrs. Wages Kosher or Polish Dill Mix

7 cups white vinegar

18 cups water

6 cups sugar

cucumbers to fit 15 qt. jars

onion slices (optional)

carrot slices (optional)

Slice cucumbers the long way. If too long break in half. If you have some little cucumbers don't slice them, just mix them in with the others. If cucumber is too thick slice the seeds off, do not peel. Bring the above mixture to a boil. Do not cook cucumber just pack them in your jars.

Fill jars with juice and cold pack. To cold pack bring your canner water to a full rolling boil. Make sure there is enough water to cover cans. When water is boiling put your jars in and immediately set your timer for 10 minutes. After 10 minutes remove jars.

— Ruth King
Narvon

Refrigerator Pickles

4 cloves garlic

4 small onions

4 pieces dill or grape leaves

4 cups vinegar

1 cup water

1/4 cup salt

2 cups sugar

2 Tbsp. pickling spices

Put vegetables in salt water overnight. Drain and rinse. Make hot and pour over vegetables. Can keep in crock in cellar or refrigerator. Ready to eat in one week. Zucchini and cucumbers are good. Green peppers are delicious too.

— GRACIE FOX
East Earl

Uncle John's Southern Bread & Butter Pickles

1 gallon cucumbers (small cucumbers work best, about 4 quarts sliced thin)

1 green pepper

1 red pepper, for color

8 small white onions

1/2 cup salt

bag of ice

7 pint jars with lids

SYRUP

5 cups white sugar

2 tsp. turmeric

1/2 tsp. ground cloves

1 tsp. celery seed

2 Tbsp. mustard seed

5 cups white vinegar

Find small, crisp, fresh cucumbers and wash, but do not pare. Slice onions and cucumbers very thin and wash and cut peppers into fine shreds. Mix salt with all your vegetables. We use an oblong roasting pan and layer 1/3 vegetables with a layer of cracked ice, more vegetables, then ice, final layer of vegetables, final layer of ice (3 layers of each total, ice will "crisp up" the pickles).

Cover with weighted lid (we use the lid of the roasting pan turned upside down) and let stand for three hours, and then drain thoroughly.

For the pickling syrup, mix dry ingredients with vinegar and pour over vegetables. Place over low heat and mix occasionally, using a wooden spoon.

Heat the mixture to scalding, but do not boil. Pack pickles into hot jars, pour liquid over pickles (pickles will absorb liquid) and seal. Process in boiling hot water bath for 10 minutes to seal. *Makes 7 pints*

"We love using a metal wide mouth funnel to get the pickles into the jars since the pickle juice can be sticky."

— ROBIN BUCKWALTER
Reinholds

Sweet Dill Pickles

dried garlic

dried dill

cucumber slices

3 cups sugar

2 cups vinegar

2 cups boiling water

2 Tbsp. salt

Place 1 teaspoon dried garlic and 1 teaspoon dried dill in bottom of jar. Fill jar with cucumbers. Place 1 teaspoon each of dill and garlic on top of cucumbers. Add syrup. Place jar in canner and bring to a rolling boil, processing for 10 minutes. *Makes 3 quarts*

— RACHAEL LAPP
Narvon

Onion Relish

2 lb. chopped sweet onions

2 stalks sliced celery

1 chopped sweet red pepper

1 Tbsp. butter

3/4 cup vinegar

1/4 cup water

2 Tbsp. brown sugar

1 tsp. celery seed

1/4 tsp. salt

Sauté onions, celery, pepper and butter for 15 minutes in Dutch oven. Add other ingredients. Bring to boil. Reduce heat and simmer uncovered 20 minutes.

Chill and store in refrigerator or double batch and put in 1/2 pint jars and cold water process for 10 minutes in boiling water bath.

— RUTH LAMBERT
East Earl

Pepper Relish

3 green peppers

3 red peppers

2 onions

1/2 cup sugar

1/2 cup butter

2 Tbsp. flour

1 tsp. mustard

1/2 cup vinegar

salt

Ground peppers and onion fine. Mix other ingredients and cook 20 minutes.

Add to peppers and onions. Seal 10 minutes in boiling water bath.

"Sister Lettie's recipe."

— FLORIBEL STYER
Narvon

Zucchini Relish

MIXTURE I

6 cups zucchini, unpeeled

2 cups sliced onion

1 red pepper

1 green pepper

2 1/2 Tbsp. salt

MIXTURE 2

1 1/4 cups vinegar

3 cups sugar

2 Tbsp. corn starch

1/2 tsp. turmeric

3/4 tsp. celery seed

1 1/2 tsp. dry mustard

1/4 tsp. nutmeg

1/4 tsp. black pepper

Mixture 1: Grind or cut fine first 4 ingredients. Mix well with salt and let stand overnight. Rinse with cold water and drain well.

Mixture 2: In a kettle cook these ingredients until slightly thickened.

Then add mixture 1 and cook slowly for 30 minutes, stirring occasionally to keep from scorching. Put into hot jars and close with dome lids that have been in hot water. Process 15 minutes in hot water bath. Makes 3 pints or 6 half pints. This is very good on ham sandwiches.

"This recipe was given to me from Mrs. Elsie Zook who with her husband owned Zook Molasses Co. in Honeybrook. She was a great person and good cook!"

— KATHY MARTIN
Narvon

Salsa

14 cups tomatoes, peeled, seeded and chopped

3 cups onions, chopped

1 1/2 cups sweet green peppers, chopped

6 or 7 small hot peppers, chopped

3 Tbsp. salt

1 Tbsp. chili powder

1 1/2 tsp. garlic powder

1 1/2 tsp. cumin

1/2 cup vinegar

1 cup tomato juice

7 Tbsp. cornstarch

Combine first nine ingredients in a large kettle. Combine tomato juice and cornstarch. Add to kettle.

Boil 20 minutes. Put in jars and process in boiling water 10 minutes. *Makes 10 pints*

— MARILYN HOOVER
East Earl

Amish Susie's Pepper Jam

18 large red peppers

1 Tbsp. salt

4 1/2 cups white sugar, or more

1 1/2 cup white vinegar

3 boxes Sure-Jell®

Wash all peppers, drain. Chop to mince in processor. Put into large pan, sprinkle salt over top. Let sit overnight. Rinse salt off; bring all ingredients to a full boil in large pan. Cook, uncovered at lower temperature for 45 minutes. Add 3 boxes Sure-Jell, stir until thickened. Pour and spoon into hot jars/lids in hot water as you tightened. Place jars in boiling water bath for 10 minutes.

To serve, spoon cold jam on relish over desired size brick of cream cheese, or an attractive dish (an abundant amount of the jam is recommended). Garnish with sprinkle of dill weed and mint leaves or fresh parsley. Spread with small knife on crackers. It is also delicious mixed into softened cream cheese.

"Pepper jam is a popular seller at Kitchen Kettle, however, this is a recent recipe given to me. We serve it over cream cheese or mixed in for a delicious snack!"

— SUSAN MARRIS
Goodville

Apple Butter

5 lb. sugar

3 qt. apple

cinnamon

allspice

hot red candies

vanilla

Peel and core apples. Add 1/2 cup water and cook till soft. Run through blender or mash with a potato masher. Add cinnamon, allspice, hot red candies, vanilla or any combination of spices to apples to taste. Add sugar. Bake at 250 degrees in oven or slow cook on top of stove or put in a large crock pot. You can do any combination of the above. When it reaches the thickness you want place in jars, pint or jelly, and cold pack 20 minutes.

"I also do pears and peaches this way. Some of my favorite combos are: Peaches, ginger and cinnamon; Pears, orange peel, and allspice; Apples, allspice and cinnamon; and Apple pear with lemon, ginger and allspice.

— LINDA BOYER
Narvon

Canned Apple Butter

11 cups applesauce,
    unsweetened

6 cups sugar

1/2 cup vinegar

1/2 cup water

3 tsp. cinnamon

2 tsp. ground cloves

1 tsp. ground allspice

Mix all ingredients and put into a large stainless steel pan. Do not cover.

Bake at 350 degrees for 2 1/2 to 3 hours, until thick, stirring frequently. Put into hot jars and seal, 15 minutes. *Makes 5 pints*

— KATHY MARTIN
  Narvon

Pepper Jam

1 dozen large red peppers,
    chopped fine

1 Tbsp. salt

2 cups white vinegar

3 cups sugar (or Splenda®)

Day 1 – Chop 1 dozen red peppers real fine. Let chopped peppers and salt sit overnight.

Day 2 – Drain and press out all liquid, it will be very dry. Add 2 cups of white vinegar and 3 cups of sugar. Cook until thick, about 1 hour or more. Put in jars and seal. Serve over cream cheese with crackers.

— SHIRLEY WEIDMAN
  Narvon

Pepper Hash

15 peppers

15 onions

1 stalk celery

1 1/2 pt. vinegar

1 pt. water

1 tsp. mustard seed

3 cups sugar

3 tsp. salt

Grind peppers, onions and celery. Pour boiling water over it and let stand 15 minutes, and then drain 15 minutes.

Add vinegar, 1 pint water, mustard seed, sugar and salt. Boil 3 minutes. Hot pack.

— REGINA CLARK
  East Earl

Rose-Petal Jam

1 cup rose petals

3/4 cup water

juice of 1 lemon

2 1/2 cups sugar

1 pkg. Sure-Jell® in 3/4 cup
water

Gather rose petals in the morning. Any pesticide-free roses will do (wild roses are best). Snip the white base from petals, as it contains a bitter substance.

Measure 1 cup of petals. Put petals into a blender along with 3/4 cup of water and the juice of 1 lemon. Blend until smooth. Gradually add 2 1/2 cups sugar with the blender still running. Blend until all the sugar is dissolved. Leave mixture in container.

Stir 1 package Sure-Jell into 3/4 cup water, bring to boil and boil hard for 1 minute, stirring constantly. Pour the pectin into the rose-sugar mixture and run the blender on slow until you are sure the pectin has been thoroughly incorporated into the other ingredients.

Pour immediately into small sterilized jars with screw caps. Process 10 minutes in boiling water bath. Jam will keep for a month in the refrigerator. Can also freeze jam. Enjoy!

— CHERYL FOX
New Holland

Bread & Butter Pickles for Freezing

2 qt. sliced cucumbers

1 big onion sliced

2 Tbsp. salt

1 1/2 cups sugar

1/2 cup vinegar

Soak cucumbers, onion and salt mixture for 2 hours. Mix well.

Bring sugar and vinegar to a boil. Add cucumber and onions and let sit until cool. Put in containers and freeze.

— SHIRLEY J. PLANK
New Holland

Freezing Corn

8 cups raw corn cut off cob

1/2 cup butter

1/2 cup margarine

1/2 cup water

3 Tbsp. sugar (or Splenda®)

salt and pepper to taste

Put all ingredients in a tall pan. Bring to a boil for 3 to 8 minutes. Put in freezer containers after cool.

— SHIRLEY WEIDMAN
Narvon

BrownHill Bites - Horse Treats

2 cups horse feed (pellets) with about 1 cup of water to make a mash

1 cup carrots

2 cups oatmeal

1/2 cup molasses

1/4 cup flour

2 Tbsp. corn oil

1 tsp. salt

Preheat oven to 350 degrees. Lightly grease cookie sheet. In a food chopper, chop carrots, oats and horse feed. Add remaining ingredients. Make small balls and put on cookie sheet. Bake 30 minutes. Flip and bake another 15 to 30 minutes. Be careful not to burn them!

"We enjoy making these treats with our students. Our dog loves them too!"

"BrownHill stables are home to 15 horses on a beautiful wooded property. We enjoy helping riders of all ages become better horsemen. We teach riding to age 3 to 93 and both able bodied and those with physical and mental challenges."

— SHERRI BROWN, BROWNHILL STABLES
Narvon

Winter Treat - Bird Suet

1 cup crunchy peanut butter

1 cup lard

2 cups cooking oats

2 cups cornmeal

1 cup flour

1/3 cup sugar

Melt peanut butter and lard. Mix in rest of ingredients. Mold in square plastic containers about 1 1/2 inch thick and place in freezer until firm.

— CHERYL FOX
New Holland

Plant Food

1 tsp. cream of tartar

1 tsp. saltpeter

1 tsp. ammonia

1 tsp. Epsom salt

1 gallon warm water

Mix together. Feed houseplants once a month.

"African violets will amaze you with continuous blooms. Ferns and other plants will be a lush green."

— VERA JANE NEWSWANGER
Morgantown

Holiday Hospitality Potpourri

2 oranges sliced into 1/4 inch rings

2 lemons sliced into 1/4 inch rings

2 apples, (1 red, 1 yellow) cut each into 8 wedges – remove core only

8 cinnamon sticks

6 to 8 whole nutmeg

6 to 8 star anise

8 to 10 whole allspice

Layer fruit in a large crock pot and add spices. Cover with hot water until ingredients just start to float. Use high setting with cover off. It can also be simmered on top of stove in a large pan.

"This can be used a few days in a row. Add water as needed during use. Enjoy the aroma!"

— HISTORIC POOLE FORGE
HOSPITALITY COMMITTEE

Contributors

Carl W. Adams, *Dedicated to Constance S. Adams*

Elwood M. Dapp, *In loving memory of Elwood Dapp, Jr.*

John David & Mary Martin and Housekeeper Anna H. (Martin)
Burkholder during the 1960's and 1970's, *In Memory of the late former
owner Dorothy Wimer and the late tenant Margaret McDowell and the
years spent and memories made on the Poole Forge property*

Marguerite Fink, *In memory of Wayne & Maude Fink*

Dwayne & Janessa Fisher, *In gratitude of the men and
women of Caernarvon Fire Company*

Sue Groff, *In memory of Bill & Dorothy Wimer, owners of Poole Forge from 1948 – 1981*

Mary & Lance Guldin, *Narvon, PA*

Brenda Martin, *In loving memory of Teanse & Abe Martin,
Churchtown & their daughter Kate Hostetter.*

Brenda Martin, *In loving memory of Freda & George Clark, Churchtown.*

Deb Martin, *In honor of my Mom & Dad, Janet & Dave Anspach,
for all their devotion to raising a great family*

Kathy Martin, *In memory of Carl & Jean Dombach*

Maryann & Joe Oestreich, *loving Grandparents of Brian, Eric & Jenna Muttik*

Martha Piotrowski, *dedicated to Charles Rex & Mary Francis Thomas*

Shirley (Plank) Weidman & Family, *In memory of Parents, Elizabeth R. & Charles
E. Plank, & Grandmother, Elizabeth E. Spece, and sister Betty Lou Plank*

The Raffensperger Family, *For all her loving kitchen memories, Lorraine Raffensperger*

Charlene Sagner, *In honor of my Parents, Charles & Verna
(Huyett) Sagner, & brother Donald Lynn Sagner*

From her children, *In memory of Grace F. Shirk, fantastic Mother,
Grandmother, Great-Grandmother, teacher and friend*

Clara (Betty) Sturla, *In memory of Fianna W. Weaver who was a fabulous cook*

Special Thanks

The Cookbook Committee members Lida Bensinger, Alex Diem, Cindy Diem, Maryann Oestreich, Kay Raffensperger, Sondra Simmers and Shirley Weidman, would like to thank the following for their help, knowledge, expertise and encouragement during the process of creating this cookbook:

- Annals of the Conestoga by Christian Z. Mast and Robert E Simpson
- Jeff Buckwalter & Family
- Caernarvon Historical Society
- Michael W. Chorazy
- Barb Diem
- Barb Garrett
- Ruth Good
- Gaynor Green
- Jack Hillard
- Mary Kauffman
- Melanie Klemas
- Jerry Martin
- John David & Mary Martin
- Kathy McClure
- Rose Newswanger
- Sara Newswanger
- Joe Oestreich
- 100 Years of Camera Scenes by Elanco Chapter of L.C.B.C.
- Quilting 101

- Zach Raffensperger
- Charlene Richardson
- Cathy & Bill Shirk & Sarah
- Bob & Paula Shirk
- George & Brenda Martin
- Sara Newswanger
- Floyd & Anna Mary Ringler
- Beth Shirk
- Harvey Shirk
- Simmers Family
- Moses & Susie Smucker
- Tom & Darlene Stauffer
- Becky Stoltzfus
- Floribel Styer
- Yvonne Styer
- Alvin Sweigart
- Fran & Lou Trego
- Maurine VanDyke
- Sarah Van Dyke
- Frank Weaver

References

100 Years Of Camera Scenes Views Of Eastern Lancaster County In Our Nation's Second Century. Lancaster, PA: Lancaster County Bicentennial Committee (Elanco Chapter). 1980.

Mast, Christian Z. and Robert E. Simpson. *Annals of Conestoga Valley in Lancaster, Berks, and Chester Counties, Pennsylvania*. 1942.

Petrofske, Mary T. *Recollections of Caernarvon Township. Portrait of a Lancaster County Community, 1930-1993*. Friends of Bangor. 1993.